# ENCODED ARCHIVAL DESCRIPTION APPLICATION GUIDELINES

## VERSION 1.0

Prepared by the
Encoded Archival Description Working Group
of the Society of American Archivists

Chicago
1999

**Encoded Archival Description Application Guidelines, Version 1.0**

EAD Technical Document No. 3

These guidelines represent version 1.0 of the Encoded Archival Description Document Type Definition (DTD), released in August 1998. This volume supersedes the beta guidelines made available via the official EAD Internet site beginning in 1996.

The SAA Encoded Archival Description Working Group is responsible for updating and editing the EAD DTD (EAD Technical Document No. 1), the *EAD Tag Library* (EAD Technical Document No. 2), and these *EAD Application Guidelines* (EAD Technical Document No. 3).

The Network Development and MARC Standards Office of the Library of Congress serves as the maintenance agency for online EAD documentation, including storage and delivery of electronic files and maintenance of the official EAD Internet site, available at: <http://www.loc.gov/ead/>.

Funding for preparation and publication of *Encoded Archival Description Application Guidelines Version 1.0* was received from the Institute of Museum and Library Services (IMLS) in September 1998.

Available from: **The Society of American Archivists**
527 S. Wells Street, 5th floor
Chicago, IL 60607

312/922-0140 Fax 312/347-1452
info@archivists.org
www.archivists.org



**Library of Congress Cataloging-in-Publication Data**

Society of American Archivists. Encoded Archival Description Working Group.
Encoded Archival Description application guidelines : version 1.0 / prepared by the Encoded Archival Description Working Group of the Society of American Archivists.
p. cm.
Includes bibliographical references (p. ) and index
ISBN 0-931828-42-2
1. Encoded Archival Description (Document type definition) Handbooks, manuals, etc. I. Title.
Z695.2.S63 1999
025.3'24--dc21 99-34876
CIP

# TABLE OF CONTENTS

# PREFACE

Encoded Archival Description (EAD) has captured the interest and imagination of archivists, librarians, software designers, and information professionals worldwide. This is because it is the first data structure standard to facilitate distribution via the Internet of detailed information about archival collections and fonds via the standard archival access tool: the finding aid. Such distribution enables finding aids to be searched with an effectiveness and thoroughness that was all but unthinkable a mere five years ago. Moreover, EAD enables digitized images of archival materials to be embedded in or linked to their corresponding finding aids, enabling a user to navigate successively more detailed layers of information.

Publication of the *EAD Application Guidelines* represents the final piece of documentation for EAD Version 1.0, which also includes the EAD Document Type Definition (DTD) and the *EAD Tag Library*. Although published last, the *Guidelines* are the part of the documentation that administrators and archivists interested in implementing EAD should turn to first. The purpose of the *Guidelines* is to introduce EAD from a number of perspectives—administrative, technical, and, most importantly, archival—and to address the need for instruction and advice that has been voiced by the archival community. The many questions that have surrounded EAD over the course of its development and implementation—from questions as broad as "Will my finding aids fit into EAD?" to specific questions relating to use of EAD elements—are addressed in the *Guidelines*.

These *Guidelines* do not, however, legislate specific encoding practices, because current international descriptive practices are divergent enough to make hard-and-fast rules impractical. Rather, the *Guidelines* illustrate and discuss the pros and cons of various options. In addition, the *Guidelines* do not attempt to articulate a content standard for finding aids, although certainly the developers of EAD hope that this work will pave the way toward a future international archival content standard.

It is also important to acknowledge that the desire to publish finding aids on the Internet is not the only reason to use EAD, since its stable yet flexible hierarchical structure is equally applicable to finding aids in any format. The same data elements that constitute a "good" Internet finding aid are equally valid for a finding aid produced by a database or a word processing program, or one printed on paper. One of the tenets of the *Guidelines* is that we need to take a hard look at our descriptive practices to ensure that we are delivering intelligible, useful information about our collections to researchers.

Bear in mind that EAD is, and likely always will be, a "work in progress." The Internet, EAD, archival descriptive practices, and digital technology are all dynamic entities in an environment that is increasingly driven toward standardization. EAD Version 1.0 was the culmination of five years of testing and refinement that began with the Berkeley Finding Aid Project, and as we learn more about how researchers locate and use our finding aids on the Web, continued refinement will be necessary.

# ACKNOWLEDGEMENTS

## From the Encoded Archival Description Working Group

The members of SAA's Encoded Archival Description Working Group would like to express our profound appreciation to the numerous institutions and individuals who assisted in the preparation of these *Guidelines*. Full acknowledgements for the overall development of Encoded Archival Description can be found in the *EAD Tag Library*.

A great debt of gratitude is owed to the Council on Library and Information Resources (CLIR), formerly the Council on Library Resources, and the encouragement of its executive director, Deanna Marcum, for providing funding to the Society of American Archivists both to develop more fully the EAD DTD and to underwrite the preparation of the beta application guidelines. The guidelines development process began with a meeting of the Bentley Fellowship Finding Aid Team[1] in November 1995 at the Library of Congress, hosted by the National Digital Library, and including Anne J. Gilliland-Swetland as the recently appointed author of the then forthcoming guidelines.

A meeting in January 1996, hosted by the University of California, Los Angeles (and funded by CLIR) was attended by a subset of the Bentley Team (Michael J. Fox, Steven L. Hensen, Kris Kiesling, Daniel Pitti, and Janice E. Ruth) in addition to Gilliland-Swetland and Thomas A. La Porte. This meeting laid the foundation for the guidelines and provided general guidance and an outline for the authors. A second CLIR-funded meeting was convened at the University of California, Berkeley, in April 1996 to examine progress and issues regarding the draft guidelines. Attendees at this meeting included Gilliland-Swetland and La Porte, the entire Bentley team (with the exception of Steven DeRose), Randall Barry of the Library of Congress, and Tim Hoyer and Jack Von Euw of the Bancroft Library.

In spring 1998, with the impending release of Version 1.0 of the EAD DTD and publication of the *EAD Tag Library*, it became clear that the beta version of the guidelines would require revision to accommodate the many changes that had occurred. An application to enable and facilitate this revision was submitted to the Institute of Museum and Library Services (IMLS) on behalf of the Society of American Archivists and the Bentley Historical Library, University of Michigan, which had agreed to host revision meetings. This application was successful, and a subset of the Society of American Archivists' EAD Working Group, consisting of Jackie M. Dooley, Michael J. Fox, Steven L. Hensen, Kris Kiesling, Bill

[1] A history of EAD's development may be found at the *Encoded Archival Description Official Web Site,* which is maintained by the Library of Congress and is available at: <http://www.loc.gov/ead>. The original Bentley team included Stephen J. DeRose (INSO, formerly Electronic Book Technologies), Jackie M. Dooley (University of California, Irvine), Michael J. Fox (Minnesota Historical Society), Steven L. Hensen (Duke University), Kris Kiesling (Harry Ransom Humanities Research Center, University of Texas at Austin), Daniel Pitti (University of Virginia, formerly University of California, Berkeley), Janice E. Ruth (Library of Congress Manuscript Division), Sharon Gibbs Thibodeau (National Archives and Records Administration), and Helena Zinkham (Library of Congress Prints and Photographs Division).

Landis, and Janice E. Ruth, along with Greg Kinney of the Bentley Historical Library, met in Ann Arbor, Michigan, in November 1998 to complete this process.

The Working Group is therefore extremely grateful to IMLS, the Society of American Archivists, the Bentley Historical Library, and the University of Michigan for their support toward the completion of this document. We are particularly appreciative of the continuing support and encouragement of Francis X. Blouin and William Wallach, director and assistant director, respectively, of the Bentley Historical Library, and to their support staff (particularly Diane Hatfield) for their good-natured tolerance of the various EAD-related invasions of their precincts over the past few years.

Editing of the draft was supervised by Jackie M. Dooley and Bill Landis of the University of California, Irvine. Members of the SAA EAD Working Group[2] and the SAA Technical Subcommittee on Descriptive Standards[3] provided feedback on a preliminary draft. A later draft was reviewed by Elizabeth Dow, Chris Powell, and Kathleen Roe, and their detailed feedback was crucial in improving many areas of the *Guidelines*. Teresa Brinati, director of publications for the Society of American Archivists, provided editorial management and moved this publication to final production and distribution.

The Working Group is indebted to the University of California, Irvine for its support and oversight of this project, and to the Society of American Archivists and its executive director, Susan Fox, for their unwavering support for this and all other work connected with the development and promulgation of EAD.

Encoded Archival Description Working Group<br>Society of American Archivists<br>April 1999

---

[2] The Society of American Archivists EAD Working Group consists of the members of the Bentley Fellowship Finding Aid Team (except DeRose), as well as Randall Barry (Library of Congress Network Development and MARC Standards Office), Wendy Duff (University of Toronto), Ricky Erway (Research Libraries Group), Anne Gilliland-Swetland (University of California, Los Angeles), Bill Landis (University of California, Irvine), Eric Miller (OCLC Online Computer Library Center), Meg Sweet (Public Record Office, United Kingdom), Robert Spindler (Arizona State University), and Richard Szary (Yale University).

[3] The Society of American Archivists Technical Subcommittee on Descriptive Standards is chaired by Bill Landis (University of California, Irvine) and also includes Nicole Bouché (Yale University), Donna DiMichele (Mashantucket Pequot Museum and Research Center), Susan Potts McDonald (Emory University), Dennis Meissner (Minnesota Historical Society), and Alden Monroe (Alabama Department of Archives).

# ACKNOWLEDGEMENTS

## From the Executive Director of SAA

The EAD Working Group, the SAA body responsible for the continuing development and maintenance of Encoded Archival Description, has labored long and hard to bring to the archival community the three major pieces of EAD Version 1.0 documentation: the Document Type Definition (DTD), the *EAD Tag Library,* and these *EAD Application Guidelines.* Individual Working Group members have contributed in various ways by writing or reviewing drafts of the documentation, providing international perspectives, and testing changes and revisions.

Within the Working Group, however, eight dedicated individuals have been the principal players in bringing Version 1.0 of EAD to fruition. Each of these SAA members has been involved with EAD since its inception and has contributed in numerous ways, including serving as the authors of individual sections of the Version 1.0 *Tag Library* and *Guidelines.* In addition, they merit individual recognition for the following contributions:

Jackie Dooley served as editor of the *Guidelines.* Ever mindful of the diverse EAD audience, she blended innumerable drafts of chapters and sections into a comprehensive document that will be useful to both EAD novices and masters. In her capacity as chair of the SAA Publications Board, Jackie also facilitated the publication of the *Tag Library.*

Michael Fox contributed his extensive knowledge of descriptive practices not only from the archival perspective, but from the library and museum perspectives as well. He also kept the group abreast of XML and other technical developments. In his role as liaison to the Working Group from the International Council on Archives Committee on Descriptive Standards, he was able to bring international concerns to the group.

Steve Hensen, in addition to his role as "elder statesman" and conscience of archival description, has been the unofficial but highly successful fund-raiser for the group. The grant applications he wrote on behalf of SAA to the Delmas Foundation and to the Institute of Museum and Library Services funded two critical meetings, enabling members of the EADWG to revise the DTD and to draft the *Guidelines.* He also coordinated final editorial work on the *Tag Library.*

Kris Kiesling, chair of the Working Group since it was established in 1995, provided key leadership during all phases of the group's work on documentation, coordinating all efforts and enforcing demanding production schedules. In addition, she was instrumental in the creation of the SAA EAD Roundtable.

Bill Landis brought not only a fresh perspective when he was added to the Working Group in 1997, but also wit and enthusiasm. Bill gathered the numerous examples that provide encoding guidance in the *Tag Library* and assisted with editing the *Application Guidelines.*

Daniel Pitti, leader of the original Berkeley Finding Aid Project, was responsible for extensive revisions and testing of the DTD. He kept the group on the SGML/XML straight and narrow and also has acted as advisor and mentor to a number of EAD implementers.

Janice Ruth brought her considerable editorial and writing skills to bear on both the *Tag Library* and the *Application Guidelines*. Her editorial perspective was particularly critical in "visioning" the *Guidelines,* and she served in many instances as the group's institutional memory for previous iterations of EAD documentation.

Helena Zinkham was a catalyst in kicking off the creation of the Version 1.0 *Tag Library*, drafting element descriptions, tracking down endless details, and checking and rechecking to ensure that nothing was missed.

SAA commends each of these individuals for their vision, dedication, and uncommon commitment to the archival profession. Their leadership represents archival history in the making.

Susan Fox
Executive Director
Society of American Archivists
April 1999

# HOW TO USE THIS MANUAL

## Overview of the *Application Guidelines*

The *Encoded Archival Description (EAD) Application Guidelines* are intended to provide archivists, manuscript curators, and others involved in the description of archives, manuscripts, or other primary research materials with the following information:[4]

- Explanation of the genesis and functionality of EAD and its role in archival description (chapter 1)
- Guidance on administrative issues and other questions associated with implementing EAD (chapter 2)
- Overview of EAD tagging, including guidance in the use of required and other key elements (chapter 3)
- Comparative overviews of tools and methods available for authoring and publishing (chapters 4 and 5)
- Basic SGML and XML concepts as they relate to EAD (chapter 6)
- Detailed instructions for use of EAD's linking elements (chapter 7)

In addition to its narrative text, the *Guidelines* include a variety of useful appendices:

- Minimum recommended elements for an effective encoded finding aid,[5] noting those that are required for machine validation of an EAD finding aid (appendix A)
- Crosswalks (translation tables) between EAD and three related descriptive standards: MARC, ISAD(G), and Dublin Core (appendix B)
- Frequently Asked Questions (FAQs) (appendix C)
- Implementation checklist (appendix D)
- Examples of EAD-encoded finding aids (appendix E)
- Glossary of technical terms (appendix F)
- Bibliography of sources on EAD, SGML, XML, and archival description, as well as of important thesauri and descriptive rules (appendix G)

These *Guidelines* are designed to assist both those considering use of EAD and those actively encoding the descriptive information commonly found in archival finding aids. They address, therefore, the various stages and levels of EAD implementation and its

---

[4] Please refer to the glossary in appendix F for the meaning of unfamiliar terms or acronyms mentioned in this introduction and throughout these *Guidelines*. Many terms are defined elsewhere in the *Guidelines* in addition to appearing in the glossary.

[5] The term "finding aid" is used throughout these *Guidelines* to refer to the types of archival descriptive tools typically known as inventories and registers. Although EAD has been optimized for such finding aids, its design precludes neither its use for other kinds of finding aids nor its further development to accommodate new forms of archival description.

associated activities from both a management and an encoding perspective. They are also intended to provide insight into the rationale, processes, and implications of EAD encoding for a very broad audience, including administrators, resource allocators, managers and supervisors, reference archivists and librarians, finding aid encoders, programmers, and systems administrators. Those needing the broadest possible understanding of EAD will want to study and use all of the chapters as thoroughly as necessary, while those with more limited and specific needs may wish to focus on specific chapters.

Chapter 1 explains EAD in the larger context of archival description and descriptive standards. The selection of SGML is justified; the relationships among EAD, SGML, HTML and XML are explained; the relationship between EAD and the General International Standard Archival Description (ISAD(G)) is outlined; and the continuing important role of MARC records is clarified. Chapter 1 should be studied by anyone considering the use or application of EAD, with the possible exception of programmers and systems administrators.

Chapter 2 focuses on topics relating to management and administration of EAD projects. It covers such issues as the relationship of EAD to institutional mission and goals; the importance of assigning priorities and resources; staffing and training issues; encoding workflow; and questions surrounding conversion of legacy data. It also addresses the possible advantages of outsourcing and of collaborating with partner institutions in cooperative ventures. Chapter 2 will be most useful to those in administrative positions.

Chapter 3, the core of the *Guidelines,* describes in detail the context within which all major EAD elements are to be applied in constructing an encoded finding aid. This chapter is designed to be used in conjunction with the *EAD Tag Library*, and one of its principal purposes is to place the *Tag Library* elements within the context of archival descriptive work. The major components of EAD are presented in a logical progression, beginning with those used to describe the collection as a whole and progressing to those that describe "components" or parts of a collection. A wide range of issues are addressed, from the importance of developing consistent descriptive practice prior to embarking on EAD encoding to specific questions relating to depth of markup. The final section describes use of EAD "metadata" elements, those that describe the finding aid itself. Chapter 3 is of central importance for staff and supervisors actually doing encoding or starting encoding programs. Once they have become familiar with EAD and the various issues and recommendations contained within these *Guidelines,* particularly as local protocols and processes are established, they will need to refer to this document less frequently. At that point, it may become more expedient to refer directly to the *Tag Library* for many purposes.

Chapter 4 addresses issues concerned with "authoring" EAD-encoded documents, which refers to the mechanics of using software to apply SGML encoding to a finding aid document. Topics include a comparative discussion of specific software alternatives and authoring approaches; specific software considerations relating to SGML and XML; the relationship of MARC data to EAD finding aids; encoding issues that affect display; and file management.

Chapter 5 describes options for "publishing" EAD documents by making them available to researchers via the World Wide Web. Issues covered here include software choices for searching and resource discovery; stylesheets and their use in both online display and hard-copy output; server- versus client-based delivery and publishing; obtaining hard-copy printouts of encoded finding aids; and systems management issues as they relate to small- and large-scale SGML servers.

Chapter 6 focuses on basic SGML and XML concepts as they relate to EAD. While a comprehensive knowledge of these topics is not essential for all EAD encoders or project administrators, an elementary understanding of them is critical for those responsible for systems design and administration. Subjects covered include the role and structure of the DTD, nesting and inheritance in SGML, character sets, elements, attributes, entities (particularly formal public identifiers), content-bearing versus "empty" elements, general information on presentation and style in both SGML and XML, and the implications of the impending full implementation of XML on SGML in general and EAD in particular.

Chapters 4, 5 and 6 may be of most interest to programmers and systems staff due to their needs to select software, administer EAD servers and systems, and understand the technical aspects of SGML and XML.

Finally, chapter 7 provides detailed information on the use of EAD's linking elements, which facilitate hypertext and navigational capabilities. A variety of useful internal and external linking features are described, including use of the Digital Archival Object <dao> element to link from finding aids to digital surrogates of archival materials. This chapter is crucial for those encoders and programmers who intend to implement EAD's rich and complex linking capabilities.

## Overview of the EAD Implementation Process

A brief overview of the implementation process is presented in this section to lay the groundwork for the ensuing chapters. In contrast with the "Overview of the *Application Guidelines,*" in which aspects of implementation were addressed in the order in which they are discussed in chapters 1 through 7 of these *Guidelines*, the present section addresses the basic steps in the order in which a repository might logically confront them.

The basic phases of EAD implementation, with all its apparent attendant complexities, can be summarized by asking three questions: [6]

- Should we implement EAD?
- How will we create electronic finding aids?
- How will we distribute them?

---

[6] Michael Fox, "Implementing Encoded Archival Description: An Overview of Administrative and Technical Considerations," *American Archivist* 60 (summer 1997): 342.

Each institution's decision to implement EAD will be influenced at least in part by practical considerations. These include such very basic concerns as whether the institution currently has or is prepared to undertake a descriptive program that produces finding aids that are consistent, both internally and with emerging national or international standards. Other questions revolve around institutional mission, goals and audience, and whether implementing EAD will in any way advance the former and serve the latter.

The big question for many institutions will be one of resources: Do we have the staff, the technical competence, and the hardware and software resources to undertake implementation of EAD? If not, is there a collaborative program we can join or develop in order to distribute the resource impact over several institutions? Finally, the question of being able to maintain an EAD program over the long term must be considered, since it will be necessary for repository staff to keep current with changes, such as the evolution of the DTD and the inevitable software upgrades and other innovations that accompany any technological tool.

Once an affirmative implementation decision has been reached, the principal stages in creating EAD-encoded finding aids will include the following:

- Evaluating your repository's descriptive practices in order to develop consistent approaches to both conversion of existing finding aids and authoring of new finding aids in EAD
- Making decisions regarding rules and protocols for descriptive conventions and style, depth of markup, assignment of controlled access headings, and the relation between EAD-encoded finding aids and MARC cataloging records
- Choosing appropriate software to author EAD files
- Acquiring (downloading) the necessary official files, such as the EAD DTD and various other files for specific software applications, and then loading these files correctly in your local environment
- Validating EAD files using SGML parsers

Finally, repositories must consider possible methods for "publication" and distribution of electronic finding aids in order to make them available to researchers. As with the authoring of encoded finding aids, a variety of scenarios and software choices are available, ranging from simple linking of finding aids to a World WideWeb site, to employing powerful (and often costly) search engines to facilitate researchers' ability to locate relevant materials. All delivery scenarios require use of a combination of conversion scripts and/or stylesheets to interpret EAD encoding for public display and retrieval purposes. Issues pertaining to making printouts of electronic finding aids may also need to be considered.

## Basic Conventions Used

To understand many aspects of these *Guidelines* you will need basic comprehension of some SGML conventions. This section is a brief introduction to these conventions; for more detailed information about SGML in an EAD context, see chapter 6.

**Elements:** The EAD structure consists of data fields, known as *elements*. Each element is assigned a unique name, abbreviation, and definition, as specified in the *EAD Tag Library*. EAD elements are represented by short alphanumeric expressions or *tag names*, which are surrounded by angle brackets (< >).

In these *Guidelines*, when each element is first introduced, both its element name and its tag name are given; thereafter, the element is referred to only by its tag name. For example, both the element name Date of the Unit and the tag name <unitdate> are given when this element is first mentioned, but in later discussions of the element, only the tag name <unitdate> is given.

Some EAD elements are known as *wrapper* elements; they must contain another element before text can be inserted. An example of a wrapper element is Scope and Content <scopecontent>, which must contain a Paragraph <p> before text can be entered. Most elements can contain other elements *or* text, but not both.

Each piece of text within an encoded finding aid is surrounded by one or more EAD tags; sometimes a specific piece of information is nested within several layers of tags. The examples in these *Guidelines* illustrate how finding aid text appears between the start-tag and end-tag of each element. For example:

```
<date>1957</date>
```

where <date> is the start-tag for the element, "1957" is the finding aid text, and </date> is the end-tag for the element. Unlike HTML, which allows you to omit end-tags for elements such as <p>, SGML permits no tag minimization; you must close every element with an end-tag.

The term *subelement* is used when the discussion focuses on a broader *parent element*. For example, within the discussion of Descriptive Identification <did>, Repository <repository>, Origination <origination>, and other elements that are available within <did> are referred to as <did> subelements. Every EAD element except <ead> is a subelement of one or more other parent elements (<ead> is the highest-level element, or *document element*, in the EAD DTD, and thus has no parent elements).

**Attributes:** Most EAD elements can be modified through the use of *attributes.* Although attributes most frequently make the meaning of an element more specific, some are instead used to control display or retrieval. For example, the Date <date> element can be used to encode dates, *except* those associated with the creation of archival materials (for which <unitdate> would be used). In some cases you may wish to specify what *kind* of date is being encoded, such as birth dates, publication dates, or acquisition dates; this is accomplished by using an attribute. Whenever attributes are applied, the attribute name and its value are noted within the start-tag of the element:

```
<date type="publication">
```

In the above example, "date" is the tag name, "type" is the attribute name, and "publication" is the attribute value. The order and syntax is always the same: tag name, followed by attribute name, followed by an equals sign, followed by the attribute value in quotation marks. Several attributes may be strung together within an element's start-tag.

Within the narrative text of these *Guidelines,* attribute names are always stated in SMALL CAPS, and attribute values always appear within quotation marks. When an attribute name is used within an example, however, it appears in lowercase to match its appearance in an encoded document (as in the example immediately above).

EAD makes extensive use of attributes, most of which are optional (the only two required attributes are LEVEL in <archdesc> and TYPE in <dsc>). For the most part, attributes make it possible to limit the number of elements needed in EAD. The developers utilized generic element names wherever possible to eliminate archival jargon that might have a specific meaning in a given institutional or international context; EAD allows more specific terms to be expressed in an attribute. For example, Component <c> has a LEVEL attribute that specifies the level within the collection's hierarchy which a given component represents--whether it is a series, a subgroup, or a subseries—in lieu of defining separate "series," "subgroup," and "subseries" elements in EAD. All attributes are fully defined in the *EAD Tag Library.*

**The DTD:** The structure of a valid EAD-encoded finding aid is controlled by the EAD Document Type Definition (DTD). The DTD defines the elements, determines the order in which they can be used and whether or not they are repeatable, and also controls which attributes are available for each element. The EAD DTD is quite flexible and will accommodate many forms of "legacy data,"[7] while also encouraging archivists to standardize their descriptive practices. This flexibility means that you will often have several options for encoding the same piece of information. When that is the case, the *Guidelines* present the options in the discussion of the element, along with any pros and cons.

**Examples:** Examples of markup are provided for each of the elements discussed in these *Guidelines*. Note that the examples focus on the element being explained and do not include required parent elements. Three fully-encoded finding aids are provided in appendix E. Note that the *EAD Tag Library* also includes one or two examples of usage for most elements.

---

[7] "Legacy data" is a term used to describe finding aids created prior to the existence of EAD. Such finding aids often must be restructured to some degree in order to fit within EAD's hierarchical structure and set of data elements.

# Chapter One

## SETTING EAD IN CONTEXT: ARCHIVAL DESCRIPTION AND SGML

## 1.1. Introduction

Encoded Archival Description (EAD) is a data structure standard for preserving the hierarchy and designating the content of descriptive guides to archival holdings worldwide. It enables Internet delivery of these guides and also ensures their permanence by providing a stable, non-proprietary data storage environment from which data can be transferred to other software environments as necessary. In technical terms, EAD comprises a Document Type Definition (DTD) for encoding archival finding aids that is written following the syntactic rules of Standard Generalized Markup Language (SGML) and Extensible Markup Language (XML).

The *EAD Tag Library*[8] identifies the names and definitions of all EAD data elements defined in the DTD. These *EAD Application Guidelines* provide interpretative guidance to enable archivists to apply the DTD accurately and effectively when encoding their repositories' finding aids. These three documents (the DTD, the *Tag Library*, and the *Application Guidelines*) together comprise complete documentation for EAD Version 1.0.

This first chapter places EAD within the broader context of other archival descriptive standards and explains the choice of SGML as its technical environment. It emphasizes that while EAD's development began in the United States and its structure is rooted in this country's descriptive practices, EAD's developers incorporated significant concepts from the international descriptive framework provided by the *General International Standard Archival Description* (ISAD(G))[9] and from national descriptive content standards such as the Canadian *Rules for Archival Description* (RAD).[10] In addition, EAD elements were assigned language-neutral nomenclature designed to circumvent terminological differences and thereby encourage international application and acceptance of the DTD.

The EAD development process has been thoroughly documented elsewhere,[11] but one point is important to emphasize in the context of these *Guidelines*, namely that both the philosophical underpinnings and the structural particulars of EAD are firmly rooted in archival principles, tradition, and theory. The EAD development group analyzed archival finding aids as documents, as well as the descriptive principles embodied in the aforementioned ISAD(G) framework, RAD, and *Archives, Personal Papers, and Manuscripts* (APPM);[12] from this the group developed and articulated a set of design

---

[8] *Encoded Archival Description Tag Library, Version 1.0* (Chicago: Society of American Archivists, 1998).

[9] *ISAD(G): General International Standard Archival Description, adopted by the Ad Hoc Commission on Descriptive Standards, Stockholm, Sweden, 21-23 January 1993* (Ottawa, Ontario: International Council on Archives, 1994). Also available at: <http://www.archives.ca/ica/isad(g)e.html>.

[10] Bureau of Canadian Archivists. Planning Committee on Descriptive Standards, *Rules for Archival Description* (Ottawa, Ontario: Bureau of Canadian Archivists, 1990).

[11] See, for example: Daniel V. Pitti, "Encoded Archival Description: The Development of an Encoding Standard for Archival Finding Aids," *American Archivist* 60 (summer 1997): 268-83. Also see the background information on the *Encoded Archival Description Official Web Site,* available at: <http://www.loc.gov/ead/>.

[12] Steven L. Hensen, *Archives, Personal Papers, and Manuscripts: A Cataloging Manual for Archival Repositories, Historical Societies, and Manuscript Libraries*, 2d ed. (Chicago: Society of American Archivists, 1989).

principles. These principles provided a conceptual foundation intended to ensure that EAD would remain grounded in the realities of past and current theory and practice. [13]

One key design principle states that EAD will accommodate both the creation of new finding aids and the conversion of existing (or *legacy*) data. EAD is indeed sufficiently flexible to achieve this, but at the same time, it seeks to foster structural uniformity across finding aids in the belief that adherence to a consistent data model increases successful document interchange among repositories and that greater standardization of finding aids would generally be a positive development. Another important design principle specifies that while a large and diverse universe of archival descriptive data exists, EAD is intended to accommodate data that supports description, control, navigation, indexing, and online or print presentation, but not necessarily data that is only intended to address local collection management needs.

---

[13] *Encoded Archival Description Tag Library, Version 1.0*, 1-3.

## 1.2. The Evolution of Archival Descriptive Standards[14]

Archives, libraries, museums, and other cultural institutions exist to preserve and protect the documentary record of human activity and to make it available for research, study, and evidentiary purposes. To carry out this mission, archival repositories have long devoted significant effort to arrangement and description of their holdings, routinely preparing detailed guides to collections so that users can locate materials relevant to their interests. Until recently, however, many of these finding aids were unpublished and therefore available only within a single repository. Archivists have long sought affordable and effective means of making their resources more widely known.

In the United States, for example, some repositories have prepared published summaries of their holdings, and during the economic depression of the 1930s, the government funded a major historical records survey as a work relief project. In the late 1950s, more systematic efforts were initiated to assemble summary descriptions of resources nationwide. The commencement in 1959 of the multivolume *National Union Catalog of Manuscript Collections*,[15] followed by the 1961 publication of Hamer's path-breaking *Guide to Archives and Manuscripts in the United States*,[16] helped identify the location and general scope of the manuscript collections within participating repositories.[17]

Helpful as these paper-based projects were, however, it was not until the advent of the MARC AMC format in the late 1970s that repositories in the United States gained the ability to disseminate information about their holdings more widely via national bibliographic systems. MARC AMC provided a *data structure standard* for sharing cataloging information about archival and manuscript holdings, enabling their integration with library bibliographic data in online catalogs. The first edition of APPM, published at roughly the same time (1983), provided a companion *data content standard* for that same cataloging information. The assignment of controlled access points[18] to the resulting catalog records enabled archival holdings to be searched with the same flexibility and precision as published materials. The advances of MARC AMC notwithstanding, the MARC records could accommodate only summary information about holdings; they could not absorb all the data in a detailed finding aid. They could, however, point to the existence of detailed paper-based finding aids. Nevertheless, it remained problematic that these detailed finding aids were not

---

[14] This section is based in part on: Steven L. Hensen, " 'NISTF II' and EAD: The Evolution of Archival Description," *American Archivist* 60 (summer 1997): 284-296.

[15] Library of Congress. Descriptive Cataloging Division. Manuscripts Section, *National Union Catalog of Manuscript Collections* (Washington, D.C.: Library of Congress, 1959-1993).

[16] Philip Hamer, *Guide to Archives and Manuscripts in the United States* (New Haven: Yale University Press, 1961).

[17] Important union lists were published in other countries as well. For example, the most comprehensive such publication in Canada was: Public Archives of Canada, *Union List of Manuscripts in Canadian Repositories = Catalogue collectif des manuscrits archives canadiennes,* edited by Robert S. Gordon (Ottawa: Public Archives of Canada, 1968).

[18] Controlled access points consist of personal, family, corporate, and geographic name headings; topical subject headings; form and genre headings; etc., that are constructed according to standards or rules or drawn from an authorized thesaurus or list.

yet part of a shared online environment. This was especially frustrating because many finding aids gradually were being produced using word processing or database systems.

Although numerous American repositories embraced the MARC AMC format, most European institutions did not, working instead toward development of ISAD(G), which was adopted by the International Council on Archives (ICA) in 1993. ISAD(G) defines twenty-six elements "that may be combined to constitute the description of an archival entity" at any level.[19] ISAD(G) also provides a set of definitions for archival terminology and formulates four general principles to guide archivists in multilevel description. The primary motivating factor behind the development of this standard was the recognition that some level of descriptive consistency would be required in order to facilitate the exchange and retrieval of archival information in unified, multirepository or multinational information systems.

EAD is a more specific structural standard than ISAD(G) in that EAD is focused on the particular type of archival finding aid typically called an inventory or register. As mentioned earlier, however, the developers of EAD looked closely at ISAD(G) and made certain that its elements were accommodated within the EAD data structure.[20] Moreover, EAD is completely compatible with ISAD(G)'s principles of multilevel description. This comfortable fit between the ISAD(G) and EAD data structures is a primary reason why interest in EAD has been strongly international in scope.

Archivists who lack experience thinking explicitly about multilevel description when implementing a hierarchical data structure such as EAD will find that ISAD(G) provides a vital framework within which to situate EAD-related decision making.

---

[19] *ISAD(G)*, rule I.2.

[20] See appendix B for a specific data element-to-data element crosswalk between ISAD(G) and EAD.

## 1.3. The Evolution of Archival Information on the Internet[21]

The emergence of EAD, in concert with the growth of the Internet, now enables repositories worldwide to disseminate more easily information about their holdings. Systems can be constructed to enable researchers to search across all the collections of a single repository (and in union systems, of multiple repositories) in order to identify and locate resources on any topic of interest. In addition, users in some environments can now navigate via hyperlinks from broad-based subject or name searches of MARC records, to EAD finding aids, to digital representations of archival materials themselves.

This new environment provides us with an opportunity to reconceptualize how we deliver information to our users, both traditional archival users and entirely new potential audiences. Archivists were quick to recognize that the Internet provided opportunities for electronic dissemination of finding aids, and many rapidly established Gopher sites for that purpose. The results of these experiments were tantalizing but ultimately discouraging. Gopher software could manage finding aids only as simple text files lacking structural or typographical formatting and important features such as footnotes; this made lengthy finding aids difficult to navigate. Moreover, no mechanism existed to link the finding aids to any corresponding MARC records. A user searching a repository's online catalog therefore had to exit the catalog and log into the Gopher site to verify whether a finding aid existed (for those still using Gophers after Web-based online catalogs became available, this particular problem was eliminated).

The emergence of the World Wide Web in the early 1990s offered significant advantages over Gophers. Hyper Text Markup Language (HTML), the SGML DTD in which Web-based documents are currently encoded, furnished the mechanism to display finding aids with additional typographical nuances and navigational techniques. Moreover, the essence of the Web—the ability to create dynamic hyperlinks among documents stored at different locations—made it possible, particularly with the appearance of Web-based online catalogs, to link a MARC record to its corresponding finding aid.

It soon became clear, however, that HTML also has significant limitations. The principal problem lies in the fact that HTML is designed to provide only *procedural* encoding to facilitate improved layout and appearance; the intellectual structure or content of documents cannot be meaningfully encoded. For example, HTML easily represents features such as differing point sizes for headings or italics for formal titles, but it cannot distinguish a scope and content note from a biographical summary, a personal name from a geographic name, or a title from a date. Thus, HTML is unable to represent visually or permanently store the complex content and structure of archival finding aids. This means that HTML cannot enable sophisticated searching or navigation, nor ensure data permanence and facilitate future data migration. Moreover, although the basic rules and structure of HTML are

---

[21] Sections 1.3 through 1.5 are based in part on: Daniel V. Pitti, "Encoded Archival Description: The Development of an Encoding Standard for Archival Finding Aids," *American Archivist* 60 (summer 1997): 268-83.

relatively stable, its development environment is quite volatile and idiosyncratic, lacking the rigor of standards that is essential to successful information exchange and data migration.

## 1.4. Why SGML?

Working as director of the Berkeley Finding Aid Project, the precursor to EAD, Daniel Pitti determined that SGML offered a promising framework for overcoming the flaws of Gopher and HTML for delivering archival finding aids via the Internet. Not only does SGML enable full structural and content encoding, but in its inherently hierarchical approach to data structure it mirrors the information hierarchies that have long been a fundamental characteristic of archival description. Moreover, through the earlier implementation of standards such as MARC AMC and the various national content standards mentioned earlier, the archival community had learned the value of using community-based open standards. Thus, SGML was compelling because it *is* a standard (ISO 8879), it is *open* (in the sense of being independent of any particular community or proprietary software application), and it is possible to design an SGML application specifically focused on the characteristics of archival finding aids, rather than having to use a more generalized scheme designed for some other type of document.

One example of a more generalized scheme is the Text Encoding Initiative (TEI), an international cooperative effort to develop an SGML DTD for scholarly texts.[22] Pitti looked closely at TEI because it was an important humanities-based computing initiative, but he ultimately found its goals incompatible with the needs of finding aids. This was because TEI was designed to encode literary and other texts as objects of study, and such documents are very different from the type of descriptive metadata that archival finding aids represent. As a result there are many elements in TEI that are not needed in EAD. More significantly, key elements required for finding aids are not available in TEI. EAD was, however, made as consistent with TEI as possible: the basic TEI header structure was incorporated into EAD,[23] and element names and attributes conflict as little as possible. Moreover, there has been active communication between the EAD and TEI developers in order to ensure that EAD remains a compatible part of the larger universe of humanities-based computing initiatives.

As noted above, SGML is inherently hierarchical. EAD reflects the ability of a well-crafted SGML DTD to identify the constituent intellectual and physical parts of a predominantly text-based document as distinct fields or *elements*, and then to *nest* component parts, or *subelements*, within them. This nesting capability allows the encoder of a finding aid (and subsequently a researcher using the encoded finding aid online) to work first with high-level elements that reflect an overview of the finding aid, and then to unfold progressively more detailed sections. Conversely, certain browser software can enable a user to search an EAD finding aid directly at item- or folder-level, then to broaden or contextualize the search by examining other items contained at the same level, or to move further up in the hierarchy to such elements as a scope and content note for a particular series or for an entire collection.

---

[22] For more information, see the Text Encoding Initiative Home Page, available at: <http://www-tei.uic.edu/orgs/tei/>.

[23] The EAD Header <eadheader> is explained in section 3.6.1.

Employing the principle of *inheritance,* SGML enables elements at a lower level in a hierarchy to inherit the information encoded in higher-level elements; this complies with the ISAD(G) rule regarding the nonrepetition of information.[24] This means that an encoder need not repeat descriptive data that already was entered at a higher level within the finding aid. Inheritance is illustrated in chapter 3, particularly in the figures in section 3.5.2.5.

[24] *ISAD(G)*, rule 2.4.

## 1.5. What is XML?

In 1996 the World Wide Web Consortium founded the XML Working Group to write a set of specifications to enable use of SGML DTDs other than HTML on the Web.[25] This need was rooted in HTML's inability to support intellectual encoding of data.

In order to be Web-deliverable, XML simplifies some of SGML's complexities; EAD included few of these complexities and so was easily made XML-compliant. The full implications of XML with respect to EAD implementation are covered in section 4.3.2 and in chapter 6.

XML was adopted by the World Wide Web Consortium as a Web standard in 1998. Version 5.0 of Microsoft's Internet Explorer browser supports XML documents, and as of early 1999, Netscape had incorporated XML into the beta versions of its next browser release.

---

[25] The formal name of the XML specification is Extensible Markup Language.

## 1.6. The Relationship between MARC and EAD

As mentioned in section 1.2, MARC records for archival materials are summaries of the more detailed information usually found in finding aids; this abridgement is necessary because a MARC record has a length limit that generally accommodates only a collection-level description. Many archivists have therefore questioned whether MARC cataloging has become redundant or unnecessary now that EAD exists. While this is a logical question, it is important to note that the inclusion of archival catalog records in integrated online catalogs enables many users to locate archival resources more easily than they might otherwise. Until cross-domain resource discovery is more developed than at present, the value of maintaining archival information (however summary it might be) in these integrated systems in order to bring primary sources to the attention of library catalog users cannot be overstated.

Some questions surrounding the coexistence of MARC and EAD derive from two aspects of MARC implementation that have concerned some archivists: first, the fact that a MARC record is just a summary, not the complete finding aid; and second, that the preparation of a MARC record adds one more resource-intensive step to the arrangement and description of archival materials. EAD seeks to address both of these concerns by identifying the relationships between MARC data elements and their corollaries within encoded finding aids. This is achieved by specifying *encoding analogs* for EAD elements that correspond directly to specific MARC fields (see section 3.5.3.1 for details).

The use of encoding analogs provides the potential for repositories to consolidate EAD encoding and MARC cataloging into a single activity by generating a basic MARC record automatically from EAD; the opposite also can be accomplished by importing a MARC record into an EAD finding aid in order to add collection-level descriptive information and controlled access points to an existing container listing. Either activity would be accomplished by means of a programming script (see section 4.3.4 for more information). A MARC record exported from an EAD finding aid potentially could be uploaded into a larger MARC system, such as RLIN, OCLC, or a local online catalog. Repositories following this course would still retain the option of further editing the resulting MARC records using whatever MARC-based editing software they normally utilize. Automated routines have not yet been developed for these processes, but repositories wishing to explore these options are advised to consult the MARC-to-EAD crosswalk found in appendix B to identify concordances between data elements.

While EAD provides a much more flexible and detailed data structure for archival description than does MARC, EAD is a data *structure* standard, not a data *content* standard, and therefore does not mandate authoritative forms of content for any of its elements. This is potentially a significant drawback for information exchange. Standardization of the content of EAD descriptive elements can be achieved, however, if repositories or consortia develop and adhere to specific data content conventions, or "best practices." The content of EAD elements that have encoding analog attributes can be chosen based on a data content standard such as RAD or APPM, or a data value standard such as the *Library of Congress Name Authority File* (LCNAF) or *Library of Congress Subject Headings* (LCSH).

## 1.7. Other Resources for Learning About EAD

In addition to the official EAD documentation comprising the *Tag Library* and these *Guidelines,* other resources are available to assist those interested in learning more about EAD.

### 1.7.1. Readings

The published literature on EAD is growing gradually, and special issues of several library and museum journals were in the planning stages as of early 1999. The first significant body of articles about EAD was published in the summer and fall 1997 issues of the *American Archivist* (vol. 60, nos. 3–4), which were special thematic issues devoted entirely to EAD.[26]

The summer issue *(Context and Theory)* contains six articles written by members of the EAD development team that provide background information on these topics: aspects of the history of archival description and of information systems that establish the context within which EAD was developed; the nature of structured information in general and of EAD's structure in particular; administrative and technical issues that must be considered prior to implementing EAD; and EAD's significance as an emerging standard for archival description.[27]

The fall issue *(Case Studies)* contains six case studies written by EAD "early implementers," which is to say archivists at institutions that implemented EAD while it was still under development, prior to publication of the Version 1.0 DTD in August 1998. The first case study describes the process of "reengineering" finding aids to conform to EAD's data structure and to maximize user comprehension within the Web environment; this article may be the very best place for an archivist contemplating EAD implementation to begin reading.[28] The other five articles detail the software, hardware, and encoding choices made by particular institutions in the course of EAD implementation. The case studies may be particularly meaningful after you have read chapters 1 through 3 of these *Guidelines,* because the significance of the various institutions' choices will then be clearer.

### 1.7.2. Web Sites

Of the many World Wide Web sites containing useful information on EAD, these two are key:

---

[26] The articles in these two issues also were reissued as: Jackie M. Dooley, ed., *Encoded Archival Description: Context, Theory, and Case Studies* (Chicago: Society of American Archivists, 1998).

[27] Several of these articles served as the basis for sections of these *Guidelines,* as indicated in the relevant footnotes.

[28] Dennis Meissner, "First Things First: Reengineering Finding Aids for Implementation of EAD," *American Archivist* 60 (fall 1997): 372-87.

The *Encoded Archival Description Official Web Site,* hosted by the Library of Congress, is the official source of the EAD DTD files. This site also includes background information on the development of EAD, instructions for subscribing to the EAD Listserv, and descriptions of major EAD implementation sites, including significant cooperative projects. The site is available at: <http://www.loc.gov/ead/>.

The *EAD Help Pages,* maintained by the EAD Roundtable of the Society of American Archivists, contain a wide variety of useful information and links to other helpful sites. Specific items include tools and helper files, descriptions of the authoring and publishing software used by various EAD implementers, readings on SGML and XML, and an "I need help!" feature in which users can write for assistance with specific questions. The site is available at: <http://jefferson.village.virginia.edu/ead/>.

Other well-maintained Web sites focusing on EAD, SGML, and XML are listed in the bibliography in appendix G.

### 1.7.3. Training Opportunities

The Research Libraries Group began offering EAD workshops to its member institutions in 1996, and the Society of American Archivists did the same starting in 1997. These two-day workshops introduce archivists to the most important structural and content elements of EAD and include numerous hands-on exercises designed to enable graduates to return to their repositories and begin adapting their finding aids to fit within EAD. Some of the SAA workshops have open registration (these are advertised in SAA's bimonthly newsletter *Archival Outlook*[29] and other archival media), while others are sponsored by regional archival societies, local consortia, or individual institutions.[30] In addition, the University of Virginia offers a five-day EAD course as part of its annual summer Rare Book School program.[31] Other organizations have sponsored EAD training courses as well.

As with most adult education, attending a workshop can be an exceptionally helpful way in which to begin learning a new standard, particularly one based in state-of-the-art information technologies. The combination of a well-informed instructor and a cadre of fellow students, eager to learn and to share their experiences, can serve both to demystify many aspects of EAD and to build confidence in your ability to succeed.[32] On the other hand, it is important to note that any complex standard takes time to master fully; a workshop can only give you the basics and get you started on the right foot. These *Guidelines* can help reinforce and expand on such instruction and lead you to additional resources to address your increasingly sophisticated learning needs.

---

[29] *Archival Outlook* (Chicago: Society of American Archivists), ISSN 1520-3379. Published six times each year.

[30] For more information about hosting an EAD workshop, contact the SAA Education Office. Email: info@archivists.org. Phone: 312/922-0140. Fax: 312/347-1452. Mail: Society of American Archivists, 527 S. Wells Street, 5th floor, Chicago, IL 60607 USA.

[31] Information is available online at: <http://www.virginia.edu/oldbooks/>.

[32] Additional training issues are discussed from a managerial perspective in section 2.5.2.

# Chapter Two

# ADMINISTRATIVE CONSIDERATIONS

## 2.1. Introduction[33]

Implementation of EAD requires consideration of the same programmatic and administrative issues that are relevant when evaluating any new initiative, particularly a new technology. Inevitably, a decision to incorporate EAD into a repository's arsenal of tools for preparing and publishing finding aids will require that a standard array of fundamental administrative issues be confronted and evaluated:

- Potential for this new technology to enhance the institution's mission and goals
- Availability of resources, possibly from new sources
- Need for careful pre-implementation planning
- Array of hardware and software choices available for use with EAD
- Staffing requirements for encoding new finding aids and converting legacy data, including training needs
- Workflow choices and methodologies
- Options for utilizing both outsourcing and cooperative ventures

In addition to the guidance provided in chapter 2, the Implementation Checklist in appendix D may be useful in helping repositories plan their approach to implementing EAD.

---

[33] This chapter is based in part on: Michael Fox, "Implementing Encoded Archival Description: An Overview of Administrative and Technical Considerations," *American Archivist* 60 (summer 1997): 330-43.

## 2.2. Mission and Goals

EAD is a fairly complex technology, and its use makes sense only if the potential benefits correspond to institutional objectives. In undertaking such an assessment, it may be helpful to focus on the essential characteristics of EAD, as described in chapter 1. To summarize that discussion, EAD is defined as the following:

- A data structure standard for finding aids that enables multiple uses of the information they contain, their interchange, and their long-term accessibility
- A communication format that enables archives to deliver finding aids electronically, including via the Internet, to distant and local users
- A technology that is standards based, computer platform independent, and that employs powerful tools for the searching, retrieval, display, and navigation of finding aids

Answers to some pointed questions about your repository's existing and potential clientele, as well as the ways in which your existing inventories are created and used, will help frame your decision making. Candor is required, but those who have previously implemented sophisticated descriptive standards or technologies, perhaps most notably MARC AMC, should feel at home with the process.

- Is digital delivery of both metadata about collections and digital surrogates of collection materials themselves an important goal for your institution?
- How might the delivery of searchable, electronic inventories fit into that objective?
- Are off-site users a target audience?
- Is it an institutional priority to attract *new* audiences, such as K-12 teachers and students?
- Who currently uses your finding aids?
- How often and in what ways (to provide contextual information about collections, to identify box numbers, to make copies for researchers) are the finding aids used?
- How many finding aids do you have?
- How many different formats (both intellectual and technological) are they in?
- How would you rate the effectiveness of your finding aids with regard to usability, quality, and completeness?
- If they are less than optimal, would you be willing to make them available electronically in their present condition?
- If not, how much revision would be required?

Your answers to questions such as these should prove helpful in determining whether the long-term benefits of EAD will be worth the effort involved in implementing it. In addition, give thoughtful consideration to the fact that for many archival repositories, adherence to standards is an increasingly important strategic goal when deploying new technology. Standards are seen as insurance that protects our investments in data creation and technology by making it possible to take advantage of a broader and more diversified marketplace, while also enhancing our ability to migrate data to future systems (an inevitable need). For decision makers such as library and archives directors who have adopted this strategy, the standards-based, community-endorsed aspects of EAD provide a convincing rationale for its adoption.

## 2.3. Resources

Assessing the benefits of EAD implementation is not enough; even highly desirable projects must be weighed against other important activities as you set priorities and allocate limited resources. Such planning decisions are subject to a complex array of local variables, one of which is the relative cost of the implementation itself. As with most institutional endeavors, the most significant costs often will be related to staffing; major tasks are outlined in section 2.5.

The investment in computer hardware and software that will be required is highly dependent on your local environment. Archives that already have the capability to produce finding aids in some sort of machine-readable form and to deliver information via the Internet are in a strong position to implement EAD encoding. On the other hand, a repository that has not yet automated its descriptive functions or integrated the World Wide Web into its public service operations would necessarily have to invest significantly in hardware and software in order to implement EAD in-house. Such institutions may wish to consider evaluating EAD's data structure for its potential to improve local finding aid practice while also investigating possibilities for identifying partners for a cooperative implementation venture.

The cost of *authoring* software ranges from trivial to somewhat significant, depending on the EAD encoding methodology selected. Similarly, software for *publishing* EAD finding aids also covers a wide spectrum of costs, depending on the approach taken. Chapters 4 and 5 provide extensive information on scenarios currently available for both authoring and publishing.

While implementation of a new technology can perhaps most readily be viewed as a sinkhole for existing resources, it is also important to recognize the very real potential for conserving resources. By defining the elements of finding aids, and by suggesting effective means of arranging and displaying those elements, EAD can save you the expense and frustration of reinventing the wheel in the context of finding aid design, not to mention the cost savings in the public service context that result from improved finding aid effectiveness. These considerations are particularly potent for a new repository or for one seeking to professionalize existing operations, but even well-established archives are likely to find in EAD some strong ideas for improving the overall effectiveness of their descriptive practices.

In addition, numerous repositories have amply demonstrated that implementation of EAD has enormous potential for attracting new sources of funding. By providing repositories with a standardized approach to including finding aids (and linked digital surrogates of collection items) within digital archives and libraries, use of EAD has been shown to raise the public profile of repositories and to give potential funders confidence in the soundness of their investments.

## 2.4. Planning

Prior planning is vital if costly missteps are to be avoided, and many issues must be resolved before the first finding aid is encoded. The six case studies written by EAD early implementers that were published in the fall 1997 issue of the *American Archivist*[34] all speak forcefully about the need to plan, and a thoughtful review of the status quo will be a good beginning. The questions you ask may include the following:

- What is the role of finding aids in your institution's reference and access system?
- Do collection-level catalog records and finding aids work together in an integrated search process?
- Does their content overlap in effective rather than redundant ways?
- Are they created in the most efficient manner, given their inherent interrelatedness?

Given that the introduction of any new technology has the potential to result in a wide variety of workflow changes, a broad review of your overall descriptive environment is highly worthwhile at the outset. For example, we may find that user access to in-depth electronic finding aids will allow us to rethink the length and level of detail of collection-level MARC catalog records.

Most centrally, however, EAD provides an opportunity to rethink the structure and presentation of your finding aids per se. Meissner has described how the Minnesota Historical Society evaluated its finding aids in the context of EAD's structure and elements before beginning markup.[35] This process included asking fundamental questions about the purpose of finding aids, their intelligibility to users when read without access to a reference archivist, their relation to collection-level catalog records in MARC, and their physical appearance. These aspects were evaluated in terms of the informational content of the finding aids, how users in the reading room perceived them, and how remote access might affect their use. Virtually every repository will find it necessary to undergo this process in order to determine how its finding aids map to EAD, both to identify relevant elements and to optimize their arrangement within a finding aid. Moreover, a thorough review of EAD is likely to suggest new techniques for inclusion and presentation of data that have not heretofore seemed necessary in a strictly local environment.

---

[34] Reissued as: Jackie M. Dooley, ed., *Encoded Archival Description: Context, Theory, and Case Studies* (Chicago: Society of American Archivists, 1998).

[35] Dennis Meissner, "First Things First: Reengineering Finding Aids for Implementation of EAD," *American Archivist* 60 (fall 1997): 372-87.

## 2.5. Major Implementation Tasks

It will come as no surprise to any administrator that staff time and other personnel-related costs are likely to be a repository's greatest expense when implementing EAD. It should also be no revelation that actual costs cannot be provided here, since they are so dependent on individual circumstances. Instead, the principal tasks that may be necessary for implementation will be described as an aid to determining the types of staffing expenses that may be incurred. The full recitation of these activities may seem overwhelming, or even discouraging at first, and perhaps beyond the reach of many archives; with forethought and planning, however, the tasks become manageable.

### 2.5.1. Selecting and Implementing Hardware and Software

Staff must evaluate hardware and software requirements and then select, acquire, and install the tools. As described in chapters 4 and 5, there are multiple options for creating EAD-encoded finding aids and delivering them to users. Because no turnkey systems are available as yet,[36] archives must assemble their own systems from a mixture of components, and it will take time to evaluate the available choices and make decisions. As always with technology, this process is complicated by rapid evolution in the computer marketplace, which makes the choice of software a moving target.

If your EAD implementation will be part of a multirepository effort or other consortial project, you must factor in the overhead attendant on decision making in a collaborative project. On the other hand, you are likely to have considerable outside expertise to draw upon as a result of working collaboratively, not to mention enormous cost savings due to sharing of hardware, software, and systems management costs.

Technology-based programs are always dynamic, subject to continuous evaluation and revision. Depending on the options chosen,[37] the level of technical expertise required to deliver finding aids electronically will range from modest to substantial. Archivists are resourceful people, and many early implementers of EAD have undertaken their projects with existing staff who have acquired new skills. Repositories that have access to in-house technical support staff, perhaps from another branch of the parent organization, may be able to tap into those resources, particularly within the context of bringing the archive into a broader digital library development effort. Purchase of support services is often a viable alternative, especially for routine activities such as setting up desktop computers and servers or installing and configuring common software such as Web browsers. SGML database search engines may, however, be less familiar to contract personnel, and so such services may be more difficult to locate or more expensive to acquire.

---

[36] The Internet Archivist software package, available from Interface Electronics, holds promise as an effective turnkey system (although some desirable features of such a system were not yet in place as of spring 1999). For more information, see the company's Web site, available at: <http://www.interface.com/ead>. See additional information in section 4.2.2.2.

[37] See section 5.2 for a description of options.

### 2.5.2. Staff Training

Staff education and training needs can be easy to underestimate or overlook when implementing a new technological standard. In addition to acquiring a working knowledge of the structure and content of EAD per se, those who will work with EAD must master specific software packages for creating, converting, and editing finding aids, and this invariably requires significant investments of time and energy.

As usual, training options range from enrolling in formal classes or workshops to turning your more self-sufficient staff loose with written EAD documentation or software manuals. As mentioned earlier, the *Encoded Archival Description Tag Library, Version 1.0*[38] is a key companion document to these *Application Guidelines*. Additional useful writings are available in print or on the World Wide Web, some of the most useful of which are listed in appendix G. The implementation case studies published in the *American Archivist*[39] describe a variety of collaborative self-education processes that are particularly effective in large or consortial environments. Whether or not you will engage in a collaborative systems implementation of EAD, joining forces with other local repositories to sponsor formal training workshops may help jump start your implementation process.

Graduate programs in archival studies have begun to incorporate EAD into their curricula on archival description and digital archives, and as a result, the job market will gradually be populated with applicants who come prepared to implement EAD. Such recent graduates will, nevertheless, often need training relevant to a repository's particular hardware and software environment. In some cases, graduate-level courses may also be available to working archivists through universities' increasingly popular distance education programs.

### 2.5.3. Encoding New Finding Aids

One hallmark of success for any new technology is its ability to incorporate new activities into existing operations and to deliver clear benefits without significantly adding to ongoing workloads. While the planning and managerial activities described above are significant, they principally represent an initial investment of time that need not be repeated, or at least continued at the same level of intensity. Ongoing operations, chiefly the encoding of finding aids and the concomitant maintenance of computing infrastructure, are where the real increase in effort is likely to occur. The most efficient implementation, therefore, will be one in which those activities can be closely integrated into, or simply replace, existing tasks on a one-for-one basis.

Most archives today create printed finding aids using word processing or database software. If one can continue to create finding aids in the same way and convert them afterwards, or

---

[38] *Encoded Archival Description Tag Library, Version 1.0* (Chicago: Society of American Archivists, 1998).

[39] Reissued as: Jackie M. Dooley, ed., *Encoded Archival Description: Context, Theory, and Case Studies* (Chicago: Society of American Archivists, 1998).

substitute an SGML editor for the word processor, the impact on workflow may be minimal. Indeed, the net effect of such changes, once implemented, may actually be greater efficiency and less work overall. Meissner reports on the use of standard word processing templates, which at the Minnesota Historical Society reduced the time needed for keying container lists and the subsequent cleanup of data entry errors.[40]

As will be described in later chapters, numerous encoding choices must be made that will determine how labor-intensive this process is. One major consideration is the level of detail to be employed in tagging, an issue discussed extensively in the Library of Congress, Harvard, and Yale case studies in the *American Archivist.* Protocols developed range from minimal content designation focusing on finding aid structural elements, to experiments with richer markup that includes tagging each instance of proper names wherever they appear in a finding aid. For example, Lacy and Mitchell describe the numerous hypertext links embedded within Library of Congress finding aids.[41] As with many descriptive practices, greater effort at the input stage offers the potential for improved performance at the retrieval stage.

### 2.5.4. Converting Existing Finding Aids

Conversion of existing finding aids raises another set of issues. While encoding of descriptions of newly processed collections will be relatively straightforward once a repository has "reengineered" its finding aids to optimize use of EAD, marking up existing ones invariably will be more complex, depending on their format and condition. At least three types of decisions are relevant, each of which will be familiar to institutions that have implemented MARC cataloging and the associated retrospective conversion of a catalog:

- Prioritization—Recognizing that conversion of existing data may continue for an extended period, how does a repository set priorities?
- Revision strategies—How much editing is feasible to match current institutional practices or to optimize use of EAD?
- Conversion techniques—What is the best method of converting existing finding aids, both those in word processing or database formats and those available only in paper form?

#### 2.5.4.1. Prioritization

Most repositories will face the issue of converting a substantial number of existing finding aids (often referred to as *legacy data*) into EAD, many of them replete with idiosyncratic practices, editorial changes, and handwritten annotations. As with any retrospective

---

[40] Dennis Meissner, "First Things First: Reengineering Finding Aids for Implementation of EAD," *American Archivist* 60 (fall 1997): 386. Examples of other institutional methodologies may be located via the *EAD Help Pages,* available at: <http://jefferson.village.virginia.edu/ead>.

[41] Mary A. Lacy and Anne Mitchell, "EAD Testing and Implementation at the Library of Congress," *American Archivist* 60 (fall 1997): 424.

conversion project, the first question is where to begin, particularly if resources for conversion are limited. In making this decision, consider two basic questions:

1. Which finding aids are the *most important* to convert, and
2. Which finding aids will be the *easiest* to convert?

To determine which finding aids are most important or urgent for your repository to convert, consider which of them describe the following:

- Your most prominent collections or collecting areas
- Your most heavily used collections
- Collections that might be used more often or more effectively, especially by new or remote users, if they were available online and could be searched electronically
- Collections that are stored off-site
- Collections that are split between multiple repositories at one or multiple institutions for which a comprehensive "virtual finding aid" might usefully be created
- Collections relating to other digital materials that are already available online

In addition to these issues, consider the fact that some finding aids offer more potential than others to enhance access, such as those whose content will yield greater rewards in response to a text search for key words or phrases. For example, searching a container list containing lengthy lists of names of correspondents or of photographic captions would significantly enhance name or subject access, while one chiefly comprising an enumeration of box numbers, volume titles, and span dates, such as are often used to describe certain types of organizational and governmental records, probably would not.

As for which finding aids will be fastest and easiest to convert, those initially created in some sort of digital format, whether using word processing software or a database management system, will almost certainly fall into this category. Two principal factors will influence how fast and simple that conversion is likely to be using a scripting tool or template:

- Whether the finding aid elements were predictably formatted (that is, as fields in a database, or through use of a word processing template), and how consistent this formatting is across all of your finding aids in digital format
- Whether the digital files are in the same version of database or word processing software, as opposed to existing in multiple software environments, each of which would require its own conversion methodology

### 2.5.4.2. Revision Strategies

By reviewing your existing finding aids in the context of EAD, you will obtain a good sense of how difficult they will be to encode and of the revision issues that lie ahead. Structural changes may be relatively easy for higher-level elements, such as bundling the basic data that describes an overall collection into the Descriptive Identification <did> area, or gathering a variety of types of administrative and access information in the Administrative Information <admininfo> area. On the other hand, will you take the time to *add* such types of information to finding aids that presently lack them? Will you encode container lists that lack any contextual biographical information or scope and content descriptions, or will you decide it is prudent to restrict access to such finding aids to local users until they can be enhanced for unmediated Internet access? Your own local considerations, such as user demands for electronic access to your finding aids, will help answer these questions.

#### 2.5.4.3. Conversion Techniques

The most appropriate and successful process for converting your existing finding aids into EAD will vary based on their format and condition. Finding aids that were created electronically using word processing or database formats can have EAD tags added one by one, be converted automatically, or most likely, be encoded by some combination of the two methods. Finding aids that exist only on paper will first have to be converted into electronic form, either by rekeying or by scanning and optical character recognition (OCR).

When considering the feasibility of OCR, the legibility of printed data is a significant issue. A printed guide published using a clear typeface and without complex formatting, or a photocopy of one created on a high-quality, fairly modern typewriter, usually can be successfully converted to digital format using OCR. On the other hand, a finding aid created using an early typewriter or existing only in a poor-quality carbon copy or photocopy would almost certainly have be to be rekeyed. Rekeying may also be preferable for some finding aids that are otherwise suitable for OCR if their layout and formatting is highly variable or inconsistent.[42]

Hard-copy finding aids that are the *easiest* to convert exhibit the following characteristics: (1) clean ribbon or carbon copy with uniform typing and clear typeface; (2) uniform density of typing throughout the document with little or no handwritten corrections or annotations; (3) consistent formatting throughout the finding aid (uniform spacing, tabs, and or columns throughout the document, in particular throughout the listings of contents). Finding aids that are lengthy and fit into this category would be obvious targets for early conversion, since they will be quicker to convert than multiple shorter finding aids.

Hard-copy finding aids that are *more difficult* to convert exhibit several of the following characteristics: (1) inconsistent formatting (tabs or spacing, especially within listings of contents, are not uniform throughout, resulting in irregular columns); (2) typeface is hard to read because of the use of carbon copies or irregular typing and typeface; (3) multiple annotations or corrections have been made throughout the document, including handwritten attachments and listings appended to the finding aid.

---

[42] The data conversion taxonomy that follows was developed by Jack Von Euw of the Bancroft Library, University of California at Berkeley.

The *most problematic* hard-copy finding aids to convert are preliminary or in-process listings, donor or dealer inventories, and card files. Generally such documents do not represent complete or otherwise fully satisfactory finding aids, and each repository will have to decide whether to expend resources to convert them "as is" or to wait until a complete finding aid can be prepared. Although converting such data may be anathema to most archivists, we are already beginning to find that many users (and administrators) have come to expect *all* our finding aids to be online, howsoever partial or imperfect, which may in turn cause a gradual shift in archivists' willingness to make imperfect finding aids available electronically.

Once your legacy data is in digital format, various characteristics of the data will affect how you convert it, as well as how difficult this process will be. As mentioned earlier, the *consistency* of the data will determine to what extent EAD tags can be inserted using macros or other automated processes, as well as whether a vendor would be able to successfully interpret the meaning of various types of information if you are considering contracting this work out. As described in more detail in chapter 4, some word processing software packages include scripting or macro languages that allow users to automate certain processes. In many cases, however, inconsistencies in formatting or descriptive practice will limit the extent to which repositories will be able to tag their finding aids in this manner. You should therefore probably assume that staff will have to spend some time doing manual editing of certain portions of your finding aids.

The *level of tagging* to be employed is another important consideration during the data conversion process, and reasons may exist to make different choices for converting legacy data than those you will use when encoding new finding aids. For example, you may be planning to reorganize aspects of your new finding aids to more clearly label specific EAD data elements (such as if your legacy data does not clearly separate biographical information from scope and content, or if details regarding acquisition and processing have been intermingled). It may or may not be feasible, however, to revisit all of your legacy finding aids at this level of detail during an EAD conversion project, and careful decisions will have to be made about which types of changes will and will not be made. A careful reading of chapter 3, in which the significance of particular groups of EAD tags is described in detail, will help you decide where to focus your efforts.

### 2.5.5. Other Ongoing Tasks

Once implementation is underway, the project must be appropriately managed. The work of purchasing equipment, contracting for services, negotiating with partners, and hiring, supervising, and/or training staff is not trivial. An ongoing EAD operation will need personnel to mark up, proof, and test the finding aids, to load and manage files on computer servers, and to handle any associated image files. Quality control is important for any work that is outsourced.

If the finding aids are to be electronically linked to an online catalog, linking data (in USMARC field 856) must be added to each corresponding MARC record as a pointer to the electronic finding aid. As described in section 5.3.2.3, the archive also may wish to supply an HTML version of each EAD finding aid for users with Web browsers that do not support SGML or XML. If so, a process for converting the EAD files into HTML must be developed and implemented.

Finally, many EAD implementers are offering explanatory materials on their Web sites describing what finding aids are, how they are used, and the methods provided for accessing them online.[43] This is an important service to provide to your electronic users to help ensure that they do not flounder for lack of a reference archivist to help them navigate your finding aids. The text of such online guides must of course be prepared, encoded, loaded, and maintained.

### 2.5.6. Publicity

Lastly, you will almost certainly want to focus some staff energy on publicizing the results of your EAD efforts to your important constituencies, given the inherent appeal of "digital archive" projects. Such constituencies may possibly include your governing board or other parent agency, existing clientele such as teaching faculty or in-house curators, and potential donors of both archival materials and monetary resources.

---

[43] Excellent examples of such sites, such as those at the Library of Congress and Yale University, are accessible via the *EAD Help Pages,* available at: <http://jefferson.village.virginia.edu/ead>.

## 2.6. Outsourcing

Contracting for services is a popular approach to special projects and may be appropriate for some aspects of EAD implementation. The choice between performing work in-house and contracting it out is usually one of trading time for money: doing the work oneself may involve lower out-of-pocket expenses, but it consumes precious staff resources. In some institutions, it may be easier to obtain special funds such as grants, gifts, or exceptional budgetary allocations for special projects such as EAD implementation than it is to hire additional regular staff. Certain tasks such as finding aid encoding, database installation and administration, and Web server maintenance are obvious choices for outsourcing.

The involvement of regular staff is crucial to several aspects of this process. Planning and operational oversight are difficult, if not impossible, to contract out, although consultants may be very helpful at the start-up phase. Moreover, the contracting process itself generates administrative overhead. Certain skills are required: (1) a knowledge of the issues involved; (2) the ability to articulate institutional objectives and convert them into clearly measurable vendor deliverables; (3) familiarity with contract negotiations; and (4) an understanding of the dynamics of contract supervision, especially where quality control is an issue. A successful vendor-customer relationship requires both parties to have a clear and detailed agreement on their objectives and requirements. This would be particularly important in outsourcing EAD encoding, for example, given the wide range of choices that EAD provides for marking up finding aids. The options exercised in this area will directly and perhaps significantly affect the time required to encode a finding aid, and consequently, the cost of conversion.

## 2.7. Cooperative Ventures

The value of seeking partnerships for a collaborative implementation of EAD has been mentioned several times in this chapter in the context of topics such as combining resources, sharing expertise, and cosponsoring training events. Early implementers of EAD, institutions large and small, have found direction, support, and funding through consortial undertakings and other joint projects. Early examples include the intra-institutional cooperative efforts at Harvard, Yale, and the Library of Congress, as well as multi-institutional projects such as the Online Archive of California (including the nine campuses of the University of California and numerous other cultural repositories within California) and the American Heritage Virtual Archive Project (involving UC Berkeley, Duke, Stanford, and Virginia).[44] While other archivists may view such repositories as large and well-staffed organizations for which EAD implementation is surely trivial, these project groups in many cases comprise a loose federation of smaller operations (as small as one to three persons) whose staff are as thinly spread across multiple responsibilities as in many small, independent repositories.

The ways in which consortial members have been able to work together to plan for, educate themselves about, and implement EAD suggests a cooperative model that others may beneficially replicate. This approach will be particularly useful for planning, procurement of hardware and software, documentation, training, and technical support. As described in chapters 4 and 5, setting in place your approaches to authoring and publishing EAD finding aids can be both costly and extremely challenging. Sharing a joint implementation of these aspects of a project can therefore make the difference between feasibility and impossibility, particularly for smaller repositories. In addition, the added value that may accrue from the high public profile of a large collaborative project, particularly for a small archives affiliated with more visible institutions, should not be underestimated. And once a large institution or consortium has its EAD implementation up and running, it may be a straightforward process to take on more partners.[45]

On the other hand, it is important to recognize that consortial activity may carry other types of overhead. Broader discussion of issues and options in order to reach consensus invariably takes longer when more partners and interests are involved. Strong leadership and expertise is important to any such group; if the project leaders are disorganized, biased toward certain partners' interests, or otherwise ineffective, the project may be in trouble. Finally, if all partners to a cooperative endeavor do not take active part and make their required contributions, frustrations will inevitably result, since freeloaders ultimately cost everyone else time and money.

---

[44] Web sites for these projects may be located via the *EAD Help Pages,* available at: <http://jefferson.village.virginia.edu/ead>.

[45] The University of California's Online Archive of California project, to name only one example, exemplifies every potential advantage of collaboration mentioned in this paragraph.

## Chapter Three

## CREATING FINDING AIDS IN EAD

## 3.1. Introduction

Although EAD is a new descriptive development emerging from the information technology of the late twentieth century, its structure, and hence archivists' ability to use EAD, rests squarely on time-honored principles of archival arrangement and description. Much of the information considered essential for creating a good EAD finding aid is data that archivists have routinely created during the process of acquiring, organizing, and describing materials. This chapter seeks to demonstrate that much about EAD is familiar ground for archivists. It is hoped that it will reveal to readers what many archivists have discovered after taking an EAD training workshop, namely that mastering EAD's intellectual framework and tagging structure is a relatively straightforward process.

Nevertheless, some of the terms, descriptive practices, and encoding concepts found herein are likely to be new to many readers, and you may find it helpful to read through the entire chapter once for a general understanding of EAD's structure, and then a second time to master some of the finer points of specific elements. Although for the most part these *Guidelines* separate the discussion of implementation issues and technical matters from the explanation of the DTD's structure and choice of elements, some overlap is unavoidable. At each point in chapter 3 where a technical term or implementation issue is relevant to the discussion of an element or group of elements, a very brief explanation is given on the spot, and a cross reference leads you to a more substantial discussion of the topic elsewhere in the *Guidelines*.

The next three sections of this chapter comprise an orientation to EAD within the context of archival description:

- Section 3.2 briefly reviews how archivists collect information about the materials they administer
- Section 3.3 analyzes how tagging approaches, depth of markup, and best descriptive practices intersect in EAD
- Section 3.4 discusses the concept of multilevel description that is central to EAD's structure

Section 3.5, the core of the chapter, provides a step-by-step description of the process of creating an EAD finding aid, focusing on the relationship between the parts of a finding aid that most archivists find familiar and their corresponding elements and attributes in EAD. When various encoding approaches are possible, the pros and cons of each are discussed. It is suggested that you also refer to the corresponding element descriptions and examples in the *EAD Tag Library* as you read this section.

Finally, section 3.6 explains how to include metadata or bibliographic information about the finding aid itself, which is essential for publishing your finding aids on the Web.

Until you are comfortable with the EAD structure and tag set, you may want to refer back to this chapter while encoding your finding aids. The chapter's section structure will assist you in locating the information you need. It may also be useful to refer to appendix A, Minimum Recommended Finding Aid Elements, to correlate the use of particular EAD elements with good descriptive practice.

## 3.2. Collecting Data for a Finding Aid

Creating a finding aid is a descriptive process that may begin before a collection ever arrives in your repository.[46] If, for example, you are a manuscript curator or archivist for a collecting repository, you will likely gather crucial data about the origins, provenance, and chain of custody of a collection during the course of identifying the materials for possible acquisition. You may meet with the creator and/or donor of the records or papers, learn something about the context in which the materials were generated, and glean from background reading, conversation, and examination, bits and pieces of information about the organization, scope, and content of the materials under consideration. A memorandum summarizing your findings may be prepared, filed away, and possibly forgotten about until months or years later when the materials arrive on your doorstep through donation, deposit, purchase, or transfer. At that time, you may pull out this memorandum and compare it to the materials before you. You will likely also review packing lists and legal documents, such as the deed of gift or purchase agreement. Through this discovery process, you will begin to piece together a rudimentary accession record or preliminary catalog record containing some of the basic content of a future EAD finding aid:

- What is the name or *title* of the collection?
- Who *created* the material and for what purpose?
- What *dates* does it cover?
- *How much* material is there?
- What *genres or formats* are represented?
- How did it come into the repository's control or possession?
- Who or what was the immediate *source* of the acquisition?
- Are there *restrictions* on access or reproduction?
- Has it been assigned a *unique identification number* for tracking within the repository?
- What *storage location* will be used for the materials?
- Have any materials been *separated* for transfer to other units in your repository?

The more information that can be captured at this stage the better, especially if the facts are based on oral sources and are unrecorded elsewhere. This initial collection-level description may be viewed by the archivist more as inventory control than an access tool, but gathering and recording the information is an investment in archival description that will reap significant rewards when the data is teased apart and easily mapped to counterpart EAD data categories. From these earliest acquisition and accessioning records, a finding aid author can begin to extract a fundamental description of the collection in its entirety (what we later refer to in section 3.5.1.1 as the "high-level <did>") and start to outline important background information about how the collection was acquired and the conditions under

[46]Throughout this chapter, the term "collection" is used to refer to the entirety of any body of archival materials, e.g., a fonds, a record group, a body of personal papers, or an artificial collection.

which it is administered by the repository and used by researchers. This latter "administrative information" (explored further in section 3.5.1.4) will help future finding aid readers know how to approach the collection and make use of the data they find.

At the outset of processing the collection, additional information suitable for inclusion in an EAD finding aid is assembled. In an effort to educate yourself about the materials, you may track down biographies, agency histories, or corporate chronologies about the creator. You may prepare a crib sheet to refer to during processing that identifies the key dates and events in a person's or organization's life. As suggested in section 3.5.1.5, this processing aid can become a public reference tool when included in an EAD finding aid as a biographical note or agency history designed to enhance researchers' understanding of the origins and context of the archival materials. Also easily accommodated in EAD are bibliographies, such as the list of sources you may have prepared during your background research, and other types of "adjunct descriptive data" described in section 3.5.4.

Background reading and consultation of external sources continues throughout processing, but the next stage of organizing and describing a collection involves studying its existing order and structure to identify its majors parts and deduce how those parts have been or could be divided into smaller components. Once the organization has been determined, the focus shifts to issues of arrangement, which relate to how the materials are filed (alphabetical, chronological, etc.) within the higher-level components. During the analysis of the collection, you will likely record information about its current organization and arrangement and may incorporate such information into a processing proposal, which outlines how the various parts will be prepared for research use. In delineating both the original and projected structure of the collection, the processing proposal lays the groundwork for building a multilevel EAD finding aid, which, as described in section 3.4, provides a summary description of the whole collection, followed by progressively more detailed descriptions of the parts.

As you work your way through the collection, you begin to build a description of its components. This accomplishes two key purposes: to reflect the components' relationship to the whole and to one another, and to assign to each component key pieces of information such as a title, date, physical location, quantity, and others. Section 3.4 discusses this whole-to-part relationship, while section 3.5.2 explores how the component descriptions are incorporated into an EAD finding aid.

At the same time that you are creating your component descriptions, you are also perhaps recording the major themes and topics covered in the collection, identifying the types of materials represented, listing people and organizations of interest, and noting the existence of alternative finding aids and access tools. All of these are important pieces of description that have clearly defined places in the EAD structure, as illustrated in later sections of this chapter.

As you read through these subsequent sections, you are likely to recognize that EAD incorporates much of what you currently do in the area of archival arrangement and description. Please note, however, that EAD is more than a structure for accommodating current descriptive practices; it has the potential to improve those practices. EAD already has begun to force archivists to think more critically about our descriptive practices and to encourage us to bring local, national, and international practices into a more rigorously conceived framework. Furthermore, EAD paves the way for finding aids to become more dynamic in an online environment and offers possibilities for building multirepository union databases of finding aids, conducting searches across multiple finding aids and repositories using one or more elements contained in EAD, and manipulating individual finding aids in new ways as we become more aware of how our researchers approach and use these tools.

## 3.3. Evaluating Descriptive Practices

EAD is a complex structure that, if fully utilized, presents your repository with opportunities to compile, search, retrieve, and otherwise customize your finding aids in an infinite number of ways—many of which might be quite nontraditional, and some of which are as yet unforeseeable. The potential for doing this derives almost entirely from consistent and extensive encoding of the intellectual content within the finding aids. By using EAD's intellectual content tags judiciously, one can create a highly flexible finding aid that can function both as the kind of linear document that we are accustomed to creating and as a structured, searchable database.

### 3.3.1. Analyze Existing Finding Aid Structure

In their eagerness to exploit this new technology, some repositories may leap into converting their old finding aids or creating new ones with little regard as to whether their existing access tools provide "good" or complete descriptions of the archival materials, or whether they provide the appropriate contextual information needed by researchers to understand the materials. Because of the need to secure funding and build staff expertise in EAD, these repositories may decide to tag existing finding aids "as is," with the intent of returning later to clean them up. Realistically, however, it is unlikely that such cleanup will actually take place. Nonstandardized finding aids will reproduce local idiosyncrasies online, where they will be encountered by inexperienced archival researchers who do not have an archivist nearby to help them interpret the information. Because EAD enables you to incorporate individual finding aids into conglomerate databases of multiple finding aids, inconsistencies in content or structure across finding aids may result in union databases that will be difficult to search or manipulate.

It is therefore essential that encoded finding aids be clear and intelligible *to remote users* who will encounter them online. If they are not clear, then you have gained nothing by encoding and disseminating your finding aids in this fashion and may actually discourage some users. Before attempting to embark on an EAD project, it is recommended that you consider the various issues raised in chapter 2 and appendix D and conduct a careful analysis of existing finding aid practices. In terms of the latter, look at each individual piece of information and how it is currently structured in your finding aids. You should then determine if this information belongs in more than one EAD data element, in which case it may be best to divide the data appropriately among elements to ensure the long-term usefulness of the information. Also be sure to ask yourself what function a piece of information serves in the finding aid and whether it would be intelligible if presented to a user in an online environment where an archivist is unavailable to elucidate its meaning. If the information included in an existing finding aid is not sufficiently self-explanatory or helpful, then it should either be revised before inclusion, or it should be eliminated.

It is equally important to consider the *completeness* of your finding aids. Oftentimes a repository has only a container list for a collection, which may be adequate as a retrieval tool within the confines of the institution, but which may be utterly useless to a researcher in an online environment due to lack of contextual information, such as a biographical sketch or agency history and a summary of the contents. Though it will take time to add this critical, even if brief, information to the encoded finding aid, untold benefits will accrue to the repository and to researchers. We need to reevaluate our assumptions about users' understanding of the information being presented in our finding aids. Even such seemingly insignificant aspects as headings for the various sections of a finding aid should be reviewed in a new light.

### 3.3.2. Structure EAD Documents Consistently

If EAD is to achieve its full potential, archivists must begin to implement "best practices" when describing archival materials. This means that we should *use national and international data structure and data content standards* to supplement the guidance given in these *Guidelines* and in the *EAD Tag Library*. One such data structure standard is ISAD(G),[47] which (as explained in sections 1.1 and 3.4) offers international guidelines for creating multilevel descriptions of archival materials similar to those found in EAD finding aids. ISAD(G) consists of two major segments: (1) a segment that identifies the essential data elements or information buckets that should be used to describe an entire archival unit or one of its components; and (2) a segment that provides rules for showing the hierarchical relationship between the whole and its parts. ISAD(G) is not as specific as EAD with respect to finding aid data, but it offers a useful model for determining both essential elements and the amount of descriptive detail an archivist may wish to gather at each hierarchical level.

In addition to consulting national and international standards, *be consistent locally* in how you create finding aids, for example, by requiring certain key elements to be completed for every finding aid or standardizing the way in which component descriptions are created. EAD does not, for the most part, require that elements be presented in a given order, but it does support a logical progression of information, as outlined in subsequent sections of this chapter. As in MARC, only a handful of elements are required to produce a valid EAD document.[48] Employing only the *required* EAD elements does not mean, however, that the MARC record or the encoded finding aid is a good or even adequate representation of the collection. It is perfectly possible to have a valid EAD-encoded document that contains nothing but empty elements;[49] the SGML authoring software can detect only that the required elements are present and that certain elements are in the correct order. There are no MARC police, as the saying goes, and there won't be any EAD police either. Each repository must be responsible for ensuring that key elements are included in every finding aid and that the elements are used as intended.

---

[47] *ISAD(G): General International Standard Archival Description* (Ottawa, Ont.: International Council on Archives, 1994).

[48] These required elements are listed in **bold** in appendix A. Note that the required elements alone do *not* comprise a complete finding aid.

[49] An empty element consists of a start-tag and an end-tag containing no text or data.

Careful reading of these *Guidelines* and the *EAD Tag Library* should help encourage responsible and effective use of the EAD element set. Both documents are intended to foster community-wide discussion and usage by providing a sound explanation of the EAD structure, identifying key options permitted by the DTD, and theorizing on potential costs and benefits of various approaches. It would be premature at this stage of EAD's development to dictate a uniform sequence of elements across repositories or to recommend a particular degree or depth of encoding. Additional analysis of how markup affects display and retrieval must be done, and greater input and feedback from the user community should be gathered. The important things for now are to make certain that you are including those elements about which the community has achieved some consensus (as recommended by these *Guidelines* and by relevant external standards), that you are using elements and attributes in accordance with the DTD, and that the data included within each element matches the element's definition.

Appendix A and subsequent sections of these *Guidelines* identify a core set of about 30 elements considered necessary to construct a *minimum* useful and logical description of a collection. While including these elements does not guarantee the quality of the information entered into each, it does at least ensure that the most important intellectual pieces of a finding aid are available to users. While all finding aids should incorporate at least the EAD elements given in appendix A, you always have the option of including more elements and may at any point revise a finding aid to add more information.

### 3.3.3. Use Content Standards and Authority Files

It is important to note that while EAD provides a standardized structure for information about finding aids and the collections they describe, it does not, in its present form, mandate the use of any standards for how the *content* of each data element is determined and entered, in other words, through the use of standard authority files. The optimal way to ensure consistency in the content of EAD elements is to use existing content standards that are relevant to a repository's country, profession, or subject area for major access points contained in finding aids. For example, construct selected name elements and the titles of archival units according to descriptive rules and conventions such as the following:

- *Anglo-American Cataloguing Rules, 2nd Edition*
- *Archives, Personal Papers, and Manuscripts*
- *Graphic Materials*
- *Rules for Archival Description*
- *Library of Congress Name Authority File*

When encoding selected personal, corporate, or geographic names, functions, occupations, subjects, or genres and forms, use controlled vocabularies such as the following:[50]

---

[50] A full bibliographic citation for each of the sources listed below can be found in the "Thesauri and Rules for Archival Description" section of appendix G.

- *Art and Architecture Thesaurus*
- *Canadian Subject Headings*
- *Dictionary of Occupational Titles*
- *Thesaurus for Graphic Materials*
- *Library of Congress Subject Headings*
- *Medical Subject Headings*
- *Moving Image Materials: Genre Terms*
- *National Council on Archives Rules for Construction of Personal, Corporate, and Place Names*
- *Revised Nomenclature for Museum Cataloging*
- *Thesaurus of Geographic Names*
- *Union List of Artists' Names*
- *UNESCO Thesaurus*

As with most things, however, there is a trade-off between the amount of time you spend identifying and entering authorized forms for data and the long-term benefits in access that accrue. The capabilities of available software may influence how you evaluate this trade-off, although you should bear in mind that system capabilities will change over time. You may decide that you will use standardized data for major access points in encoded finding aids, but not for minor ones, especially if your system is likely to search and display high-level elements first. For example, the title of a collection, its span dates, and personal, corporate, and place names appearing in the highest level scope and content note (which reflect the major aspects of the collection) might be controlled, but not those appearing at lower levels in finding aids.

As an alternative, you might choose to add controlled access points such as names and subject headings only at those points where such names or subjects appear in the materials being described, at the series, file, or even item level. The benefit of this approach would be that users' searches could take them *directly* to relevant materials in a finding aid. For repositories that are already creating authority-controlled subject and added entries for their MARC records, specifying these same terms in the finding aid does not entail additional work. These and others issues concerning the use of controlled vocabulary terms are discussed in greater detail in section 3.5.3.

Section 3.5.3 also describes another means by which EAD-encoded finding aids can interact with existing standards, namely through the use of *encoding analogs*. Encoding analogs are attributes on EAD elements that correspond in type and function to fields or subfields found within other data structure standards such as MARC. Encoding analogs have been included in EAD to permit the exchange of finding aid data in systems that conform to relevant national and international data structure standards. As described in section 1.6, a potential benefit for repositories heavily invested in MARC cataloging is to be able to extract a skeletal MARC record from the encoded finding aid, or conversely, to build the framework of an encoded finding aid from an exported MARC record.

### 3.4. Understanding Multilevel Description

As suggested in section 3.2, archivists typically gather and compile information that describes both the entirety of a unit of archival materials and the unit's component parts. EAD fully enables expression of these multiple descriptive levels that are central to most archival finding aids and that reflect the levels of hierarchy present in the materials being described.

The EAD structure was formulated in an environment that was fairly independent of technical considerations. EAD's developers focused much of their discussion on the content of finding aids, that is, the types of information that are conveyed about a body of archival materials. The group never lost sight of the fact that the structure had to be translated into SGML at some point, but much of the analysis involved teasing apart and identifying the structural components of archival description. Through this analysis, the group determined that the same types of information recur throughout a single finding aid at all levels of description. Steve DeRose, the group's SGML consultant, looked at a sample finding aid and remarked that there were actually three finding aids in that document: one that describes the collection as a whole, one that describes the large groupings of materials within the collection, and one that describes the files or items within the groupings.[51] This led to conceptualizing different "views" of a collection as represented in a finding aid.

A typical finding aid has two or three views of a collection, each of which describes the same body of materials, but at varying levels of detail. The first level describes the entire collection in a very general way. It usually gives an overview of the types of material present, points out significant people and subjects represented, and provides provenance and access information. This first level of description may include a biographical sketch or agency history and a scope and content note that describes the collection in its entirety.

The next level might focus on groupings of material within the collection, describing each in more detail than was done at the first level, highlighting more specific material types and additional individuals and subjects represented. This mid-level description may be represented in a finding aid by narrative descriptions of series or subseries within the whole. Depending on the complexity of the collection and institutional practices, this mid-level description may be unnecessary.

Finally, each file, or possibly each item, may be described. This description often takes the form of a container or folder list, which explicitly lays out the intellectual hierarchy of the materials and is used by researchers to request materials.

As explained more fully in subsequent sections of this chapter, the Archival Description <archdesc> element encompasses these unfolding, hierarchical levels by first allowing a descriptive overview of the whole, followed by more detailed views of the parts, or Components <c> (see section 3.5.2). The descriptions of the parts are bundled inside one or

---

[51] Bentley Fellowship Finding Aid Team discussions, July 1995.

more Description of Subordinate Components <dsc> elements (see section 3.5.2.5), which represent the mid-level and file-level views noted above. Data elements used to describe the whole unit at the <archdesc> level are available or repeatable at all the <c> levels within the <dsc> (see Figure 3.4a). In addition, information is inherited at each level from the higher levels that precede it.

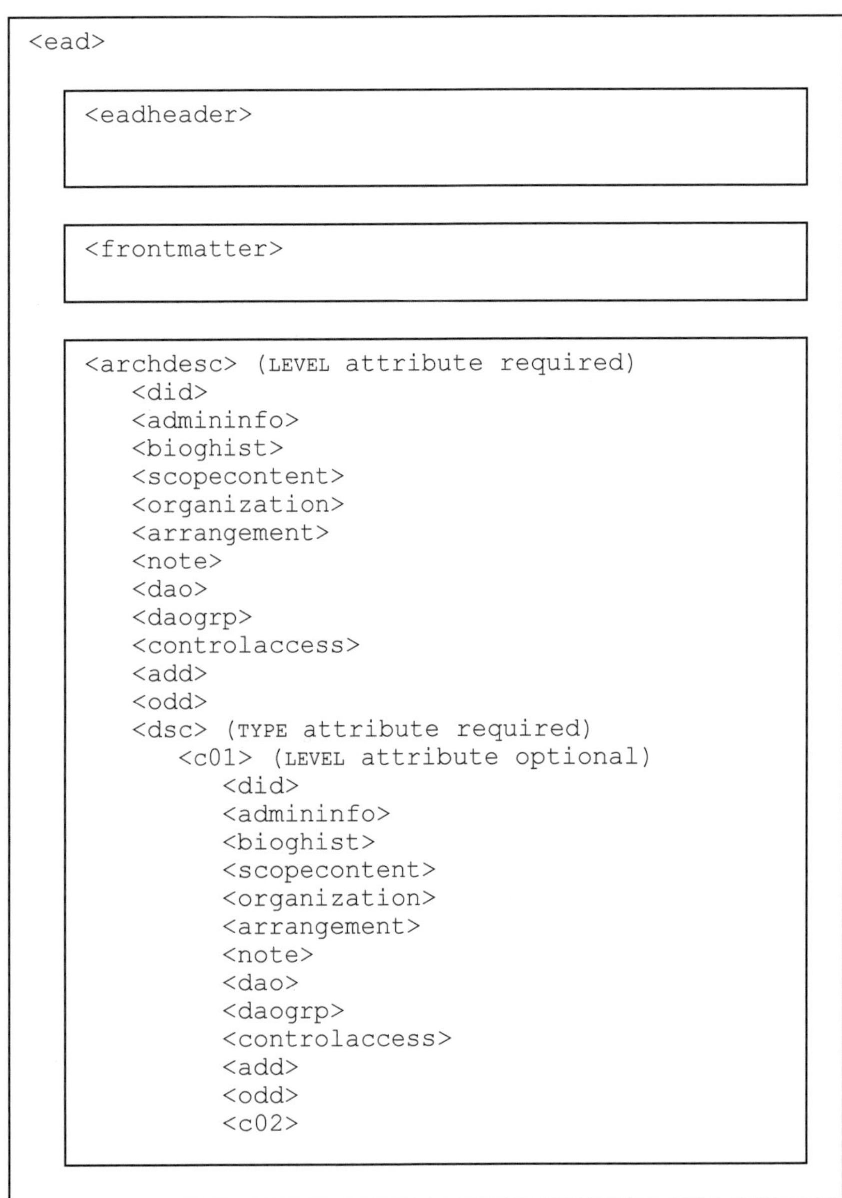


**Figure 3.4a.** *High-Level Model for the Encoded Archival Description (EAD) DTD.*

In embracing the concept of multilevel description, EAD captured the spirit and intent of two other important archival standards: ISAD(G) and the Canadian *Rules for Archival*

*Description* (RAD). As noted in section 3.3.2, ISAD(G)[52] provides a mechanism for first describing an entire body of archival materials and then proceeding to describe the parts of the fonds or collection using the same areas of description or elements that were used at the top level. The sum total of these descriptions, presented in a hierarchy, constitute "multilevel description." This whole-to-part relationship is also directly addressed in RAD, a national data content standard that reflects the ISAD(G) structure. RAD states: "The description of the fonds as a whole constitutes the highest or first level of description and the descriptions of its parts constitute lower levels of description. The description of the fonds in these rules consists of a set of descriptions which show the fonds as a dynamic and organic whole, consisting of series which in turn may consist of files which in turn may contain items. Each of these parts becomes (or has the potential to become) an object of description, resulting in multiple descriptions that need to be linked hierarchically to represent the part-to-whole structure of a fonds."[53]

The rules expressed in ISAD(G) and RAD are intended to encompass complete finding aid systems, including archival inventories and registers, MARC records, databases, and any other type of descriptive mechanism employed by archivists.

---

[52] ISAD(G), section 1.0.

[53] *Rules for Archival Description.* (Ottawa, Ont.: Bureau of Canadian Archivists, 1990), section 1.0A1.

## 3.5. Building an EAD Finding Aid

The preceding sections of this chapter have attempted to lay the theoretical foundation for the more detailed examination of EAD elements in section 3.5. The order in which we discuss these elements does not necessarily correspond to the order in which you might draft various sections of a finding aid, nor does it follow strictly the structure of the EAD DTD, which requires that a valid EAD instance[54] begins with the outermost EAD <ead> tag, followed first by metadata (in the mandatory EAD Header <eadheader> and optional Front Matter <frontmatter> elements) and next by the Archival Description <archdesc> (see Figure 3.4a). We elected instead to begin with <archdesc>, since it embodies the bulk of the finding aid and contains the information archivists are most accustomed to including in their inventories and registers. Yet before we become immersed in <archdesc>, it may be helpful to say a few words about the other high-level elements, which would appear before <archdesc> in an encoded finding aid.

The document element <ead> encloses all other elements. It indicates to a computer that what follows is a machine-readable version of a finding aid that has been encoded using the SGML document type definition known as Encoded Archival Description. Setting the AUDIENCE attribute in <ead> to "external" will display the contents of all of the subelements, unless the attribute in an individual subelement is set to "internal." The element <ead> also has a RELATEDENCODING attribute that can be used to declare a descriptive encoding system, such as MARC, Dublin Core, or ISAD(G), to which many EAD elements can be mapped using the ENCODINGANALOG attribute. <eadheader> and <frontmatter>, the other two high-level elements inside <ead>, are discussed in detail in section 3.6 at the end of this chapter.

The required <eadheader> is an essential part of a properly encoded finding aid; it contains metadata about the title, author, and creation date of the finding aid, as well as information about the language in which the finding aid is written and details about its encoding. The optional <frontmatter> element includes subelements that can be used to create nicely formatted title pages and other publication-type prefatory material such as acknowledgements and introductions.

Since EAD permits a great deal of flexibility in the order of information within <archdesc>, these *Guidelines* discuss the <archdesc> subelements in an order that matches a suggested sequence for the information in an online finding aid. This order is unlikely to correspond exactly to the manner in which you collect and compile the information in your finding aids. As mentioned in section 3.2, information for portions of a finding aid may have been gathered over a long period of time. When processing a collection, particularly one that is large and complex, you may draft descriptions of discrete and possibly noncontiguous parts as you complete their organization and arrangement. Presenting this information in the most "logical" order for your researchers offers a challenge that these *Guidelines* aim to help you address.

---

[54] In SGML parlance, "instance" is the term used to refer to a particular SGML-encoded document, such as a single EAD-encoded finding aid.

### 3.5.1. Describing the "Whole": Collection-Level Information <archdesc>

As you read through the following sections that discuss application of specific EAD elements, it might be a good idea to have a copy of the *EAD Tag Library* close at hand. These *Application Guidelines* provide options and guidance for use of important elements and attributes, and the *Tag Library* supplements this by specifically defining each element, listing all possible attributes, and providing additional tagged examples. If you find the examples in the following sections difficult to follow, review the basic conventions in the "How to Use This Manual" section of these *Guidelines*.[55]

Note that some of the tagged examples in this chapter omit required elements when the additional tagging would obscure the point being made in the accompanying text. Whenever you have a question as to where an element is available or which parent elements are required, consult the *EAD Tag Library*.

As noted in section 3.5, the EAD element that encompasses the text of the archival finding aid is <archdesc>, within which are nested all other descriptive elements. The <archdesc> element is a wrapper; it holds the other elements together in a cohesive package. In addition, its required LEVEL attribute identifies the highest level of description represented in the finding aid, which is usually set to "fonds," "collection," or "record group." Occasionally a finding aid may relate to only one "series," "subgroup," "subseries," "file," or "item," and those alternative values could also be selected for the <archdesc> LEVEL attribute. Although EAD accommodates such instances, these *Guidelines* have been written with the assumption that most inventories and registers will capture at least a basic description of the highest-level fonds, collection, or record group before describing individual components, and that the <archdesc> LEVEL attribute should therefore reflect the highest tier in the collection's hierarchy. Lower tiers in the hierarchy are identified by setting the LEVEL attribute in the component descriptions, as explained in section 3.5.2.

There are several other attributes in <archdesc> that can be used to control or provide information for the entire finding aid:

- Setting the AUDIENCE attribute to "external" renders the text in all <archdesc> subelements viewable by all users, unless the attribute is set to "internal" on specific subelements *and* your server has the ability to hide the specified text from users outside your repository.
- Likewise, if MARC will be the only encoding analog used for elements in the finding aid, the RELATEDENCODING attribute can be set to "marc" in <archdesc>, and that value will apply to all the subelements.
- The LANGMATERIAL attribute specifies the language of the collection materials. These *Guidelines* recommend that you use the appropriate 3-letter code for that

[55] You should also consult later chapters of these *Guidelines* for certain technical issues affecting encoding. For example, see section 4.3.5 regarding the use of Headings <head>, whitespace, and punctuation.

language, as listed in ISO 639-2, *Codes for the Representation of Names of Languages*.

- Some repositories hold collections for which the legal status of the materials is controlled by statute; the LEGALSTATUS attribute can be used to declare this fact.
- The TYPE attribute in <archdesc> indicates whether the finding aid is of the inventory or register style.

An <archdesc> start-tag that includes this full complement of attributes may look like this (the attributes may be arranged in any order):

```
<archdesc audience="external" relatedencoding="marc"
langmaterial="eng" legalstatus="public" level="fonds"
type="register">
```

Having specified this control information in <archdesc>, the archivist then proceeds to identify some basic facts about the collection by using the Descriptive Identification <did> element.

#### 3.5.1.1. Basic Description: The High-Level <did>

The elements available within the Descriptive Identification <did> element represent the basic building blocks for *any level* of description in a multilevel archival finding aid. These fundamental elements answer such questions as those below:

- Which *repository* holds the material?
- *Who created* the material?
- What is the *title* of the material?
- *When* was the material created?
- *How much* material is there?
- What is the material's *subject* matter?

Because these questions apply to all levels of archival groupings, from the fonds, record group, or collection, down to the item, <did> is available at all levels of description. While a single occurrence of <did> is required (usually as the first element within <archdesc>), specific elements within <did> are not, because not all will be needed at every level of description. For example, once Origination <origination> or Repository <repository> data has been specified for an entire body of materials, it may not need to be repeated at the series or file level.

One of the advantages of bundling such information in <did> is that it serves as a wrapper for these essential pieces of information in an online environment, where retrieval of coherent chunks of descriptive information about a given archival unit is critically important to the end user's understanding of a search result. It may also encourage good descriptive practice by reminding archivists to include the same basic data at all levels of description.

The first occurrence of <did>, which represents the highest level of description for a given body of materials, should allow a researcher to determine whether the materials are pertinent to his or her line of inquiry without having to read far down into the finding aid. To facilitate this resource discovery and recognition, the first <did>, referred to hereafter as the "high-level <did>," should include the following elements, which are discussed in greater detail below:

- Repository <repository>
- Origination <origination>
- Title of the Unit <unittitle>
- Date of the Unit <unitdate>
- Physical Description <physdesc>
- Abstract <abstract>

At its most basic, the high-level <did> might therefore look like this (with the sequence of <did> subelements determined by the repository):

```
<did>
   <repository>Harry Ransom Humanities Research Center</repository>
   <origination>Stoppard, Tom</origination>
   <unittitle>Tom Stoppard Papers</unittitle>
   <unitdate>1944-1995</unitdate>
   <physdesc>68 boxes (28 linear feet)</physdesc>
   <abstract>The papers of British playwright Tom Stoppard (b.
   1937) encompass his entire career and consist of multiple
   drafts of his plays, from the well-known
   <title render="italic">Rosencrantz and Guildenstern Are
   Dead</title> to several that were never produced,
   correspondence, photographs, and posters, as well as
   materials from stage, screen, and radio productions from
   around the world.</abstract>
</did>
```

Other elements such as ID of the Unit <unitid> and Physical Location <physloc> should also be included if the repository assigns a unique identifier (perhaps an accession number) to the materials, and if a physical location of the entire collection is specified in the finding aid. It is also recommended that the high-level <did> be given a Heading <head> and be encoded fairly specifically with various subelements and ENCODINGANALOG attributes; this will enable search engines to retrieve a basic description about the collection or to facilitate the extrapolation of a skeletal MARC record. Again, each of these subelements and attributes are explained in the sections which follow. A fully encoded <did> might look like this:

```
<did>
   <head>Summary Description of the Tom Stoppard Papers</head>
   <repository>
      <corpname>The University of Texas at Austin
      <subarea>Harry Ransom Humanities Research Center</subarea>
      </corpname>
   </repository>
   <origination>
      <persname source="lcnaf" encodinganalog="100">Stoppard,
      Tom</persname>
   </origination>
   <unittitle encodinganalog="245">Tom Stoppard Papers, </unittitle>
   <unitdate type="inclusive">1944-1995</unitdate>
   <physdesc encodinganalog="300">
      <extent>68 boxes (28 linear feet)</extent>
   </physdesc>
   <unitid type="accession">R4635</unitid>
   <physloc audience="internal">14E:SW:6-8</physloc>
   <abstract>The papers of British playwright Tom Stoppard (b.
   1937) encompass his entire career and consist of multiple
   drafts of his plays, from the well-known
   <title render="italic">Rosencrantz and Guildenstern Are
   Dead</title> to several that were never produced,
   correspondence, photographs, and posters, as well as
   materials from stage, screen, and radio productions from
   around the world.</abstract>
</did>
```

Such detailed markup, which includes subelements and attributes, is recommended at the highest level of your multilevel description but may not be necessary or even desirable at the component level. Conversely, other <did> subelements such as Container <container>, Note <note>, Digital Archival Object <dao>, or Digital Archival Object Group <daogrp> are often unnecessary in the high-level <did>. The subelement <container> is discussed in section 3.5.2.4; the latter three elements are mentioned briefly in the discussion of the high-level <did> and are discussed more thoroughly in sections 3.5.1.7 and 7.3.6.

All subelements within <did> have a LABEL attribute. This attribute functions somewhat like the Heading <head> element (which is used in lieu of LABEL for non-<did> elements; see section 3.5.1.7.1) in that it can be used to generate print or display constants. The <did> subelements carry a LABEL attribute instead of a <head> subelement primarily because the information contained in the <did> subelements tends to be brief—frequently only a few words—in contrast to such elements as <scopecontent> and <bioghist>, which tend to consist of longer narrative chunks of text. If each <did> subelement contained <head>, a Paragraph <p> would also be necessary in order to enter the text of the element; this would effectively double the amount of tagging for such small bits of information.

The LABEL attribute is especially useful at the highest-level <did> to aid readers in interpreting the collection summary description, while LABEL or <head> information may be less frequently necessary elsewhere in the finding aid. For example, this markup

```
<did>
   <repository label="Repository:">
      <corpname>The University of Texas at Austin
         <subarea>Harry Ransom Humanities Research
            Center</subarea>
      </corpname>
   </repository>
   <origination label="Creator:">
      <persname source="lcnaf" encodinganalog="100">Stoppard,
         Tom</persname>
   </origination>
   <unittitle label="Title:">Tom Stoppard Papers,
      <unitdate type="inclusive">1944-1995</unitdate>
   </unittitle>
</did>
```

can generate the following display based on specifications in a stylesheet:

| | |
|---|---|
| **Repository:** | The University of Texas at Austin<br>Harry Ransom Humanities Research Center |
| **Creator:** | Stoppard, Tom |
| **Title:** | Tom Stoppard Papers, 1944-1995 |

A stylesheet is a text file or output specification that is used by a processing system in conjunction with the encoded finding aid to control how the document will be displayed or formatted.[56] Stylesheets define the appearance of each element in each of its contexts within the document. Any element can be assigned specific display features, such as font size, style, and color. A stylesheet also can be used to insert preceding characters or spacing to an element, rather than using the LABEL attribute as noted in the example above. A stylesheet allows you to modify the element's display or formatting features in relation to where the element appears in the finding aid. For example, in certain contexts, such as in the high-level <did>, you may want the <unittitle> of the collection or fonds to appear on a separate line, in a certain font size and style, and preceded by the word "Title," followed by a colon. Elsewhere in the finding aid, you may want the <unittitle> of a component to appear inline and in a smaller font size than that of the higher-level <unittitle>. The stylesheet allows you to control those decisions so you need not hardwire formatting codes into a document in the same way that you do in a word processing or HTML document.

Omitting such "formatting" instructions from your data allows you to change the appearance of all your finding aids by simply changing the stylesheet; this also will simplify the encoding of each individual EAD finding aid. Keep in mind, however, that an end user can choose to replace the stylesheet you created with a different stylesheet. Use of the LABEL attribute may better ensure that words you designate will stay with the finding aid regardless of the stylesheet attached to it.

---

[56] See section 5.3.3 for more information on stylesheets.

Note also that it is possible to create multiple stylesheets to use with your EAD finding aids. For example, you may create one stylesheet for online display and another for printed output. Creating your finding aid in EAD allows you to separate what the text actually is from how the text is rendered, thereby making it possible to process or format the same text in different ways.

### 3.5.1.2. Using the <did> Subelements

#### 3.5.1.2.1. Repository <repository>

In the distributed online environment in which many EAD finding aids will reside, inclusion of the repository's name in the finding aid is critical. This information may or may not have been recorded in finding aids in the paper environment. The <repository> element identifies the institution or agency responsible for providing intellectual access to the materials being described. As shown in the Tom Stoppard example in section 3.5.1.1, the Corporate Name <corpname>[57] and Subordinate Area <subarea> elements may be used within <repository>. This more precise markup facilitates flexible display and retrieval of the information. (You may want your parent institution's name to display in 18 point bold Times New Roman and your repository's name in 14 point bold Times New Roman, or you may want to facilitate the ability to restrict searches to collections located in specific divisions or subunits of an institution.)

Note that in most instances the repository that provides intellectual access to the materials is also the institution that holds physical custody, but when that is not the case, the name and other pertinent information about the physical custodian should be encoded in the <physloc> element.

#### 3.5.1.2.2. Origination <origination>

The <origination> element specifies the individual, family, or organization responsible for the creation, accumulation, or assembly of the described materials before their incorporation into an archival repository. As with <repository>, it is possible to embed specific name elements (Personal Name <persname>, Family Name <famname>, or Corporate Name <corpname>) within <origination> to improve specificity. Further, the ROLE attribute can be used to indicate whether the originator was a "creator" or "collector" or had some other function relative to the materials. It is also possible, as noted earlier in section 3.5.1.1, to supply such information by using the LABEL attribute in <origination> and having a stylesheet display or print the word "creator" or "collector" before or after the text that appears in <origination>. For example, the markup

```
<origination label="creator">Mary Hutchinson</origination>
```

[57] See section 3.5.3 for a discussion of controlled vocabulary elements.

in combination with stylesheet instructions, could result in either of the following outputs:

Creator: Mary Hutchinson
Mary Hutchinson, creator

In addition to the LABEL attribute, <origination>, like many EAD elements, has an ENCODINGANALOG attribute that enables you to specify a MARC or other encoding scheme field that relates to this element (in this case, the MARC 100 field). Either of the following options is valid in EAD, but the latter is more specific:

```
<origination encodinganalog="100" label="creator">Mary
Hutchinson</origination>

<origination label="creator">
   <persname encodinganalog="100">Mary Hutchinson</persname>
</origination>
```

It would also be possible to invert the <persname> data (Hutchinson, Mary) to match the formatting of a MARC 100 field for retrieval purposes. Using the NORMAL attribute would accomplish the same purpose:

```
<origination label="creator">
   <persname encodinganalog="100" normal="Hutchinson,
   Mary">Mary Hutchinson</persname>
</origination>
```

For more information about "name" subelements, see the discussion of <controlaccess> in section 3.5.3.

### 3.5.1.2.3. Title of the Unit <unittitle>

Archivists typically assign titles to collections, since no bibliographic entity such as a title page exists from which to transcribe the information for descriptive purposes. The <unittitle> element is used to provide the title of the materials, either formal or supplied, at any level of description. National descriptive content standards such as APPM or RAD often provide the best guidance for archivists in determining how to construct supplied titles for archival materials.

In the high-level <did>, the <unittitle> is the title of the collection, or perhaps of a subgroup or series, depending on what the highest level of description in the finding aid is. If the title of the body of materials includes a formal title, it may be desirable to nest the Title <title> element within <unittitle> for display or retrieval purposes. For example:

```
<unittitle encodinganalog="245">Stuart Johnson Collection of
<title>Alice in Wonderland</title> Memorabilia</unittitle>
```

This markup would permit the display or printing of the title *Alice in Wonderland* in any fashion desired by the repository, including but not limited to italics, through use of the RENDER attribute in <title> or a stylesheet. In addition, it would facilitate the retrieval of the phrase "alice in wonderland" in a <unittitle> or <title> search, and, through the use of the ENCODINGANALOG attribute, the export of the text within the <unittitle> element to a MARC record for the archival collection.

### 3.5.1.2.4. Date of the Unit <unitdate>

The inclusive dates of a collection are considered a basic part of most finding aids. In EAD it is possible to embed the dates of the materials within <unittitle> by using <unitdate>. The <unitdate> element is also available outside of <unittitle>, so both of the examples shown below are valid. Note that <unitdate> has an optional TYPE attribute that allows you to specify whether the dates are inclusive dates, bulk dates, or a single date.

```
<unittitle>Stuart Johnson Collection of <title>Alice in
Wonderland</title> Memorabilia, <unitdate type="inclusive">1905-
1928</unitdate></unittitle>

<unittitle>Stuart Johnson Collection of <title>Alice in
Wonderland</title> Memorabilia, </unittitle>
<unitdate type="inclusive">1905-1928</unitdate>
```

Each repository should *choose one of the above methods* of encoding with regard to the relative placement of <unittitle> and <unitdate> and be consistent both within an individual finding aid and across all finding aids. National descriptive standards may provide guidance on this point. Archivists who catalog their materials using APPM are accustomed to thinking about span and bulk dates for a body of materials as part of the title, while RAD users treat such dates as a separate data element in the Dates of Creation Area.[58] In either case, <unittitle> and <unitdate> information may be displayed together.

The element <unitdate> also has a NORMAL attribute that allows dates to be stated in a standardized form: YYYYMMDD. Use of this attribute would facilitate retrieval of date information if implemented consistently. However, date information is provided in numerous formats in finding aids, as in the following examples:

March 17, 1946
17 March 1946
1946 March 17
ca. 1946
1946?
1940s
n.d.
undated

[58] *Rules for Archival Description,* section 1.4.

Because of this the additional markup required to supply normalized dates for searching purposes may be prohibitively time consuming.

#### 3.5.1.2.5. Physical Description <physdesc>

Archivists use many different expressions of extent for their holdings, such as linear or cubic feet, number of boxes or other containers, or perhaps number of items. Frequently this is a very simple expression; sometimes it is a series of statements delineating quantities of various formats of material within a collection. In other cases, the physical description of a collection may include information about the method of creation.

It is possible to put a basic statement of extent into the <physdesc> element without using any subelements:

```
<physdesc>149 cubic feet</physdesc>

<physdesc>3800 photographs</physdesc>
```

In many cases, this level of markup is sufficient. The use of subelements, such as Extent <extent> and Genre/Physical Characteristic <genreform>, as well as attributes in <physdesc> can, however, render the physical description much more specific:

```
<physdesc encodinganalog="300">149 cubic feet</physdesc>

<physdesc>
   <extent>3800</extent> <genreform>black and white prints
   (photographs)</genreform>
</physdesc>

<physdesc>
   <extent>46</extent> <genreform>sound recordings</genreform>
</physdesc>
```

What is the benefit of such additional encoding? Any time information is encoded at a more granular (detailed) level, the ability to manipulate and reuse the data is enhanced. For retrieval purposes, you might want to search for a particular type of photograph, such as albumen prints, salted paper prints, or hand-colored prints. While this can be done using a keyword search, searching for these types of terms within a <physdesc> or <genreform> element improves the relevance of the search result.

#### 3.5.1.2.6. Abstract and Note <abstract> and <note>

In an online environment, it can be extremely helpful to the end user if a brief statement describing the context and content of a body of materials appears on the first or second screen of a finding aid. This can help the user immediately determine the relevance of the collection to his or her research. The <abstract> element was created for this purpose. In the high-level <did>, <abstract> may be a hybrid of a creator sketch and a scope and content note; in other words, it may contain a brief statement about the creator or collector of the materials as well as a very general summary of their scope. Summarize as briefly as possible, while still providing pertinent information; the Biography or History <bioghist> and Scope and Content <scopecontent> elements, described in sections 3.5.1.5 and 3.5.1.6, are used for more expansive information.

```
<abstract>The archive comprises records mainly from the pre-1837
Archdeaconry before its removal from the jurisdiction of York to
that of Lincoln. Most of the documents stem from the Archdeacon's
twice-yearly visitations and the cases pursued in his court, the
earliest dating from the 16th century. The Archdeaconry of
Nottingham joined with the county of Derby [from the Diocese of
Lichfield] to form the Diocese of Southwell.</abstract>
```

The <abstract> element could easily be confused with <note>, which also is available within <did>. The <note> element should not be used for summary descriptive information, but rather to cite the source of a quotation (as in a footnote), provide a short explanatory statement or user directive, or for miscellaneous purposes such as to indicate the basis for an assertion. In general, the generic text element <note> should never be used when a more specific structural EAD element is more appropriate.

```
<note><p>Note to researchers:  To request materials, please note
both the location and box numbers shown below.</p></note>
```

In the high-level <did>, a <note> also could be used to alert the reader to the fact that the materials described in the high-level <did> are in fact a component of a larger body of materials that had to be described in separate EAD instances because of the difficulties encountered in parsing and downloading a single large finding aid file for the entire fonds or record group. The creation and linking of separate finding aids for a single large collection is discussed in greater detail in connection with the Archival Reference <archref> element in section 7.3.3.

Because of its utility as explanatory text, the <note> element is also available outside <did>, as explained in section 3.5.1.7.3.

#### 3.5.1.2.7. ID of the Unit <unitid>

Archivists often assign unique identifying numbers or alphanumeric strings to units of archival material for control and citation purposes. Such identifiers include accession numbers, lot numbers, classification numbers, or entry numbers in a bibliography or catalog. The <unitid> element is used to encode such numbers; do not confuse it with <physloc> or <container>, which encode information about the physical location or housing of the material.

Two attributes are available in <unitid> that are not available anywhere else in EAD and which should be used only in the high-level <did>: COUNTRYCODE and REPOSITORYCODE. COUNTRYCODE provides the unique code, taken from the ISO 3166 *Codes for the*

*Representation of Names of Countries*, for the country in which the archival materials are held. REPOSITORYCODE contains another unique code, taken from the official repository code list for the country in which the repository is located, for the repository responsible for the intellectual control of the materials being described.[59] These two attributes relate specifically to the ISAD(G) reference codes in the Identity Statement Area[60] and guarantee uniqueness of the <unitid> in a multinational finding aid database. If desired, the attribute values could be manipulated by a stylesheet to display or print the name of the country and the name of the repository as part of the <unitid> information. At the highest level of description, a <unitid> might look like this:

```
<unitid countrycode="gbr" repositorycode="067">ES</unitid>
```

#### 3.5.1.2.8. Physical Location <physloc>

Some finding aids may include information about the location of materials within the repository. This information is encoded using the <physloc> element, which may refer to an actual shelf location or instead indicate that a collection is stored off-site, warning the researcher that the material may not be immediately available.

```
<physloc>14E:SW:6-8</physloc>

<physloc>The Mary Hutchinson Papers are stored offsite, and 24-
hour notice is required to retrieve the materials.</physloc>
```

<physloc> is repeatable, so both types of information can be provided when needed. If the repository chooses to include the shelf location in the finding aid for its own internal use, the information can be encoded but shielded from public access by using the AUDIENCE attribute (if your server is capable of suppressing information coded as "internal" when delivering your EAD files to users):

```
<physloc audience="internal">14E:SW:6-8</physloc>
```

#### 3.5.1.2.9. Digital Archival Object and Digital Archival Object Group <dao> and <daogrp>

One of the exciting features of EAD is its ability to connect the finding aid to electronic representations of the described materials. Two special linking elements, <dao> and <daogrp>, are used for this purpose. The <dao> element is used to point to individual images, and <daogrp> is used to bundle multiple versions of the same images (for example, a thumbnail and a reference copy). Since these elements may be used in many places throughout a finding aid, they are described in more detail, along with other widely available

---

[59] If your country has no official list, do not use this attribute. For U.S. repositories, cite code from: *USMARC Code List for Countries* (Washington: Library of Congress Cataloging Distribution Service, 1993).
[60] ISAD(G), section 3.1.

elements, in section 3.5.1.7. Aspects of their use are also covered in the discussion of linking elements in section 7.3.6.

### 3.5.1.3. Collection-Level Access Terms <controlaccess>

Hundreds of names and subjects can appear in a finding aid, but prominence can be given to the major ones that relate to the entire collection, or that highlight the collection's principal strengths, by grouping them together within the Controlled Access Headings <controlaccess> element under <archdesc>. These headings often are the same as the terms included in the 1xx, 6xx, and 7xx fields of the MARC catalog record for the collection. Because of their value as search terms, some repositories are grouping them near the front of their finding aids, immediately after the high-level <did>, so that a researcher landing in the <controlaccess> area as the result of a search will be in close proximity to the collection summary provided in the high-level <did>. Some of these headings also can be embedded in <did> subelements, as described in section 3.5.1.1. For a detailed discussion of authority-controlled access terms and their placement and use in EAD finding aids, see section 3.5.3.

### 3.5.1.4. Administrative Information <admininfo>

Finding aids often contain information about the acquisition, custodial history, processing, and archival management of the collections they describe. Statements about the conditions of access, use, and duplication, or the availability of microfilm or other surrogates also may be included to give the user essential information about how to approach and make use of the archival materials. The <admininfo> element provides a place to assemble such information in an EAD finding aid. This optional wrapper element is for background information that users may need to gain access to the archival materials, place them in context, and make use of the information they contain. The element <admininfo> can also contain information that will assist repositories in some aspects of collection management.

At the highest level of description in <archdesc>, <admininfo> can be used to provide collection management information for the entire body of materials. It also can be used at the <c> level to provide information specific to a subgroup, series, or lower component. Unlike the <did> subelements, <admininfo> cannot contain text directly; it can only contain other elements. The subelements available within <admininfo> include generic text elements such as Heading <head>, Paragraph <p>, and List <list>, as well as nine content-specific elements:

- Acquisition Information <acqinfo>
- Custodial History <custodhist>
- Restrictions on Access <accessrestrict>
- Restrictions on Use <userestrict>
- Alternate Form Available <altformavail>

- Preferred Citation <prefercite>
- Appraisals <appraisal>
- Accruals <accruals>
- Processing Information <processinfo>

Each of these subelements is described in the sections that follow. Use of the generic text elements is described in section 3.5.1.7.

Like all <did>-level elements, <admininfo> is recursive, meaning one <admininfo> can contain another; this is a useful capability if you need a different array of <admininfo> details for distinct parts of a collection, such as multiple accessions. Recursion also facilitates the use of multiple headings or subheadings within <admininfo>. Headings should be constructed with users in mind; using only the element name or archival terminology may not be meaningful to a user. In addition, <admininfo> is repeatable, so information that is critical to a user, such as restrictions on access, can be provided near the beginning of the description, while information that is principally useful to repository staff, such as who processed the collection and when, can be provided after <scopecontent> or elsewhere in the finding aid.

The <admininfo> element can be entered as a single narrative in one or more <p>s rather than as specific subelements. This may be appropriate if individual administrative data elements cannot be easily parsed out of existing text when converting legacy data, but it leaves you with a rather undifferentiated block of text, which limits your ability to manipulate or reuse the data. Individually tagging the content-specific elements available within <admininfo> will, on the other hand, make the information much more useful in an online system. Each <admininfo> subelement contains an optional <head> and required <p>s in which you can enter text.

If an element contains standard pieces of text that apply to a range of finding aids, consider using a pointer element to display boilerplate text stored outside the finding aid (see section 6.5 on entities for more detail). This is especially useful for text that may change in future, such as the repository's address, a set of access conditions, or instructions for ordering microfilm copies.

None of the <admininfo> subelements are required and all are repeatable. Some, such as <acqinfo>, <accessrestrict>, <userestrict>, and <prefercite> may be useful in all finding aids, while others may only be needed for particular collections. The subelements can appear in any order within <admininfo>, but you should adopt a *consistent* order within all of your finding aids. Consider placing first those elements deemed most important to users (as opposed to staff). For example, you might place <accessrestrict> and <altformavail> in an <admininfo> immediately following the high-level <did>, and then open another <admininfo> that contains <appraisal> and <processinfo> after <scopecontent> or elsewhere in the finding aid. The sequence of subelements as presented in this section suggests one such possible order, but other logical or display considerations may prevail for your environment.

Each of the subelements has AUDIENCE and ENCODINGANALOG attributes. The AUDIENCE attribute can be set to "internal" to limit display of designated elements to repository staff (note, however, that the ability to suppress display of this attribute is dependent on your software environment, as mentioned elsewhere in these *Guidelines*). The ENCODINGANALOG attribute can be used to map the <admininfo> subelements to corresponding data elements in MARC or other encoding systems. (See the crosswalk in appendix B for MARC and ISAD(G) equivalents.)

### 3.5.1.4.1. Acquisition Information and Custodial History <acqinfo> and <custodhist>

Repositories have widely varying practices for recording information about the chain of custody for a body of materials and documenting their own acquisition of the materials. EAD accommodates this information in two <admininfo> subelements:

- Acquisition Information <acqinfo>
- Custodial History <custodhist>

The <acqinfo> element encodes information about the immediate source of the materials being described and the circumstances (donation, transfer, purchase, or deposit) under which they were received. It may be useful to document further details about an acquisition using elements available within Paragraph <p>. For example, an acquisition or donor number can be tagged as <num type="donor"> and the donor name tagged using <persname> or <corpname>, with the ROLE attribute set appropriately:

```
<acqinfo>
   <p>The collection, <num type="accession">77-135</num>, was
   given to the repository in <date type="accession">1977</date>
   by <persname role="donor">Georgia O'Keeffe</persname>.</p>
</acqinfo>
```

In addition to documenting the immediate source of acquisition in <acqinfo>, the <custodhist> element can be used to encode information about the previous chain of custody. This type of information often has been incorporated into biographical and historical sketches or scope and content notes. <custodhist> provides a designated area for describing both the physical possession and intellectual ownership of the material and details of changes in ownership and/or custody that may be significant for its authority, integrity, and interpretation. For example, a body of materials may have been transferred and added to by different agencies within a corporate body, or family papers may have been handed down from generation to generation; understanding this chain of custody may assist a researcher in interpreting the materials and may affect the authenticity of the materials. (See also section

3.5.1.4.5 for information about accruals and appraisals, and section 3.5.4.4 for information about separated materials.)

```
<custodhist>
   <p>The Ocean Falls Corporation records remained in the custody of
   Pacific Mills Ltd., and its successor companies, until the mill
   and townsite were taken over by the B.C. provincial government in
   1973.  In 1976 the records were transferred to the Ocean Falls
   Public Library, which began the rearrangement of the records in
   their current form.  The project was never completed, however,
   due to lack of funding and the collection lay in basement storage
   of the library until the Crown Corporation, B.C. Cellulose,
   announced the closing of the mill in 1980.  Abandoned over a
   period of several years, the records were moved from one
   temporary storage location to another as buildings were
   demolished, and suffered extensive losses and water damage due to
   neglect.  When the final dismantling of the Ocean Falls facility
   was announced in 1986, a team of curators from the Royal British
   Columbia Museum retrieved what remained of the records from the
   townsite.  These were transferred to the Provincial Archives in
   late 1986.</p>
</custodhist>
```

It is recommended that you not bog down the beginning of your finding aid with extensive acquisitions statements and custodial histories that researchers are unlikely to read immediately. Provide only as much information as your users may need when initially trying to orient themselves to a collection and to determine whether it is relevant to their research. More detailed statements about the acquisitions process or the custodial history of the materials may be better placed after information of greater immediate interest to researchers, such as the Scope and Content <scopecontent> note and Component <c> descriptions (see sections 3.5.1.6 and 3.5.2, respectively).

#### 3.5.1.4.2. Restrictions on Access and Use <accessrestrict> and <userestrict>

Limitations on researchers' access to archival materials may be imposed due to donor agreements, sensitivity of the content of the materials, physical condition of the materials, off-site storage, or statutory regulations. The Restrictions on Access <accessrestrict> element contains information about conditions that affect the availability of the materials described in the finding aid. It also can be used to state the absence of any access restrictions.

```
<accessrestrict>
   <p>This collection is open for research with the exception
   of one box of tapes and diaries, which is sealed until
   Plunkett's death or until explicit permission for use is
   given by the Plunkett family. </p>
</accessrestrict>
```

After a researcher has seen the archival materials, there may be restrictions on reuse of the information for purposes of quotation, publication, or other reproduction; these can be stated in the Restrictions on Use <userestrict> element. The use conditions may be imposed by the repository, donor, or legal statute. The <userestrict> element also can be used to indicate the absence of such restrictions.

```
<userestrict>
   <p>Materials are in the public domain. </p>
</userestrict>

<userestrict>
   <head>Ownership and Literary Rights</head>
   <p>The Gertrude Stein and Alice B. Toklas Collection is the
   physical property of the Beinecke Rare Book and Manuscript
   Library, Yale University.  Literary rights, including copyright,
   belong to the authors or their legal heirs and assigns.  For
   further information, consult the appropriate curator.</p>
</userestrict>
```

### 3.5.1.4.3. Alternate Form of the Materials Available <altformavail>

It is useful for researchers to be aware of the fact that all or portions of a collection are available in multiple formats, that they may be required to use a format other than the original, or that they may be able to use the materials without visiting the repository. The existence of copies—microforms, digital images, videotape copies of motion pictures, or paper facsimiles—can be stated in <altformavail>. Information about the copies might include the format of the alternate form, its extent, identifying number or code, location, and the source or procedure for ordering copies. If only portions of the material have been duplicated, <altformavail> can be used at the Component <c> level and should include a brief statement about what is included in the duplicate version. If copies exist in more than one format, for example, both microform and digital copies, separate <altformavail> elements can be used for each, using the TYPE attribute to distinguish between them.

```
<altformavail type="microfilm">
   <p>The Correspondence Series in this collection is
   available on microfilm through Interlibrary Loan.</p>
</altformavail>

<altformavail>
   <p>The original handwritten draft of <title
   render="italic">Women in Love</title> is extremely fragile.
   Researchers are required to use a photocopy unless special
   arrangements are made.</p>
</altformavail>
```

### 3.5.1.4.4. Preferred Citation of the Material <prefercite>

Repositories frequently supply standard statements to be used for citing their holdings; these can be encoded in <prefercite>. The text can provide an example of a generic citation for the repository, or the example can be specific to the material being described. If you have varying preferred citation formats for different original media or modes of publication, examples of all the citations relevant for a collection should be provided. Alternatively, a pointer element could be used to call an entity file that states your repository's citation policies and preferred formats (see the discussion of entities in section 6.5).

```
<prefercite>
   <p>[identification of item]. California Gold Rush Mining
   Towns, BANC PIC 1987.021 -- PIC, The Bancroft Library,
   University of California, Berkeley.</p>
</prefercite>
```

### 3.5.1.4.5. Additional Receipts, Appraisals, and Dispositions <accruals> and <appraisal>

Government and corporate archives typically receive regular, scheduled additions to record groups or series. Manuscript repositories also sometimes receive personal papers in installments, particularly if the creator is alive at the time the donations begin. Repositories may simply wish to indicate that future additions to a collection are expected. The Accruals <accruals> element contains information about anticipated additions to the materials being described, indicating the date, frequency, or quantity of anticipated additions, or conversely, that no further additions are expected. This information may be useful to researchers, but could also be used by the repository to track and plan for accessions.

```
<accruals>
   <p>Additions to the Department of Game and Fish records are
   expected annually.</p>
</accruals>
```

Your repository may document appraisal decisions in your finding aids. The Appraisal <appraisal> element contains information about the process of determining the archival value and thus the disposition of records; it can be used to describe both original appraisal decisions and reappraisals that led to significant weeding or deaccessioning. It is recommended that you document appraisal decisions in cases where users might have reason to expect to find material in your repository, either because they were familiar with it prior to accessioning into the archives or because it had been described in a finding aid prior to reappraisal. If necessary, additional information about weeding and any resulting changes in the organization or arrangement of the material can be provided in the Separated Materials <separatedmaterial>, Organization <organization>, or Arrangement <arrangement> elements in other parts of the finding aid.

```
<appraisal>
   <head>Appraisal statement:</head>
   <p>Mental health facility patient case files are an important
   route to documenting significant developments in mental health
   services in New York, particularly therapies and treatments used,
   research conducted on the nature and causes of mental conditions,
   the development of diagnostic criteria, and the experiences of
   patients and families in the facilities.</p>

   <p>The State Archives will obtain all pre-1920 patient case
   files.  For post 1920 patient case files, the State Archives will
   obtain a representative sample of patient case files in their
   entirety from the following facilities:  Binghamton, Pilgrim,
   Central Islip, Kings Park, Buffalo, Middletown, St. Lawrence,
   Mohawk Valley, and the Manhattan Psychiatric Center.   The Office
   of Mental Health will microfilm case files for Pilgrim, Central
   Islip, Kings Park, and Mohawk Valley and transfer microfilm
   masters to the State Archives.  The sample captures specific
   patient populations and treatments as defined in the detailed
   appraisal report, as well as providing for geographic coverage.
   The sample is necessary because over 110,000 cubic feet of
   patient case files currently exist, and cannot either be
   microfilmed in their entirety or retained in paper form.
   Admission and discharge ledgers for all patients will be retained
   by the State Archives to ensure core information survives on all
   patients for all facilities.</p>
</appraisal>
```

### 3.5.1.4.6. Processing Information <processinfo>

The name of the processor and the date the collection was processed is frequently included in archival finding aids.[61] While you may choose not to document routine processing activities beyond this basic information, <processinfo> also can be used to encode a range of information regarding accessioning, arranging and describing, preserving, or otherwise preparing the described materials for research use.

```
<processinfo>
   <head>Processing Information</head>
   <p>These records were originally organized and processed in
   1977 by Lydia Lucas. In 1993, Michael Fox refined the
   arrangement prior to microfilming.</p>
</processinfo>
```

For electronic records, <processinfo> may be the most appropriate place to describe file conversions, media migrations, and other maintenance and preservation actions that do not result in alternative formats being made available for public use (such formats would be encoded in <altformavail>; see section 3.5.1.4.3).

[61] When the processor is also the author of the finding aid, consider repeating the individual's name within the <filedesc> element of the <eadheader> (see section 3.6.1.2).

```
<processinfo>
   <head>Processing Information</head>
   <p>Duderstadt created many of his speeches and other
   documents using MORE 3.0, an outlining/text editing program
   for Apple computers that is no longer commercially
   available or supported.  During processing of the
   collection the MORE files were converted to WordPerfect
   files.</p>
</processinfo>
```

### 3.5.1.5. Biographical Sketches and Agency Histories <bioghist>

Contextual information about the creation or formation of a body of archival materials is typically found in finding aids in some kind of creator sketch—a biographical sketch or agency history—which provides background information about the individual, family, or organization which created or collected the materials. The information may be presented as narrative text and/or as a chronology, in which dates are paired with one or more events in a columnar format. In EAD, such contextual information is encoded in <bioghist>.

Several encoding options exist. If you prefer to present the biographical sketch in narrative form, you might use the optional <head> followed by a series of paragraphs. Within <p> it is possible to encode <persname>, <famname>, <corpname>, and <occupation> access terms, as well as dates. Such detailed content encoding could be useful if these kinds of access points, such as the name of an agency's predecessor, do not appear in other parts of the finding aid or are not grouped together in <controlaccess> (see section 3.5.3). Remember, however, that it is advisable to mark up only those pieces of text that relate to information contained in the collection itself so that users do not obtain irrelevant search results.

```
<bioghist>
   <head>Organizational History</head>
   <p><title render="italic">The Quest</title> was founded in the fall
   of 1965 by <persname>Alexis Levitin</persname>. The original
   editorial staff and board comprised--like Levitin--graduate students
   at <corpname>Columbia University</corpname>. Levitin created a
   literary magazine that attempted to avoid a narrowly-defined focus
   and to encourage good writing from contributors of many viewpoints.
   <blockquote><p>"We expect (read the magazine's entry in the
   <title render="italic">Directory of Little Magazines</title>) of the
   artist not only a well-wrought structure, but, within it, a creative
   and meaningful reflection upon the essential truths of our existence
   as well."</p></blockquote></p>

   <p>After Levitin left New York in 1968 for a teaching position at
   Dartmouth, most of the work of editing the magazine was carried on
   by <persname>David Hartwell</persname> and <persname>Tom
   Beeler</persname>, who ultimately purchased the magazine from
   Levitin in late 1969.  Hartwell and Beeler had never liked the name
   <title render="italic">Quest</title> and renamed it
   <title render="italic">The Little Magazine</title>, under which
   title it first appeared with the spring 1970 issue.</p>

   <p>After Beeler's departure in 1971 the principal burden of
   continuing the magazine was borne by David Hartwell, working with a
   constantly changing cast of editors and editorial board members.</p>

   </p>Throughout its twenty-one year life <title render="italic">The
   Quest</title> and <title render="italic">The Little Magazine</title>
   published new poetry and short fiction from primarily younger
   American writers.  Circulation never rose much above a thousand,
   even with national distribution by <persname>Bernhard
   DeBoer</persname>, and in the face of steeply rising production
   costs publication became increasingly irregular in the late 1970s.
   By the end of the decade Hartwell was heavily involved in science
   fiction editing but was able to continue publication with the help
   of the volunteer editorial board.  Eventually the end came, and with
   the appearance of v. 15, no.3-4 in 1987 <title render="italic">The
   Little Magazine</title> ceased publication.</p>
</bioghist>
```

If you prefer to present contextual information in the form of a structured chronology, the Chronology List <chronlist> element is available within <bioghist>. The element <chronlist> contains the wrapper element Chronology List Item <chronitem>, which bundles a date with a single event or a group of events:

```
<bioghist>
   <head>Biographical Note</head>
   <chronlist>
      <chronitem>
         <date>1919, Dec. 14</date>
         <event>Born, <geogname>San Francisco, Calif.</geogname>
         (Due to discrepancies concerning its authenticity, the
         year of Jackson's birth is also cited as 1916 by some
         authorities.)</event>
      </chronitem>
      <chronitem>
         <date>1940</date>
         <eventgrp>
            <event>A.B., <corpname>Syracuse
            University</corpname>, <geogname>Syracuse,
            N.Y.</geogname></event>
            <event>Married <persname>Stanley Edgar
            Hyman</persname></event>
         </eventgrp>
      </chronitem>
   </chronlist>
</bioghist>
```

The <bioghist> element is recursive (i.e., it can be nested within itself). As mentioned earlier, recursion permits bundling of the parts of a logical component of the finding aid, while at the same time allowing subcomponents to be separately identified. For example, the finding aid for the records of the Alfred A. Knopf Inc. publishing firm contains three sections of contextual information.[62] Both Alfred and Blanche Knopf were intimately involved in the running of the firm, and the records contain much personal correspondence and information about their other interests and travels; it is therefore appropriate for the finding aid to contain an agency history for the firm itself, as well as separate biographical sketches for both Alfred and Blanche Knopf. The markup would look like this:

[62] This collection is at the Harry Ransom Humanities Research Center at the University of Texas at Austin.

```
<bioghist>
   <bioghist encodinganalog="545">
      <head>Organizational History</head>
      <p>The Alfred A. Knopf Inc. publishing firm was founded in
      1915....</p>
   </bioghist>
   <bioghist encodinganalog="545">
      <head>Biographical Sketch of Alfred Knopf</head>
      <p><persname encodinganalog="700" source="lcnaf"
      normal="Knopf, Alfred A., 1892-1984">Alfred Knopf
      </persname>....</p>
   </bioghist>
   <bioghist encodinganalog="545">
      <head>Biographical Sketch of Blanche Knopf</head>
      <p><persname encodinganalog="700" source="lcnaf"
      normal="Knopf, Blanche W., 1894-1966"> Blanche Knopf
      </persname>....</p>
   </bioghist>
</bioghist>
```

This markup allows the use of multiple <head>s for formatting purposes (<head> is not repeatable within an individual element), as well as the extraction of the three sections for individual MARC 545 (Biographical or Historical Data) fields and added entries for Alfred and Blanche Knopf, if so desired. See also section 3.5.3.1 for discussion of attributes for name elements.

### 3.5.1.6. Scope and Content Notes <scopecontent>

Finding aids frequently contain a section that summarizes the range and topical coverage of the described materials, often mentioning their form and organization, and naming significant individuals, organizations, events, places, and subjects represented in the materials. Generally such sections are called scope and content notes, and in EAD they are encoded in <scopecontent>. Within <scopecontent>, you can separately encode <organization>, which describes the manner in which the materials have been subdivided into smaller units such as series, and <arrangement>, which designates the filing sequence of the materials such as alphabetical, chronological, or numerical. The <organization> and <arrangement> elements also are available within <archdesc> outside of <scopecontent> to accommodate finding aids in which this information is stated elsewhere. As in <bioghist> and other <did>-level elements, it is also possible to encode a variety of access points within <scopecontent>, such as <persname>, <subject>, and <genreform>.

```
<scopecontent>
   <head>Collection Scope and Content Note</head>
   <scopecontent encodinganalog="520">
      <p>The records of the Detroit Japanese American Citizens League
      <abbr>(JACL)</abbr> document mainly the social activities of this
      Detroit area ethnic group. Some of the files pertain to the
      lasting effect of the relocation of American citizens of Japanese
      descent during World War II.</p>
      <organization><p>The records are organized in three series:
      Topical Files, Photographs, and Scrapbooks.</p></organization>
   </scopecontent>

   <p>The Topical Files series contains papers spanning 1947 through
   1995 that document the Detroit chapter's meeting minutes,
   installation banquets, preparation for various conventions, and
   relationship with the national JACL organization. Also contained in
   this series are copies of the chapter's newsletter and <title
   render="italic">The Beacon</title>, a monthly Detroit publication of
   Nisei-Caucasian fellowship. The Miscellaneous folders hold mostly
   correspondence along with other Detroit JACL records that may be
   duplicated in the Minutes and Treasurer's Reports groups. Peter
   Fujioka's correspondence is also available and filed under his
   name.</p>

   <p>Photographs of installation banquets, picnics, conferences, teen
   events, and other activities can be found in the Photograph Series.
   Individuals in these photographs are mostly unidentified; however,
   the photographs are generally labeled and arranged according to
   event. Photographs stored in folders should be examined for
   identification markings on the back. Some photographs were removed
   from the scrapbooks for the exhibit entitled <title
   render="quoted">From Manzanar to Motor City. A History of Michigan's
   Japanese American Community</title> and are labeled with a number
   designating which scrapbook originally contained the photograph.</p>

   <p>The Scrapbook Series most clearly demonstrates the activities of
   the Detroit JACL chapter. Most scrapbooks contain information about
   the overall chapter activities, while others focus on the activities
   of the youth groups and the golf club. Each book contains
   photographs and documentation of events and publications and has
   been kept intact if possible. Materials which have become detached
   have been transferred to folders. Some duplication appears between
   the Scrapbook and Topical Files series.</p>
</scopecontent>
```

Like <bioghist>, <scopecontent> is recursive, facilitating the use of multiple <head>s and enabling the extraction of a summary paragraph, via the ENCODINGANALOG attribute, from a longer scope and content note for use in the 520 field of a MARC record.

### 3.5.1.7. Generic Text, Formatting, and Linking Elements

Most EAD elements focus on markup of the structural components of a finding aid, but some generic text and formatting elements also are necessary for coherent formatting of the document; these include <head>, <p>, <blockquote>, <emph>, <list>, and a variety of other elements. In addition, subelements within <p> enable further formatting, linking, and vocabulary control options. Not all of these elements will be discussed in this section, but you should be aware of their availability and check their proper use in the *EAD Tag Library*. Linking elements and tabular display elements are described more specifically in chapter 7 and section 4.3.5.4, respectively.

These *Guidelines* emphasize the desirability of omitting some formatting elements from the markup and allowing the stylesheet to control online display (see section 5.3.3 for more information on stylesheets). A good rule of thumb is that if the content of an element should be displayed consistently in a particular way (such as in italics) across all of your finding aids (or in all finding aids of a particular type), then it is best to let the stylesheet control the display. On the other hand, if a single word in a paragraph needs special treatment, such as to be italicized, use the appropriate formatting element (in the case of italics, use <emph>).

Most of EAD's textual and formatting subelements are optional, a certain amount of generic textual markup is necessary. One reason for this is that SGML syntax prefers that each element be defined to contain either other elements or text, but not both. This is why, for example, you must open <p> to type text into <scopecontent>, which cannot directly contain text (referred to in SGML as parsed character data, or PCDATA).

#### 3.5.1.7.1. Heading <head>

Headings are frequently used in finding aids to identify blocks of text. The <head> element is available for all of the <did>-level elements, such as <admininfo> and <scopecontent>, as well as for all components <c> and many other elements for which a heading of some sort is desirable. If <head> is used, it must appear as the first subelement, before <p> or another subelement. Headings can easily be manipulated with a stylesheet to control display. Examples illustrating the use of <head> abound in this chapter, such as in sections 3.5.1.5 and 3.5.3.7.

There are circumstances in which it is *not* appropriate to use <head> for heading-like information. As explained in section 3.5.1.1, <did> subelements use a LABEL attribute instead of <head>. It is also important to avoid using <head> when a more specific EAD structural element such as <unittitle> is more appropriate, as described in section 3.5.2.3.1.1.

#### 3.5.1.7.2. Paragraph <p>

The Paragraph <p> element is used to designate what we think of as a simple paragraph—one or more sentences that form a logical prose passage. A paragraph may be a subdivision of a larger narrative, or it may stand alone. It is usually typographically distinct: a blank line often appears before and after it; the text begins on a new line; and the first letter of the first word is often indented, capitalized, or both.

The <p> element is an important element that is used frequently. It is available, and its use often required, within more than 30 EAD elements. Unlike most elements, it may contain a combination of text and other elements. More than thirty subelements are available within <p>, including all of the subelements that are available in <controlaccess> (described in section 3.5.3). An advantage of having these elements available within <p> is that you can encode names, subjects, and form and genre terms in natural language and also provide their authority-controlled forms for search and retrieval purposes. The latter is accomplished by using the NORMAL attribute.

```
<p><persname source="lcnaf" normal="Knopf, Alfred A., 1892-
1984">Knopf</persname> entered <corpname source="lcnaf"
normal="Columbia College (Columbia University)">Columbia
College</corpname> in 1908, where he became interested in the
fields of history and literature.</p>
```

Several generic textual subelements are available within <p> as well, such as Abbreviation <abbr>, Emphasis <emph>, Expansion <expan>, Line Break <lb>, List <list>, and Table <table>. In some instances, it will be preferable to have the stylesheet control the display of such things, but in others it will be more practical to include them in the markup. Some of these elements also can be used to facilitate searching. For example, using <abbr> in the following sentence may enhance the retrievability of references to ISAD(G).

```
<p>In the General International Standard Archival Description
<abbr>ISAD(G)</abbr> ...</p>
```

A number of citation and linking elements are available in <p>, including Archival Reference <archref>, Bibliographic Reference <bibref>, Extended Pointer <extptr>, Reference <ref>, and Title <title> (the linking elements are discussed in chapter 7). The use of <title> in <p> is particularly useful for display and retrieval purposes. For instance, it may not be possible to have a stylesheet control the display of every <title> within a <p>, because the stylesheet would not be able to distinguish a journal article title that should appear within quotation marks from a title of a novel that should appear in italics. To control this type of display, the RENDER attribute would be necessary:

```
<title render="italic">Alice in Wonderland</title>
```

Keep in mind that when <p> is available within an element it is often *required* before you can insert text, unless another structural subelement is used first. For example, both of the following examples are valid, but the latter is more precise in its markup due to inclusion of the subelement <acqinfo>:

```
<admininfo>
   <p>The record group was donated by the Detroit Japanese American
   Citizens League in February 1998. Donor no. 8691</p>
</admininfo>

<admininfo>
   <acqinfo>
      <p>The record group was donated by the Detroit Japanese
      American Citizens League in February 1998. Donor no. 8691</p>
   </acqinfo>
</admininfo>
```

### 3.5.1.7.3. Note <note>

As mentioned in section 3.5.1.2.6, <note> is available many places other than <did> because of its utility as explanatory text. The <note> element can be used within all of the <did>-level elements (<admininfo>, <bioghist>, <scopecontent>, <c>, Adjunct Descriptive Data <add>, and Other Descriptive Data <odd>), as well as within the <admininfo> subelements, generic textual elements, and linking elements. They can be placed as footnotes at the bottom of each page if desired for hard-copy printouts; in an online environment, they may be placed either at the end of a document or embedded within the text. The ACTUATE and SHOW attributes can be used to suppress online display of <note>s until they are requested by a finding aid user; details on using these attributes are in section 7.4.1.

### 3.5.1.7.4. Digital Archival Object <dao>

The online environment facilitates the inclusion of digital representations of archival materials embedded within a finding aid or linked to it. EAD provides many linking elements, but the <dao> and <daogrp> elements are intended specifically for digital representations from the collection described by the finding aid. These representations might include graphic images, audio or video clips, images of text pages, and electronic transcriptions of text. The <dao> and <daogrp> elements are available within <did>, as mentioned in section 3.5.1.2.9, but they are also available within a number of other EAD elements, including <bioghist>, <scopecontent>, and <c>. In a biographical sketch you might provide photographs of the creator or images of other items from the collection that relate to an event or activity connected to the creator's life; in a scope and content note or within components, you might either link to or embed thumbnail images or clips of materials from the collection. These might represent the contents of entire files, selected items that are frequently requested, or items that are fragile and cannot be handled in the original. Detailed instructions for using <dao> and <daogrp> are in section 7.3.6.

### 3.5.2. Describing the "Parts": Nested Components

Once an archivist has finished describing in a general way the "whole" of a body of records or papers, the focus typically shifts to describing one or more of the collection's parts, as explained in the discussion of multilevel description in section 3.4. In EAD, these parts are known as Components <c>. In the following sections, we explore the nature of components and address such questions as these:

- What exactly is a component?
- Where should a component description begin and end?
- What is the difference between EAD's numbered and unnumbered components?
- Can I use the same rich content tags to describe the components that I used to describe the collection as a whole?
- How do I include information about the physical arrangement of the materials within particular boxes and folders?
- How can I group component descriptions to format them as a series description or contents list?

To those archivists accustomed to building hierarchical finding aids, especially those familiar with ISAD(G) and RAD, the answers to these questions will be familiar. In the spirit of ISAD(G), component descriptions in EAD inherit information from both the description of the whole and from any preceding hierarchical component levels. At every level, the descriptions can utilize the same essential data elements.

#### 3.5.2.1. What Is a Component? <c>

A component may be an easily recognizable archival entity such as a series, subseries, file,[63] or item, or, as the examples below illustrate, it may simply be any level or stage within the descriptive hierarchy. Components not only are nested under the <archdesc> element, they usually are nested inside one another. For example, archivists would agree that series are parts or components of collections, fonds, or record groups. Similarly, subseries are parts not only of their parent series but of their "grandparent" unit as well. Subseries, in turn, are comprised of files, which subsequently consist of other files and/or items. The description of any single archival component inherits the description of its parents, grandparents, great-grandparents, and so on. Also inherited are layers or components of description that may reflect information shared by files within a given place in the hierarchy, but that do not necessarily correlate to an intellectual grouping to which the archival profession has assigned a specific name.

---

[63] The term "file" is used here to mean an intellectual unit of archival materials, not the contents of a physical housing such as a folder.

For example, in organizing a novelist's personal papers, you may identify several large groups or series of materials, one of which you name the Literary File and another Scrapbooks. Within the Literary File you may arrange the materials by type of writing such that all the files relating to the novelist's books are grouped together, as are the files relating to the writer's short stories and articles. Depending on the size and significance of the groupings, you may consider these three categories ("Articles," "Books," and "Short stories and other writings") as subseries and identify them as such in the finding aid. These subseries or types of writings may be further arranged by title, date, or another organizing principle, with additional subheadings applied as needed to complete the classification. The varying specificity of the classification often reflects the quantity of material in the category; the more material there is, the more likely the need for subcategories. Each category and subcategory of description is a component. A finding aid may depict this nesting as follows:[64]

LITERARY FILE, 1943-1970, n.d.
- Articles, 1951-1966
- Books
  - *Raising Demons* (1957)
    - Reviews, 1956-1957, n.d.
    - Royalty statements, 1956-1969
  - *The Road Through the Wall* (1948), 1947-1970, n.d.
- Short stories and other writings
  - "The Lottery"
    - Dramatic adaptations
      - Correspondence, 1949-1953, 1967-1970
      - Scripts and screenplays, n.d.
    - Royalty statements, 1950-1953, 1964-1970
  - "Lover's Meeting," n.d.

SCRAPBOOKS, 1933-1968
- College plays, 1933-1937
- "The Lottery," 1949-1952

In this much abbreviated and somewhat fictionalized example, the Literary File and the Scrapbooks are both series-level components in a collection of novelist Shirley Jackson's papers.[65] The Literary File component begins with the word "Literary" and ends after the file "Lover's Meeting." You might think that the component would end on the first line, after the span dates of the Literary File, but it does not; the description of the series-level component includes the description of all of its subcomponents, not simply the title and dates of the series. The component tags for the series would appear thus:

[64]All examples in section 3.5.2 and its subsections are adapted from: Janice E. Ruth, "Encoded Archival Description: A Structural Overview," *American Archivist* 60 (summer 1997): 310-29.

[65] This collection is held by the Library of Congress.

```
<c>LITERARY FILE, 1943-1970, n.d.
      Articles, 1951-1966
      Books
            Raising Demons (1957)
                  Reviews, 1956-1957, n.d.
                  Royalty statements, 1956-1969
            The Road Through the Wall (1948), 1947-1970, n.d.
      Short stories and other writings
            "The Lottery"
                  Dramatic adaptations
                        Correspondence, 1949-1953, 1967-1970
                        Scripts and screenplays, n.d.
                  Royalty statements, 1950-1953, 1964-1970
            "Lover's Meeting," n.d.</c>
<c>SCRAPBOOKS, 1933-1968
      College plays, 1933-1937
      "The Lottery," 1949-1952</c>
```

Both the Literary File and the Scrapbooks contain subcomponents, and these too would be tagged with beginning <c> and ending </c> component tags (see next example). In the Literary File, the archivist has identified three subcategories, two of which (books and short stories) have been further subdivided.

In determining how to encode a subcomponent, observe where its description begins and ends. In the case of the Jackson articles, the finding aid author decided that no further specification of the file's contents was needed other than a listing of the span dates. Consequently, the component begins before the word "Articles" and ends after the date range "1951-1966." With respect to the books and short stories, however, further levels of description were deemed appropriate to assist the researcher in locating material relating to a particular work by Jackson. Consequently, the books component begins just before "Books," but does not end until after the dates for *The Road Through the Wall.* Similarly, the short stories component begins immediately before "Short," and ends after the dates for "Lover's Meeting."

The process of identifying the beginning and end of each descriptive component would be followed throughout the descending hierarchy, as illustrated below. Note that the description of a lower-level component inherits the description of all its ancestors, such that a researcher reading the component title "Scripts and screenplays, n.d." will follow the hierarchy up and deduce that the file contains scripts and screenplays for dramatic adaptations of "The Lottery," which is a short story found in the literary file of the Shirley Jackson Papers.

```
<c>LITERARY FILE, 1943-1970, n.d.
      <c>Articles, 1951-1966</c>
      <c>Books
            <c>Raising Demons (1957)
                  <c>Reviews, 1956-1957, n.d.</c>
                  <c>Royalty statements, 1956-1969</c></c>
            <c>The Road Through the Wall (1948), 1947-1970,
            n.d.</c></c>
      <c>Short stories and other writings
            <c>"The Lottery"
                  <c>Dramatic adaptations
                        <c>Correspondence, 1949-1953,
                        1967-1970</c>
                        <c>Scripts and screenplays,
                        n.d.</c></c>
                  <c>Royalty statements, 1950-1953,
                  1964-1970</c></c>
            <c>"Lover's Meeting," n.d.</c></c></c>
<c>SCRAPBOOKS, 1933-1968
      <c>College plays, 1933-1937</c>
      <c>"The Lottery," 1949-1952</c></c>
```

Note that regardless of their positions in a hierarchy, all components share the same generic element name and tag. Although each component identifies a hierarchically specific section of the described materials, no attempt was made in EAD to assign unique element names to various types or levels of component; all are simply tagged as <c>s. That does not mean that every <c> is of equal significance, or that an archivist may not wish to differentiate <c>s when displaying or searching a finding aid. Such differentiation is possible through the use of a LEVEL attribute, which, as explained in section 3.5.1., carries values of "collection," "fonds," "recordgrp," "series," "subgrp," "subseries," "file," "item," and "otherlevel." It is recommended that a LEVEL attribute be assigned for the highest <c>; the tags before "LITERARY FILE" and "SCRAPBOOKS" might therefore be expanded to <c level="series">. Elsewhere, the attribute may be used when the repository deems it useful for searching, display, navigation, or another purpose. Since many components are not likely to match any of the specific values available for the LEVEL attribute, little would be gained by identifying all of them as "otherlevel."

### 3.5.2.2. Unnumbered versus Numbered Components <c> and <c01>

Using the generic <c> to tag components, as shown in the above example, is perfectly valid, and most SGML authoring tools have no difficulty keeping track of the nested hierarchy when creating this encoded finding aid. Human comprehension may, however, be more problematic. When attempting to insert tags or proofread encoded documents prior to publication or dissemination, an archivist can easily become lost in a sea of <c> tags.

To address this authoring and editing problem, EAD offers an alternative encoding scheme of numbered components (<c01>, <c02>, <c03>, etc.), designed to assist an encoder in nesting up to 12 component levels accurately. Often the first series in a collection becomes the first <c01> in an EAD finding aid. The first <c02> is not the second series in the collection; rather, it is the next hierarchical level within that first <c01>.

It is crucial to realize that the numbers carry no intellectual significance and that their values are not absolute; in other words, a particular numbered <c> level invariably will correlate to a variety of intellectual levels, both within a single finding aid and across finding aids. For example, a <c02> in one part of a finding aid may be a file, while elsewhere, a <c02> may be a subseries. As with the unnumbered components, intellectual distinctions among components are made by using the LEVEL attribute. The example below illustrates the same section of the Jackson Papers finding aid seen earlier, but this time utilizing numbered components:

```
<c01 level="series">LITERARY FILE, 1943-1970, n.d.
      <c02>Articles, 1951-1966</c02>
      <c02>Books
            <c03>Raising Demons (1957)
                  <c04>Reviews, 1956-1957, n.d.</c04>
                  <c04>Royalty statements,
                  1956-1969</c04></c03>
            <c03>The Road Through the Wall (1948), 1947-1970,
            n.d.</c03></c02>
      <c02>Short stories and other writings
            <c03>"The Lottery"
                  <c04>Dramatic adaptations
                        <c05>Correspondence, 1949-1953,
                        1967-1970</c05>
                        <c05>Scripts and screenplays,
                        n.d.</c05></c04>
                  <c04>Royalty statements, 1950-1953,
                  1964-1970</c04></c03>
            <c03>"Lover's Meeting," n.d.</c03></c02></c01>
<c01 level="series">SCRAPBOOKS, 1933-1968
      <c02>College plays, 1933-1937</c02>
      <c02>"The Lottery," 1949-1952</c02></c01>
```

Many EAD users feel that numbered <c>s are easier to use, but some prefer unnumbered <c>s, principally because less retagging of components is necessary if errors are spotted during editing or if an additional layer of description needs to be added at any level other than the lowest level. On the other hand, some EAD users have found that their search engines have been unable to process nested unnumbered <c>s, resulting in retrieval problems.

For this reason, these *Guidelines* recommend using numbered <c>s. Whichever approach is selected, you cannot switch between numbered and unnumbered <c>s within a single Description of Subordinate Components <dsc>, an element described in section 3.5.2.5.

### 3.5.2.3. Intellectual Content of Components

We have defined what components are and have explored the value of numbering them for proofreading and other purposes. We will next describe how to encode fully the intellectual content of individual components. Following the approach used in capturing information at the highest level of description, we will first focus on the use of the required <did> element and its subelements to ensure a sound basic description of each component <c>. Much of what was written about the <did> subelements in section 3.5.1.2 also applies to the component <c> descriptions and will not be repeated here. Tagged examples will illustrate how to utilize the full complement of elements previously described under <archdesc> (see section 3.5.1), while supplementary explanations will direct the reader's attention to specific attributes and uses not explored in the earlier <archdesc> discussion.

#### 3.5.2.3.1. Basic Description of Each Component <did>

As noted earlier, information captured at the highest level of description is inherited by the subordinate components. Certain <did> subelements such as <repository> and <origination> therefore are rarely necessary at the component level. In contrast, other <did> subelements, such as <unittitle>, <unitdate>, <physdesc>, and <container>, are used frequently within components to encode more detailed description at a lower hierarchical level. These elements may be supplemented by others that are not <did> subelements, such as <scopecontent>, <arrangement>, and <organization>, or perhaps even <admininfo> and <bioghist>. A typical use of some of these elements is illustrated below in a series description taken from a Minnesota Historical Society finding aid for the records of that state's Game and Fish Commission, shown first without EAD encoding and then with sample tags:[66]

> Record of Prosecutions, 1916-1927. 3 volumes.
>
> Information provided in each entry: date of report, name and address of person arrested, locations where offense was committed, date of arrest, nature of offense, name of judge or justice, result of trial, amounts of fine and court costs, number of days served if jailed, name of warden, and occasional added remarks. Types of offenses included hunting or fishing out of season or in unauthorized places, exceeding catch of bag limits, taking undersized fish, illegal fishing practices such as gill-netting or dynamiting, illegal hunting practices such as night-lighting, killing non-game birds, fishing or hunting without a license, and hunting-related offenses against persons such as fraud and assault.

---

[66] Examples throughout this section on components do not necessarily include all possible or even all required elements. The examples are intended to illustrate the use of certain specific elements, which full tagging might obscure. Note also that date information is not specifically encoded below the series (<c01>) level. Because such a variety of date formats are used in finding aids (see also section 3.5.1.2.4), the encoding of date information at the file or item level is of questionable utility for retrieval purposes. See appendix E for fully tagged examples.

```
<c01 level="series">
  <did>
      <unittitle>Record of Prosecutions, <unitdate>1916-1927.
      </unitdate>
      </unittitle>
      <physdesc>
         <extent>3 volumes.</extent>
      </physdesc>
   </did>
   <scopecontent>
      <p>Information provided in each entry: date of report,
      name and address of person arrested, locations where
      offense was committed, date of arrest, nature of
      offense, name of judge or justice, result of trial,
      amounts of fine and court costs, number of days served
      if jailed, name of warden, and occasional added remarks.
      Types of offenses included hunting or fishing out of
      season or in unauthorized places, exceeding catch of bag
      limits, taking undersized fish, illegal fishing
      practices such as gill-netting or dynamiting, illegal
      hunting practices such as night-lighting, killing non-
      game birds, fishing or hunting without a license, and
      hunting-related offenses against persons such as fraud
      and assault.</p>
   </scopecontent>
</c01>
```

A series component from a manuscript collection, such as the Shirley Jackson Papers, would be encoded in a similar manner. The next example, however, illustrates not only the similarity in encoding descriptions of government records and personal papers, but also displays the unfolding hierarchy of EAD by showing how a description of a series component may be followed immediately by the description of its subcomponents.

LITERARY FILE, 1943-1970, n.d.

Correspondence, manuscript drafts, royalty statements, printed matter, notes, outlines, research material, screenplays, and miscellaneous items and enclosures relating to books and short stories by Jackson. Organized alphabetically by type of material and arranged alphabetically by title or topic therein. Publication dates of books are given in parentheses.

- Articles, 1951-1966
- Books
  - *Raising Demons* (1957)
    - Reviews, 1956-1957, n.d.
    - Royalty statements, 1956-1969
  - *The Road Through the Wall* (1948), 1947-1970, n.d.
- Short stories and other writings
  - "The Lottery"
    - Dramatic adaptations
      - Correspondence, 1949-1953, 1967-1970
      - Scripts and screenplays, n.d.
    - Royalty statements, 1950-1953, 1964-1970
  - "Lover's Meeting," n.d.

```
<c01 level="series">
   <did>
      <unittitle>Literary File, <unitdate>1943-1970,
      n.d.</unitdate></unittitle>
   </did>

   <scopecontent>
      <p>Correspondence, manuscript drafts, royalty
      statements, printed matter, notes, outlines, research
      material, screenplays, and miscellaneous items and
      enclosures relating to books and short stories by
      Jackson.</p>
      <arrangement><p>Organized alphabetically by type of
      material and arranged alphabetically by title or topic
      therein.  Publication dates of books are given in
      parentheses.</p></arrangement>
   </scopecontent>

   <c02><did><unittitle>Articles, 1951-
   1966</unittitle></did></c02>
   <c02><did><unittitle>Books</unittitle></did>
      <c03><did><unittitle><title render="italic">Raising
      Demons </title>(1957)</unittitle></did>
         <c04><did><unittitle>Reviews, 1956-1957,
         n.d.</unittitle></did></c04>
         <c04><did><unittitle>Royalty statements,
         1956-1969</unittitle></did></c04></c03>
      <c03><did><unittitle><title render="italic">The Road
      Through the Wall </title>(1948), 1947-1970,
      n.d.</unittitle></did></c03></c02>
   <c02><did><unittitle>Short stories and other
   writings</unittitle></did>
      <c03><did><unittitle><title render="quoted">The
      Lottery</title></unittitle></did>
         <c04><did><unittitle>Dramatic
         adaptations</unittitle></did>
            <c05><did><unittitle>Correspondence, 1949-1953,
            1967-1970</unittitle></did></c05>
            <c05><did><unittitle>Scripts and screenplays,
            n.d.</unittitle></did></c05></c04>
         <c04><did><unittitle>Royalty statements, 1950-1953,
         1964-1970</unittitle> </did></c04></c03>
      <c03><did><unittitle><title render="quoted">Lover's
      Meeting, </title>n.d. </unittitle></did></c03>
   </c02>
</c01>
```

#### 3.5.2.3.1.1. Unit Title and Unit Date <unittitle> and <unitdate>

Note in the above examples that every component description includes the required <did> element, as well as a <unittitle>, which is optional but recommended within each <did>. It is also good descriptive practice to include the <unitdate> of each component. As mentioned in section 3.5.1.2.4, the <unitdate> may be placed either within or outside the <unittitle>. Many archivists in the United States (especially those who catalog using APPM) consider span dates to be part of the title, while descriptive practice in the United Kingdom dictates using <unitdate> outside <unittitle>. Each of the following examples is valid in EAD, but it is important that each repository *select one method and use it consistently:*

```
<c04>
   <did>
      <unittitle><unitdate>1950-1961</unitdate></unittitle>
   </did>
</c04>

<c04>
   <did>
      <unitdate>1950-1961</unitdate>
   </did>
</c04>

<c04>
   <did>
      <unittitle>1950-1961</unittitle>
   </did>
</c04>
```

Note that it is important *not* to use <head> as a substitute for <unittitle>. The <head> element is used to designate the title or caption for a section of text within the finding aid, such as "Contents List" or "Scope and Content Note." Never use <head> to identify the title of an archival unit or component. For example:

CORRECT ENCODING:
```
<c01 level="series"><did><unittitle>I.
Correspondence</unittitle></did></c01>
```

The above encoding correctly identifies Correspondence as the title of the first series. The encoding shown below, *which should not be used,* simply creates a heading for the first component; it does not designate the intellectual content of the component:

INCORRECT ENCODING:
```
<c01 level="series"><head>I. Correspondence</head></c01>
```

Note that it is *not* necessary to use <head> to tag all text that you want to designate for display in a browser; a well-developed stylesheet should be able to pull in both <head>s and <unittitle>s for this purpose. See section 3.5.1.7.1 for information on the correct use of <head>.

As a general rule, do not use generic elements in any situation for which a specific element exists to designate the intellectual content of the described materials.

### 3.5.2.3.1.2. Physical Description <physdesc>

In the high-level <did> you will record the overall extent of the collection and may provide other general statements relating to the physical description of the whole (see section 3.5.1.2.5). In a component description, you are much more likely to take advantage of the four <physdesc> subelements:

- Dimensions <dimensions>
- Extent <extent>
- Genre/Physical Characteristics <genreform>
- Physical Facet <physfacet>

Some of these elements may be further subdivided. For example, museums and archival repositories that hold three-dimensional objects or describe their materials at the item level will undoubtedly find the <physdesc> subelements extremely useful for encoding detailed item-level information.

The subelement <dimensions> may be used to record the size of an item in whatever unit of measurement the archivist selects. The UNIT attribute can specify the type of measurement, for example inches or centimeters, while the TYPE attribute can specify the kind of dimensions being measured, such as height or circumference.

```
<dimensions>80 x 50 cm.</dimensions>

<dimensions>
   <dimensions type="height" unit="inches">25</dimensions> x
   <dimensions type="width" unit="inches">38.5</dimensions>
</dimensions>
```

The subelement <physfacet> encodes information about an aspect of the appearance of the described materials, such as their color, style, marks, substances, materials, or techniques and methods of creation. It is used especially to note aspects of appearance that identify or limit use of the materials. Again, the TYPE attribute specifies which aspect of the physical appearance is being designated. The <physfacet> element, like the controlled access elements described in section 3.5.3, also has a SOURCE attribute that identifies the thesaurus or other controlled vocabulary from which the term may be taken.

```
<physfacet type="sealdesc">Rounded oval, a squirrel sitting on a
tree, at the foot of which is a lion asleep.</physfacet>

<physfacet type="medium">Paper, backed with linen.</physfacet>
<physfacet type="scale">4 chains to 1 inch.</physfacet>
```

See section 3.5.1.2.5 for examples illustrating use of <extent> and <genreform>. A very detailed <physdesc> at the item level might look like this:

```
<physdesc>
   <physfacet type="medium">Parchment, with inserted paper
   leaves</physfacet>
   <extent>3 paper leaves; 1 parchment on paper leaf; 175 leaves, 4
   inserts, 2 schedules, parchment; 4 paper leaves</extent>
   <dimensions>230 x 163 mm.</dimensions>
   <physfacet type="binding">Modern, not later than
   1824.</physfacet>
   <physfacet type="foliation">i-iv, 1-20, 20*, 21-37, 37*, 38-116,
   116*, 117-180 (Fifteenth century foliation: 1-84, on ff 125-158,
   11-60).</physfacet>
</physdesc>
```

### 3.5.2.3.1.3. Abstracts <abstract>

We noted in section 3.5.1.2.6 that an <abstract> within the high-level <did> is often extracted from longer descriptions found in <bioghist> and <scopecontent>. Within a component-level <did>, the abstract may describe particular characteristics of the individual component. This information usually has aspects of <arrangement>, <bioghist>, <physdesc>, and <scopecontent> that are not substantive enough to tag individually under those elements. Using <abstract> may be simpler, and is no less valid, than closing <did> and opening <scopecontent> and <p> outside <did>.

```
<c02>
   <did>
      <container type="box">2</container>
      <unittitle>July 1925-June 1927</unittitle>
      <abstract>Includes an unexplained recapitulation of selected
      seizures for Oct. 1923 to 1925.  May have been people
      delinquent in paying fines.</abstract>
   </did>
</c02>
```

### 3.5.2.3.1.4. ID Numbers and Physical Location Information <unitid> and <physloc>

In the high-level <did>, we noted that in addition to the recommended use of <repository>, <origination>, <unittitle>, <unitdate>, <physdesc>, and <abstract>, some repositories are also electing to include <unitid> and <physloc> with information about the collection as a whole (see sections 3.5.1.2.7 and 3.5.1.2.8). These same two elements also may be used at the component level if the information is different from that recorded in the high-level <did>. For example, a collection may be identified by a specific accession number or tracking number, and each component within that collection may be assigned a derivative of that parent number. Or the collection may consist of a group of lots, each of which is assigned a unique ID even if the collection as a whole does not carry any ID number.

```
<c04>
   <did>
      <unittitle>Groups (includes Belafonte Singers), nos. 916-925
      (F)</unittitle>
      <unitid>LOT 13074, nos. 767-987</unitid>
   </did>
</c04>
```

In the high-level <did>, a building name, shelf location, or off-site storage address may be recorded in <physloc>. The same is true in <c><did><physloc>, which can be used to specify physical locations for individual components that are different from the rest of the collection, such as oversize items or films, sound recordings, or other types of materials that are likely to have special storage designations.

```
<c06>
   <did>
      <unittitle><title render="italic">Women in Love</title>,
      </unittitle>
      <physdesc>page proofs </physdesc>
      <physloc>(Removed to galley file)</physloc>
   </did>
</c06>
```

Most archival materials are housed inside file folders, boxes, and/or cabinets, and this storage locator information is often included in the finding aid. It is *not,* however, encoded using <physloc>. Another <did> subelement, <container>, is used to indicate the types of storage devices used and any sequential numbers assigned to those devices. Because this <container> information is of such a different character than most of the other information in the finding aid, section 3.5.2.4 is devoted to discussing its role and relationship to the intellectual markup.

### 3.5.2.3.2. Expanded Description of Components

As we noted several times in this chapter, all elements available to describe the collection as a whole are also available to describe the components. This means that, in addition to the <did> subelements, you may also use <admininfo>, <bioghist>, and <scopecontent> (discussed in sections 3.5.1.4 through 3.5.1.6). Also available are <arrangement> and <organization> (discussed in section 3.5.1.6 in connection with <scopecontent>, and illustrated at the component level in the last example under 3.5.2.3.1), as well as <add> (see section 3.5.4).

Any of these elements may be used whenever the description of the components differs from the parent collection or when the description given at the parent level needs additional detail. It may sometimes be appropriate to encode such data at the component level to which it most directly applies, such as the subgroup, series, file, or item. For example, information about restrictions may appear at the specific points in a container list where restricted items are described.

```
<c01 level="series">
   <did>
      <unittitle>Search Files</unittitle>
   </did>
   <c02 level="file">
      <did>
         <unittitle>College of Engineering Dean Search
            <unitdate type="single">1986</unitdate>
        </unittitle>
         <physdesc>
            <extent>2 folders</extent>
         </physdesc>
      </did>
     <admininfo>
         <accessrestrict><p>Closed until <date type="restrict"
         normal="20100101">January 1,
         2010</date></p></accessrestrict>
      </admininfo>
   </c02>
</c01>
```

In such a situation, a high-level <accessrestrict> will explain the general nature of the access restriction and rolling opening dates. Specifically tagging the closure information will facilitate automated updating of finding aids as closure dates expire.

A <scopecontent> element at the <c> level might consist of a brief paragraph describing the topics and types of material reflected in an individual series. In other cases, an individual file or item may merit a longer description than is appropriate for the <abstract> element within <did>. In many cases, the decision to use <scopecontent> as opposed to <arrangement>, <organization>, or <abstract> will depend on the nature and length of text to be encoded. Aim for consistency in tag application within and across your finding aids, as such consistency will enhance both system design and researcher familiarity.

As mentioned in section 3.5.1.7.4, the <dao> and <daogrp> elements also are available at the <c> level. You might use these to embed or link to the contents of an entire file or selected items within a file, such as those that are frequently requested or that are fragile and cannot be handled in the original. Details on how to accomplish this are in section 7.3.6.

### 3.5.2.4. Physical Location and Container Information <container>

After describing the intellectual arrangement of a collection, you may add to this description other information for physically locating the materials within the repository. The materials typically reside in boxes and folders, or they may be reproduced on microfilm reels or stored in electronic form. This packaging or storage information, which sometimes may be a control or accession number rather than an actual container number, helps staff physically locate the particular files needed. Although in some cases this storage information may help researchers comprehend the size and extent of the materials relevant to their topics, it is principally of use to them only when submitting requests for materials.

Adding container or control number information expands the role of a finding aid by enabling it to serve not only as the access tool to the intellectual content of the materials, but also as the device for identifying their physical location. In traditional paper-based finding aids, these dual roles often are conveyed typographically through the use of columns. For example, an intellectual hierarchy may run down one side of a page, and a listing of container numbers, microfilm locations, or other control numbers may appear on the opposite side, as illustrated in the next example, in which container numbers have been added to the nested hierarchy previously shown. This container information is inherited in the same way that intellectual information is inherited. Even though each container number may appear only once in the finding aid, we assume the reader intuitively understands that the container number remains the same for all subsequent components until the next container number is listed. Within each container, folder numbers also are sometimes listed, creating a nested hierarchy of physical description parallel to the intellectual hierarchy.

These dual intellectual and physical hierarchies usually shift or break at different points. This is because a single container rarely holds all the materials described in a high-level component; it would be impractical to leave containers partially unfilled simply in order to isolate physically materials described as different intellectual components. By comparing the figure below with the preceding ones, you will see that the previously identified component descriptions span across containers, and that any single container may house materials that are intellectually part of different components. For example, the Literary File component begins in container 46 and ends in container 48, while the Books component starts in container 46 and ends at the beginning of container 47. Conversely, container 47 includes materials at various subcomponent levels within both Books and Short stories.

| | | | | | |
|---|---|---|---|---|---|
| | LITERARY FILE, 1943-1970, n.d. | | | | |
| 46 | | Articles, 1951-1966 | | | |
| | | Books | | | |
| | | | *Raising Demons* (1957) | | |
| | | | | Reviews, 1956-1957, n.d. | |
| 47 | | | | Royalty statements, 1956-1969 | |
| | | | *The Road Through the Wall* (1948), 1947-1970, n.d. | | |
| | | Short stories and other writings | | | |
| | | | "The Lottery" | | |
| | | | | Dramatic adaptations | |
| | | | | | Correspondence, 1949-1953, 1967-1970 |
| | | | | | Scripts and screenplays, n.d. |
| 48 | | | | | Royalty statements, 1950-1953, 1964-1970 |
| | | | "Lover's Meeting," n.d. | | |
| | | | | | |
| | SCRAPBOOKS, 1933-1968 | | | | |
| 49 | | College plays, 1933-1937 | | | |
| 50 | | "The Lottery," 1949-1952 | | | |

SGML does not accommodate simultaneous hierarchies effectively, and the EAD developers therefore had to choose which hierarchy the DTD would be optimized to handle. It seemed clear that intellectual arrangement is more important and more permanent than physical order, and that container information therefore should be secondary to the intellectual hierarchy rather than the reverse. In other words, the boxes and folders in which the materials are housed are not the components of a collection. The series, subseries, files, items, etc., are the components, and the container or packaging information is simply associated data that assists in retrieving those components. As a result, each new physical housing has no bearing on where a component begins or ends.

In EAD encoding, the container information "follows" the intellectual structure around; it is tagged as part of the description of the first component housed in that container. The example below illustrates this concept. It also illustrates the use of the TYPE attribute on <container>, the use of which is strongly recommended to clarify the nature of the storage device. Typical values include "box," "folder," and "reel." When an assigned number combines box and folder identification, the "box-folder" attribute value can be used. *Please note that the example omits the <did> and <unittitle> tags required for valid markup in order to focus on the placement of the <container> tags.*

```
<c01 level="series">LITERARY FILE, 1943-1970, n.d.
      <c02><container type="box">46</container>Articles, 1951-
      1966</c02>
      <c02>Books
            <c03>Raising Demons (1957)
                  <c04>Reviews, 1956-1957, n.d.</c04>
                  <c04><container type="box">47</container>
                  Royalty statements, 1956-1969</c04></c03>
            <c03>The Road Through the Wall (1948), 1947-1970,
            n.d. </c03></c02>
      <c02>Short stories and other writings
            <c03>"The Lottery"
                  <c04>Dramatic adaptations
                        <c05>Correspondence, 1949-1953, 1967-
                        1970</c05>
                        <c05>Scripts and screenplays,
                        n.d.</c05></c04>
                  <c04><container type="box">48</container>
                  Royalty statements, 1950-1953, 1964-1970
                  </c04></c03>
            <c03>"Lover's Meeting," n.d. </c03></c02></c01>
<c01>SCRAPBOOKS, 1933-1968
      <c02><container type="box">49</container>College plays,
            1933-1937</c02>
      <c02><container type="box">50</container>"The Lottery,"
            1949-1952</c02></c01>
```

The dispersal of components across containers is even more pronounced when you consider the scenario of the lowest-level component being housed in more than one container. The example below illustrates what might happen if there were five folders of reviews for *Raising Demons,* and all five could not be boxed in container 46. In this fictional case, the text appearing to the right of container 47 does not represent a new component, but merely an additional extent statement for the previous component ("Reviews, 1956-1957, n.d."). (Note: In converting existing finding aids, be careful not to assume that all typographical indentations represent the start of a new component. Sometimes, as in this example, indented text is simply a continuation of a previous component description.)

```
Container Nos.  Contents

          LITERARY FILE, 1943-1970, n.d.

46              Articles, 1951-1966
                Books
                        Raising Demons (1957)
                                Reviews, 1956-1957, n.d.
                                        (2 folders)
47                                      (3 folders)
                                Royalty statements, 1956-1969
```

The figure below shows how this section would be encoded to reflect that the <c04> component "Reviews" spans containers 46 and 47. *Please note that the figure omits the necessary <did>, <unittitle>, and <physdesc> elements required for valid markup.*

```
<c01 level="series">LITERARY FILE, 1943-1970, n.d.
      <c02><container>46</container>Articles, 1951-1966</c02>
      <c02>Books
            <c03>Raising Demons (1957)
                  <c04>Reviews, 1956-1957, n.d.
                        <extent>(2 folders)</extent>
                        <container>47</container><extent>
                        (3 folders)</extent></c04>
                  <c04>Royalty statements, 1956-1969</c04></c03>
                  </c02></c01>
```

As the previous two encoded examples illustrate, EAD accommodates the traditional way in which container numbers have appeared in many finding aids—a single occurrence of the container number at the point in the finding aid where that container's contents begin. Archivists have believed that this minimalist approach has been sufficient and implicitly understood by readers. Unfortunately, as finding aids have moved into the electronic environment, a reader's ability to infer inherited container information has become more difficult. Whereas before a reader might have quickly skimmed a page of text or flipped back to a previous printed page, one must now scroll or jump through an electronic file, which may or may not display on the reader's computer as originally formatted by the creator.

In using EAD, it is important not to fixate on recreating the formatting of your existing paper guides. Some changes may be necessary to make finding aid information intelligible via electronic display to off-site users, who will not have ready access to a reference archivist. For example, some EAD users have concluded that to accommodate remote users, the container number should display for every component. Other archivists find this approach too labor intensive, dislike the repetitive display that results, and are unconvinced that the benefits are worth the increased file size caused by the additional tagging. As with any issue concerning the level of tagging employed, archivists need to consider not just the current display and navigation of online finding aids, but also whether they may want to manipulate and reuse information in an EAD document for various other purposes, both now and in the future.

One such immediate purpose, for example, would be to generate brief hit lists of materials across collections related to a specific topic or term. Although it would be helpful if this type of search returned to the reader a list of collection titles, imagine how pleased the same reader would be to receive a list that identifies not only the collection, but also the container location and specific component description within that collection. The ease with which a computer system can deliver such results will depend to some degree on the amount of EAD encoding explicitly provided, since computers are not able to interpret the many implicit connections between data that humans routinely make. While a human may deduce that a box number applies to all subsequent items until a new box number is given, a computer will have a far more difficult time making such an inference. Therefore, for the sake of machine-processing, you may wish to consider encoding the container and/or folder information for each component. As an alternative, you may wish to explore using the PARENT attribute, which is available on the <container> and <physloc> elements (see section 7.2.5.)

As with many aspects of EAD implementation, you should weigh the anticipated *value* of encoding container information for every component against the *cost* of doing so. Also consider the system's ability to suppress information not desired for display or retrieval. For example, you may want the container information to display in the brief "hit list" format, but not on every line of the electronic finding aid. One could probably write a stylesheet that would cause only the first instance of a physical location and container to display, but the ability to support such conditional scripting will likely vary from browser to browser. A more appealing (but more difficult) approach would be for the system to generate a dynamic or running header at the top of the screen that would display container location and higher-level component data that change as you move through the finding aid. Since the ability to generate such displays may be dependent upon the level of encoding, archivists should consider encoding data more extensively than current software supports or than existing needs require.

### 3.5.2.5. Formatting Component-Level Descriptions: The Description of Subordinate Components <dsc>

The previous sections have shown how an EAD finding aid can capture the unfolding hierarchical structure of an archival collection, in which the description of each component inherits the description of the higher-level components that have preceded it. Think of it, for a moment, as a steady but changing stream of water, in that the information flows downward from the <archdesc> to the various <c>s, with fluctuations in depth occurring as the number of nested components rises and falls throughout the hierarchy. As the information courses its way downward from the whole to the parts, it must first, however, pass through another element, the Description of Subordinate Components <dsc>. The <dsc> element is a formatting construct, not unlike an aqueduct, that redirects the information flow along several possible routes in an attempt to accommodate the anticipated navigation of information along the way.

The <dsc> element must be opened before any <c> element is accessible. The <dsc> is a required wrapper that surrounds the subordinate component <c> elements within <archdesc> and helps alert the computer to the special formatting and structural features that may appear as the information stream changes course. As discussed in previous sections, the description of the whole generally consists of short phrases of text in the high-level <did> subelements, followed by longer prose statements encoded as <admininfo>, <bioghist>, <scopecontent>, <organization>, and <arrangement>. For most of the latter elements, the content model is a <head>, which serves to help users interpret the data, followed by text composed of <p>s or various types of <list>. Although <admininfo>, <bioghist>, <scopecontent>, and other narrative-based elements are also available at the <c> level, traditional finding aid practice is such that most component-level descriptions consist of relatively brief <did>-like information arranged in indented columns or outlines.

The need to accommodate such legacy formats led the EAD developers to create the <dsc> in order to meet several needs:

- To identify the type of presentation given to the information
- To restrict the places in the EAD document where special tabular display elements such as <drow> and <dentry> are available (see discussion of EAD tables in section 4.3.5.4.)
- As a mechanism to help restrict searches within a finding aid either to the higher-level descriptions of the whole or to the lower-level descriptions of the parts

A TYPE attribute is *required* with <dsc> to identify the direction or course the information stream will follow, and four possible values are available:

- Combined
- Analytic overview
- In-depth
- Othertype

The most natural flow (and the one that these *Guidelines* recommend) is to set the TYPE attribute to "*combined*." This signals an information sequence similar to figure 3.5.2.5a, in which a description of a series or subseries is immediately followed by the descriptions of its component parts.

LITERARY FILE, 1943-1970, n.d.

Correspondence, manuscript drafts, royalty statements, printed matter, notes, outlines, research material, screenplays, and miscellaneous items and enclosures relating to books and short stories by Jackson. Organized alphabetically by type of material and arranged alphabetically by title or topic therein. Publication dates of books are given in parentheses.

- Articles, 1951-1966
- Books
  - *Raising Demons* (1957)
    - Reviews, 1956-1957, n.d.
    - Royalty statements, 1956-1969
  - *The Road Through the Wall* (1948), 1947-1970, n.d.
- Short stories and other writings
  - "The Lottery"
    - Dramatic adaptations
      - Correspondence, 1949-1953, 1967-1970
      - Scripts and screenplays, n.d.
    - Royalty statements, 1950-1953, 1964-1970
  - "Lover's Meeting," n.d.

**Figure 3.5.2.5a.** *Combined Model <dsc type = "combined"> Formatted Description of Series.*

```
<dsc type="combined">
   <c01 level="series">
      <did>
         <unittitle>Literary File, <unitdate>1943-1970,
         n.d.</unitdate></unittitle>
      </did>

      <scopecontent>
         <p>Correspondence, manuscript drafts, royalty
         statements, printed matter, notes, outlines, research
         material, screenplays, and miscellaneous items and
         enclosures relating to books and short stories by
         Jackson.</p>
         <arrangement><p>Organized alphabetically by type of
         material and arranged alphabetically by title or
         topic therein.  Publication dates of books are given
         in parentheses.</p></arrangement>
      </scopecontent>

      <c02><did><unittitle>Articles, 1951-
      1966</unittitle></did></c02>
      <c02><did><unittitle>Books</unittitle></did>
         <c03><did><unittitle><title render="italic">Raising
         Demons </title>(1957)</unittitle></did>
            <c04><did><unittitle>Reviews, 1956-1957,
            n.d.</unittitle></did></c04>
            <c04><did><unittitle>Royalty statements,
            1956-1969</unittitle></did></c04></c03>
         <c03><did><unittitle><title render="italic">The Road
         Through the Wall </title>(1948), 1947-1970, n.d.
         </unittitle></did></c03></c02>
      <c02><did><unittitle>Short stories and other writings
      </unittitle></did>
         <c03><did><unittitle><title render="quoted">The
         Lottery</title></unittitle></did>
            <c04><did><unittitle>Dramatic adaptations
            </unittitle></did>
               <c05><did><unittitle>Correspondence, 1949-1953,
               1967-1970</unittitle></did></c05>
               <c05><did><unittitle>Scripts and screenplays,
               n.d.</unittitle></did></c05></c04>
                  <c04><did><unittitle>Royalty statements,
                  1950-1953, 1964-1970</unittitle></did>
                  </c04></c03>
         <c03><did><unittitle><title render="quoted">Lover's
         Meeting, </title>n.d. </unittitle></did></c03>
      </c02>
   </c01>
</dsc>
```

**Figure 3.5.2.5b.** *Combined Model <dsc type = "combined"> Encoded Description of Series.*

The *analytic overview* model (type="analyticover") is for encoding a high-level component overview, such as when each of a collection's series (and possibly subseries) is individually described at its highest level, one right after the other, for collective display (see figures 3.5.2.5c and 3.5.2.5d). In other words, a <c01> is opened, the first series is briefly described, and then the <c01> is closed without its subcomponents yet having been described. Then the second <c01> is opened, the second series is briefly described, and this <c01> is closed, to be followed in the same manner by all subsequent <c01> components. As in the "combined" model, the descriptive overview of each series is encoded using the component <c> or <c01> tags, with the LEVEL attribute set to "series."

The *in-depth* model (type="in-depth") is designed to encode a contents list separate from any narrative series descriptions. Each series, subseries, file, or item represented in the contents list is tagged as a recursive, nested component, possibly with an optional LEVEL attribute set to identify its hierarchical order within the collection or record group. (See figures 3.5.2.5e and 3.5.2.5f)

The last <dsc> value, *othertype* (type="othertype") is for use with models that do not follow any of the three specifically defined formats, to which you may assign any appropriate name.

More than one type of <dsc> may be used within a single EAD finding aid. Encoding a <dsc type="analyticover"> followed by a <dsc type="in-depth"> is a common approach found in many legacy finding aids. This "two-<dsc> approach" has both advantages and disadvantages. It accommodates a legacy data structure without requiring the shifting or rekeying of text. In addition, it preserves the functionality that the legacy structure provided by assembling in one spot all the first-level component descriptions so that they may be quickly scanned by a researcher. It would be less convenient to flip through a long paper guide, or to scroll and jump through an electronic finding aid, to locate all the first-level summaries encoded under the combined <dsc>.

On the other hand, the two-<dsc> approach has drawbacks. Because you are encoding the same first-level components (<c01>) more than once (first in the analytic overview and then in the in-depth presentation), you are creating potential confusion for a computer trying to process identical information. Depending on the sophistication of a system's searching and processing capabilities, the two-<dsc> approach may hamper the ability to show a relationship between the description of the <c01> and the description of its parts. The next generation of Web browsers may offer a solution by accommodating scripts that would locate and display or print together all the series-level descriptions in a combined <dsc>. In such a scenario, the functionality of the analytic overview could be preserved without having to split a collection's natural hierarchical description between two <dsc>s.

In the meantime, archivists using the two-<dsc> approach may want to provide hypertext links from the description of the series in the analytic overview to the description of its components in the in-depth <dsc> in lieu of encoding the same first-level components twice.

| Container Nos. | Series |
|---|---|
| 1 | Diary and Diary Notes, 1932-1934, n.d.<br>A high-school diary and an undated, single-page diary fragment kept by Jackson. Arranged chronologically. |
| 2 | Family Papers, 1938-1965, n.d.<br>Letters received, notes, and cards. Arranged alphabetically by family member and chronologically therein. |
| 3-12 | Correspondence, 1936-1970, n.d.<br>Letters received and occasional copies of letters sent, telegrams, postcards, and miscellaneous enclosures. Arranged alphabetically by correspondent and chronologically therein. |
| 13-19 | Literary File, 1943-1970, n.d.<br>Correspondence, manuscript drafts, royalty statements, printed matter, notes, outlines, research material, screenplays, and miscellaneous items and enclosures relating to books and short stories by Jackson. Arranged alphabetically by type of material and alphabetically by title or topic therein. Publication dates of books are given in parentheses. |

**Figure 3.5.2.5c.** *Analytic Overview Model <dsc type = "analyticover"> Formatted Description of Series.*

```
<dsc type="analyticover">
   <head>Description of Series</head>
   <thead><row><entry>Container Nos.</entry><entry>Series
   </entry></row></thead>

   <c01 level="series">
      <did>
         <container>1</container>
         <unittitle>Diary and Diary Notes, <unitdate>1932-1934,
         n.d. </unitdate></unittitle>
      </did>
      <scopecontent><p>A high-school diary and an undated,
      single-page diary fragment kept by Jackson.</p>
      <arrangement><p>Arranged chronologically.</p></arrangement>
      </scopecontent>
   </c01>
   <c01 level="series">
      <did>
         <container>2</container>
         <unittitle>Family Papers, <unitdate> 1938-1965, n.d.
         </unitdate></unittitle>
      </did>
     <scopecontent><p>Letters received, notes, and cards.
     </p><arrangement><p>Arranged alphabetically by family member
     and chronologically therein.</p></arrangement>
     </scopecontent>
   </c01>
   <c01 level="series">
      <did>
         <container>3-12</container>
         <unittitle>Correspondence, <unitdate> 1936-1970, n.d.
         </unitdate></unittitle>
      </did>
      <scopecontent><p>Letters received and occasional copies of
      letters sent, telegrams, postcards, and miscellaneous
      enclosures. </p> <arrangement><p>Arranged alphabetically by
      correspondent and chronologically
      therein.</p></arrangement>
      </scopecontent>
   </c01>
   <c01 level="series">
      <did>
         <container>13-19</container>
         <unittitle>Literary File, <unitdate>1943-1970,
         n.d.</unitdate></unittitle>
      </did>
      <scopecontent><p>Correspondence, manuscript drafts, royalty
      statements, printed matter, notes, outlines, research
      material, screenplays, and miscellaneous items and
      enclosures relating to books and short stories by Jackson.
      </p><arrangement><p>Arranged alphabetically by type of
      material and alphabetically by title or topic
      therein.</p></arrangement><p>Publication dates of books are
      given in parentheses.</p></scopecontent>
   </c01>
</dsc>
```

**Figure 3.5.2.5d.** *Analytic Overview Model <dsc type = "analyticover"> Encoded Description of Series.*

LITERARY FILE, 1943-1970, n.d.
Container Nos.  Contents

46 Articles, 1951-1966
Books
*Raising Demons* (1957)
Reviews, 1956-1957, n.d.
Royalty statements, 1956-1969

47 *The Road Through the Wall* (1948), 1947-1970, n.d.
Short stories and other writings
"The Lottery"
Dramatic adaptations
Correspondence, 1949-1953, 1967-1970
Scripts and screenplays, n.d.

48 Royalty statements, 1950-53, 1964-70
"Lover's Meeting," n.d.

**Figure 3.5.2.5e.** *In-Depth Model <dsc type = "in-depth"> Formatted Container List.*

```
<dsc type="in-depth">
   <head>Container List</head>
   <thead><row valign="top"><entry colname="1">Container
   Nos.</entry><entry colname="2">Contents</entry></row></thead>

   <c01 level="series">
      <did>
         <unittitle>LITERARY FILE, <unitdate
         type="inclusive">1943-1970, n.d.</unitdate></unittitle>
      </did>
      <c02><did><container>46</container><unittitle>Articles, 1951-
      1966</unittitle></did></c02>
      <c02><did><unittitle>Books</unittitle></did>
         <c03><did><unittitle><title render="italic">Raising
         Demons</title> (1957)</unittitle></did>
            <c04><did><unittitle>Reviews, 1956-1957,
            n.d.</unittitle></did></c04>
            <c04><did><unittitle>Royalty statements,
            1956-1969</unittitle></did></c04>
         </c03>
         <c03><did><container>47</container><unittitle>
         <title render="italic">The Road Through the Wall</title>
         (1948), 1947-1970, n.d. </unittitle></did></c03></c02>
      <c02><did><unittitle>Short stories and other writings
      </unittitle></did>
         <c03><did><unittitle><title render="quoted">The
         Lottery</title></unittitle></did>
            <c04><did><unittitle>Dramatic
            adaptations</unittitle></did>
               <c05><did><unittitle>Correspondence, 1949-1953,
               1967-1970</unittitle></did></c05>
               <c05><did><unittitle>Scripts and screenplays,
               n.d.</unittitle> </did></c05></c04>
            <c04><did><container>48</container><unittitle>Royalty
            statements, 1950-1953, 1964-1970</unittitle></did></c04>
         </c03>
         <c03><did><unittitle><title render="quoted">Lover's
         Meeting, </title> n.d.</unittitle></did></c03>
      </c02>
   </c01>
   [...]
</dsc>
```

**Figure 3.5.2.5f.** *In-Depth Model <dsc type = "in-depth"> Encoded Container List.*

### 3.5.3. Controlled Vocabulary Terms <controlaccess>

Many archivists have become accustomed to assigning authority-controlled access terms in MARC catalog records describing their holdings. Use of controlled terms provides standardized, authoritative versions of personal, corporate, and geographic names, subjects, form and genre terms, and other access points that facilitate searching and retrieval in bibliographic databases. In EAD, such formal access terms may be grouped in <controlaccess> or distributed throughout the finding aid. Some of these access term elements have already been mentioned in conjunction with <origination>, <physdesc>, <bioghist>, and <scopecontent> (see subsections of 3.5.1).

The <controlaccess> element is a wrapper element that groups key access points for the described materials and enables authority-controlled searching across finding aids on a computer network, serving a function similar to the added entries and subject headings in a catalog record (1xx, 6xx, and 7xx fields in MARC). Hundreds of names and subjects can appear in a finding aid; processors and catalogers identify the most significant ones for special encoding as controlled access terms. Finding aid searches limited to <controlaccess> subelements will improve the likelihood of locating strong sources of information on a desired topic, because access terms will have been entered in a consistent form across finding aids. At a minimum, the same controlled access terms should be encoded in EAD as in the MARC record for the collection. The elements contained in <controlaccess> are these (listed here in the order in which they will be discussed):

- Personal Name <persname>
- Corporate Name <corpname>
- Family Name <famname>
- Geographic Name <geogname>
- Name <name>
- Genre/Physical Characteristic <genreform>
- Function <function>
- Occupation <occupation>
- Subject <subject>
- Title <title>

The <controlaccess> element can be used directly in <archdesc> to provide access terms for an entire collection. It also can be used in <c>s to provide access points to specific components of a collection. There are advantages and disadvantages to each approach. Grouping all of the access term elements inside a parent <controlaccess> in <archdesc> will make searching, display, and browsing of the access terms easier. The potential disadvantage is that retrieval will be rather imprecise, particularly for a large collection. The search results will tell the user merely that there is material relevant to the search term somewhere in the collection. Placing <controlaccess> within multiple <c>s, on the other hand, will take the user to more specific points in the finding aid. It is even possible to use

<controlaccess> for item-level description, if that is the most appropriate level at which to provide access points for a particular collection. A potential disadvantage to placing <controlaccess> terms so deeply within a finding aid, however, is that such an approach is more time consuming and therefore more costly.

The archival principle of multilevel description, the SGML concept of inheritance, and the EAD <controlaccess> element can all work together to provide a very sophisticated access system. The trade-offs are the need for a very sophisticated search engine to take advantage of the tagging and the added cost of marking up the text. Each institution will need to weigh the costs and benefits of depth of indexing based on availability of appropriate search and display mechanisms, the size and research value of a collection, and the expense of doing more complex markup. For many collections, and in many repositories, bundling all the controlled access terms in <archdesc> will be the most practical approach.

#### 3.5.3.1. Use of Attributes in <controlaccess> Subelements

The content of each of the specific <controlaccess> subelements can be further specified through the use of attributes. While none of the attributes are required, their utilization will enhance the precision and reusability of the information.

The SOURCE attribute designates the source of a specific controlled vocabulary term or the rules that were used to formulate it. For each of the index term subelements available in <controlaccess> the SOURCE attribute is a semiclosed list.[67] The source list includes acronyms for several types of sources:

- Thesauri, such as *Art & Architecture Thesaurus* (aat) and *Thesaurus for Graphic Materials I and II* (lctgm and gmgpc)
- Authority lists, such as *Library of Congress Name Authority File* (lcnaf), *Union List of Artists Names* (ulan), *National Council on Archives Rules for Construction of Personal, Corporate, and Place Names* (ncarules)
- Cataloging rules, such as *Anglo-American Cataloging Rules*, 2nd ed. (aacr2), *Archives, Personal Papers, and Manuscripts* (appm), and *Rules for Archival Description* (rad)

If the appropriate thesaurus, authority list, or cataloging rules source is not included in the semi-closed list enumerated in the *EAD Tag Library,* a code for it can be specified in the OTHERSOURCE attribute (the SOURCE attribute is set to the value "other", and then the code for the source being used is supplied in the OTHERSOURCE attribute). Note that "local terms" may be encoded as one type of OTHERSOURCE, but just as is the case in an online catalog, extensive use of local terms will greatly reduce the effectiveness of cross-finding aid or cross-institutional searching.

---

[67] For a complete list of SOURCE attribute values see *Encoded Archival Description Tag Library, Version 1.0* (Chicago: Society of American Archivists, 1998): 29.

The AUTHFILENUMBER attribute can be used to specify an authority record number for a name or term. If AUTHFILENUMBER is used, the SOURCE attribute also should be used to identify the authority file from which the record number was taken. By including the AUTHFILENUMBER attribute, it may become possible to pull an authority record into a finding aid dynamically in order to make cross references available for searching. This is especially useful when, for example, an individual is the subject of a body of materials, since it is not possible to encode <persname> within <subject> (see also section 3.5.3.5).

The ROLE attribute is available in <corpname>, <famname>, <persname>, <geogname>, <name>, and <title> to specify the relationship of the named entity to the materials. Examples of such usage are illustrated in section 3.5.3.2.

The ENCODINGANALOG attribute specifies a field or area in another descriptive encoding system to which an EAD element or attribute is comparable. Mapping elements from one system to another may help build a single interface that can index comparable information in bibliographic records and finding aids. ENCODINGANALOGs also could be used to arrange access terms for display purposes. Perhaps most significantly, it may be possible to generate a basic MARC record from a finding aid based on ENCODINGANALOG values.

MARC encoding analogs are specified in the *EAD Tag Library* for each relevant element.[68] The name of the related encoding system may be designated in one of two ways. First, it can be specified with the RELATEDENCODING attribute in <archdesc>, the value of which would be inherited by every ENCODINGANALOG attribute throughout the finding aid.

```
<archdesc langmaterial="eng" level="collection"
relatedencoding="marc">
   <controlaccess>
      <head>Topics</head>
      <subject encodinganalog="650" source="lcsh">Fishery law
      and legislation--Minnesota.</subject>
   </controlaccess>
</archdesc>
```

Alternatively, if multiple encoding systems will be referred to within <archdesc>, the name of the specific encoding system may be encoded in each occurrence of the ENCODINGANALOG attribute value. If MARC is the related encoding system, the value for the ENCODINGANALOG attribute is the appropriate MARC field number.

[68] In addition, a USMARC-to-EAD crosswalk is provided in appendix B.

```
<archdesc langmaterial="eng" level="collection">
  <controlaccess>
      <head>Topics</head>
         <subject encodinganalog="marc650"
         source="lcsh">Fishery law and legislation--
         Minnesota.</subject>
   </controlaccess>
</archdesc>

<archdesc langmaterial="eng" level="collection">
   <controlaccess>
      <head>Index Terms</head>
      <controlaccess>
         <head>Topics</head>
         <subject encodinganalog="marc650"
         source="lcsh">Fishery law and legislation--
         Minnesota.</subject>
      </controlaccess>
   </controlaccess>
   <dsc type="combined">
      <c01 level="series" encodinganalog="isad3.1.4">
         <did><unittitle>Correspondence</unittitle></did>
      </c01>
   </dsc>
</archdesc>
```

### 3.5.3.2. Personal, Corporate, Family, and Geographic Names <persname>, <corpname>, <famname>, and <geogname>

Finding aids contain many personal, corporate, family, and geographic names. Each of these name types corresponds to a specific EAD element, and each element correlates to specific MARC fields.

The <persname> element is used for a proper noun designation for an individual, including any or all of that individual's forenames, surnames, honorific titles, and added names, as well as birth and death dates:

```
<persname encodinganalog="600" source="lcnaf">Ferry, Dexter
Mason, 1833-1907.</persname>
<persname encodinganalog="600" source="lcnaf"
role="correspondent">Mason, Darius.</persname>
```

The <corpname> element is used for a proper noun designation that identifies an organization or a group of people that acts as an entity. Examples include names of associations, institutions, business firms, nonprofit enterprises, governments, government agencies, projects, programs, religious bodies, churches, conferences, athletic contests, exhibitions, expeditions, fairs, and ships. The <subarea> element can be used to code explicitly the subordinate units of a corporate body, if desired. It is not necessary to repeat the SOURCE attribute within the <subarea> element:

```
<corpname encodinganalog="610" source="lcnaf" role="subject">
University of Detroit.
   <subarea encodinganalog="610">Department of Chemistry.
   </subarea>
</corpname>
<corpname encodinganalog="610" source="lcnaf">University of
Detroit.
   <subarea encodinganalog="610">Department of Mathematics.
   </subarea>
</corpname>
```

The <famname> element is used for a proper noun designation for a group of persons who form a household or are closely related, including both single families and family groups:

```
<famname encodinganalog="600" source="lcnaf">Patience Parker
family.</famname>
<famname encodinganalog="600" source="lcnaf">Parker
family.</famname>
```

The <geogname> element is used for a proper noun designation for a place, natural feature, or political jurisdiction:

```
<geogname encodinganalog="651" source="lcsh">Chinatown (San
Francisco, Calif.)</geogname>
<geogname encodinganalog="651" source="lcsh">Appalachian
Mountains.</geogname>
<geogname encodinganalog="651" source="lcsh">Baltimore
(Md.)</geogname>
```

The <name> element may be used instead of one of the four specific name elements when it is not known what kind of name is being described, when a high degree of precision is unnecessary or unaffordable, or if it is not practical to train your encoders to distinguish among the more specific name types. For example, <name> might be used in <indexentry> when it is not clear if the name "Bachrach" refers to a person or a photographic firm. While <name> is technically valid within <controlaccess>, the ambiguous nature of both the <name> element and the data it contains render its use far less powerful than the more specific proper name elements.

### 3.5.3.3. Form and Genre Terms <genreform>

Researchers may try to access collections by the type of materials they contain, such as diaries, photographs, or holiday or greeting cards. The element <genreform> is used to encode such types of material by naming the style or technique of their intellectual content (genre), order of information or object function (form), or physical characteristics:

```
<genreform encodinganalog="655" source="gmgpc">Architectural
drawings.</genreform>
<genreform encodinganalog="655" source="aat">Photographs.
</genreform>
```

### 3.5.3.4. Function and Occupation Terms <function> and <occupation>

Terms for the spheres of activities and organizational processes that generated the described materials are encoded in <function>. Such terms often provide useful access points, especially for corporate, government, or institutional records:

```
<function encodinganalog="657" source="aat">Enforcing
law.</function>
<function encodinganalog="657" source="aat">Convicting.</function>
```

Terms identifying a type of work, profession, trade, business, or avocation that is significantly reflected in the materials are encoded in <occupation>:

```
<occupation encodinganalog="656" source="aat">Dramatists.
</occupation>
<occupation encodinganalog="656" source="aat">Librarians.
</occupation>
```

### 3.5.3.5. Subjects and Titles <subject> and <title>

Finding aids contain broad and narrow terms that identify topics associated with or covered by the described materials; these are encoded in <subject>. Note, however, that personal, corporate, family, and geographic *names* being used as the *subject* of the materials are tagged as <persname>, <corpname>, <famname> and <geogname>, respectively. In such cases, the ROLE attribute may be set to "subject" to specify that a name has a subject relationship to the materials being described (setting the ENCODINGANALOG to the appropriate MARC subject field is another option):

```
<subject encodinganalog="650" source="lcsh">Alien and Sedition
laws, 1798.</subject>
<subject encodinganalog="650" source="lcsh">American
Confederate voluntary exiles.</subject>
<persname encodinganalog="600" source="lcnaf"
role="subject">Williams, Robert Franklin, 1925- </persname>
```

Formal names of works such as monographs, serials, or paintings occur in many finding aids, and <title> may be used to encode such information. The RENDER attribute in <title> is particularly useful for specifying how a title should be presented for display purposes, such as in italics or quotation marks. Titles that are topics of correspondence or other materials in a collection should be encoded as <title> with a ROLE attribute of "subject." Subtitles of such works are not separately encoded, but a publication date may be encoded in <date> within <title>.

```
<title encodinganalog="630" role="subject" render="italic">
Huckleberry Finn</title>
```

Do *not* use <title> for the informal titles of units of archival description, such as series or file titles, for which <unittitle> is instead the correct element.

#### 3.5.3.6. Use of Grouped Controlled Vocabulary Terms

Headings and explanatory text can be incorporated into <controlaccess> using <head>, <note>, and <p>. Several formatting elements also are available, including <list>, <table>, and <blockquote>, but it is also possible (and often preferable) instead to control display of a block of access terms using a stylesheet.

The <controlaccess> element is recursive, which permits nested index terms to be grouped and labeled in units that will be meaningful to users in an online display. A repository might choose to group terms by MARC field equivalent (600s as Personal Names, 650s as Topics, 655s as Form and Genre). If the repository creates separate MARC records for different formats of materials that have been physically arranged in distinct series or other groupings, such as photographs or sound recordings, separate nested <controlaccess> elements may be opened to group the terms for each general type of material. The following example illustrates groupings of <controlaccess> terms based on MARC field equivalents:

```
<controlaccess>
   <head>Index Terms</head>
   <controlaccess>
      <head>Personal Names</head>
       <persname encodinganalog="600" source="lcnaf">Anderson,
       Jane, 1929-1937.</persname>
      <persname encodinganalog="600" source="lcnaf">Smith,
      Charles Spencer, 1852-1923.</persname>
   </controlaccess>
   <controlaccess>
       <head>Organizations</head>
       <corpname encodinganalog="610" source="lcnaf">African
       Methodist Episcopal Church.</corpname>
   </controlaccess>
   <controlaccess>
       <head>Topics</head>
       <subject encodinganalog="650" source="lcsh">Clergy--
       United States.</subject>
       <subject encodinganalog="650" source="lcsh">Education--
       United States.</subject>
   </controlaccess>
   <controlaccess>
       <head>Contributors</head>
       <persname encodinganalog="700" source="lcnaf">Smith,
       Charles S. (Charles Spencer),  Jr.</persname>
       <persname encodinganalog="700" source="lcnaf">Smith,
       Christine Shoecraft.</persname>
   </controlaccess>
   <controlaccess>
       <head>Forms of Material</head>
       <genreform encodinganalog="655" source="aat">
       Photographs.</genreform>
   </controlaccess>
</controlaccess>
```

### 3.5.3.7. Use of Controlled Vocabulary Outside of <controlaccess>

As noted earlier, only a small portion of the names and subjects represented in a collection typically will be encoded within <controlaccess>, usually those identified as the most significant. EAD also permits in-depth indexing outside of <controlaccess>, and all 10 of the access term elements discussed above are available within a variety of textual elements, including <p>. Names, subjects, form and genre terms, and others can be tagged in direct, natural language order within the flow of text, and where desired, the NORMAL attribute can be used to add a controlled vocabulary version of the name or term for retrieval purposes.

The following example illustrates in-depth markup of names, subjects, and form and genre terms within a biographical note and a container list:

```
<archdesc level="collection">
   <bioghist>
      <p><persname normal="Winchell, Alexander">Alexander
      Winchell</persname> was professor of
      <subject>geology</subject> and
      <subject>paleontology</subject> at the
      <corpname>University of Michigan</corpname>, director of
      the <corpname>Michigan Geological Survey</corpname>, and
      chancellor of <corpname>Syracuse University</corpname>,
      but he was most noted as a popular lecturer and writer on
      scientific topics and as a Methodist layman who worked to
      reconcile traditional religious beliefs to nineteenth-
      century developments in the fields of
      <subject>evolutionary biology</subject>,
      <subject>cosmology</subject>, <subject>geology</subject>,
      and <subject>paleontology</subject>. ... </p>
   </bioghist>

   <dsc type="in-depth">
      <c01 level="series">
         <did>
            <unittitle><genreform normal="diaries">Accounts of
            Geological Expeditions and Travel</genreform>
            </unittitle>
         </did>
         <c02>
            <did>
               <container>23</container>
               <unittitle>Expedition to <geogname>Lake Superior
               </geogname><unitdate>1867</unitdate>
               </unittitle>
            </did>
         </c02>
         <c02>
            <did>
               <container>23</container>
               <unittitle>Excursion to <geogname>New England
               </geogname><unitdate>1867-1868</unitdate>
               </unittitle>
            </did>
         </c02>
      </c01>
   </dsc>
</archdesc>
```

No consensus exists as yet regarding the utility and practicality of doing such extensive markup of proper names in the narrative and container list sections of finding aids. The range of practice includes the following:

- Marking up all occurrences and variations of personal and corporate names
- Marking up one occurrence of every name in a finding aid
- Marking up only those names deemed to represent significant content in a collection
- No markup of name elements outside of <controlaccess>

Some institutions are encoding access terms without using the NORMAL attribute to provide a standardized version of the name, relying instead on search engines to find combinations of first and last names within a single tag, or simply encouraging users to be creative in constructing searches on variant versions of a name. Tagging every occurrence of a name may actually mislead researchers or search engines that report weighted results. The frequent occurrence of a name in a biographical sketch, for example, may suggest that a collection is more relevant to a search than the overall substance of the collection actually merits. Or the reverse may happen: a collection containing a wealth of information on an individual may be underreported in search results because that individual is referred to by initials rather than full name, or because the individual's name is implicit throughout much of the finding aid.

The value of encoding access term elements in the narrative and container list sections of finding aids is a question that requires more research on user needs and search strategies, the capabilities of search engines, and advances in natural language searching. Ultimately each institution must develop policies on the level to which it will mark up access terms outside of <controlaccess> based on current practice, research value of a collection, and available staff resources. Is it more important to have a few finding aids encoded at great depth, or to have many finding aids online with fewer access points encoded?

### 3.5.4. Adjunct Descriptive Data <add>

Archivists frequently append to finding aids ancillary access tools that may not describe the collection in the same direct manner as <scopecontent> or other <archdesc> elements. Such tools may include file plans, bibliographies, indexes, and lists of related or separated materials. The Adjunct Descriptive Data <add> element is a wrapper for such information; it is available within <archdesc> and also within <c> to enable placement of such information at any level. The <add> subelements are:

- Bibliography <bibliography>
- File Plan <fileplan>
- Index <index>
- Other Finding Aid <otherfindaid>
- Related Material <relatedmaterial>
- Separated Material <separatedmaterial>

Within each of these subelements, generic textual features such as Bibliographic Reference <bibref>, Block Quote <blockquote>, Heading <head>, List <list>, Paragraph <p>, and Table <table> are available. If a tool applies to the entire finding aid, it should be encoded at the end of <archdesc> following all <c>s. If it applies only to one component, however, it may be placed within the appropriate <c>. For example, a file plan may relate to all the components in a finding aid, but an index of correspondents may relate only to a correspondence series.

### 3.5.4.1. Bibliographies <bibliography>

Finding aids may contain citations to works of any type, such as books, articles, television or radio programs, or Web sites that are about, based on, or would be of special interest when using the described materials. The <bibliography> element can be used to group such citations, and it contains subelements that permit special formatting (<list>, <table>), linking (<archref>, <extref>), or simple narrative text (<p>). Within <bibliography>, <bibref> permits the tagging of publication information (<edition>, <imprint>) as well as access points (<persname>, <corpname>).

```
<bibliography>
   <head>Bibliography</head>
   <bibref><title>Annual Reports</title>. New York: National
   Association for the Advancement of Colored People.
   1910- .</bibref>
   <bibref>Finch, Minnie. <title>The NAACP, Its Fight for
   Justice</title>. Metuchen, N.J.: Scarecrow Press, 1981. </bibref>
   <bibref>Hughes, Langston. <title>Fight for Freedom: The Story of
   the NAACP</title>. New York: Norton, 1962.</bibref>
</bibliography>
```

### 3.5.4.2. File Plans and Other Finding Aids <fileplan> and <otherfindaid>

Corporate and government archives frequently utilize classification schemes that were developed to arrange, store, and retrieve materials. The <fileplan> element can be used to encode any filing scheme used by the individuals or organizations originally responsible for creating or compiling the materials.

```
<fileplan>
   <head>File Index - Central Records - Irvine Campus</head>
   <note><p>Seventh revision: March 1985</p></note>
   <table>
      <tgroup cols="2">
         <tbody>
            <row>
               <entry>100-149</entry>
               <entry>University Affairs</entry>
            </row>
            <row>
               <entry>150-299</entry>
               <entry>Personnel</entry>
            </row>
            <row>
               <entry>300-399</entry>
               <entry>Administrative Activities and
               Operations</entry>
            </row>
            [...]
         </tbody>
      </tgroup>
   </table>
</fileplan>
```

The element <otherfindaid> describes additional or alternative guides to the described material, such as card files, donor or dealer lists, or lists generated by the creator or compiler of the materials. This element simply indicates the existence of such tools that are external to the finding aid; it does not encode their contents.

```
<otherfindaid>
   <p>The donor's card file, which contains descriptions of
   the individual items in the collection, is located in Box
   16.</p>
</otherfindaid>
```

### 3.5.4.3. Indexes <index>

The <index> element is used to encode any list of key terms and reference pointers that has been compiled to facilitate access to the materials. In some cases, terms and names found elsewhere in the finding aid are simply gathered in <index>. In other situations, <index> may be the only place where the name or term is found, such as when the letters are located in a file entitled "Correspondence, R-T" and each individual correspondent's name is not specifically mentioned in the folder list. Within <index>, <indexentry> contains the same access point elements that are available within <controlaccess>, which can be used to incorporate authority information into the index through use of the SOURCE and ENCODINGANALOG attributes (see section 3.5.3.1). An empty linking element, <ptr>, and <ref>, a linking element that can also contain text, also can be used to take the user back to the appropriate file in the container list (see section 7.2.1 for more information on these linking elements).

```
<index>
   <head>Index of Correspondents</head>
   <indexentry>
      <corpname>A.P. Watt & Son</corpname>
      <ref>47.5</ref>
   </indexentry>
   <indexentry>
      <corpname>Abbey Theatre</corpname>
      <ptrgrp>
         <ref>47.5</ref>
         <ref>55.5</ref>
      </ptrgrp>
   </indexentry>
   <indexentry>
      <persname>Achurch, Janet</persname>
      <ptrgrp>
         <ref>32.5</ref>
         <ref>32.6</ref>
      </ptrgrp>
   </indexentry>
   <indexentry>
      <persname>Adam, Ronald, 1896-1979</persname>
      <ref>32.4</ref>
   </indexentry>
   <indexentry>
      <corpname>American Mercury</corpname>
      <ref>47.6</ref>
   </indexentry>
</index>
```

#### 3.5.4.4. Related and Separated Materials <relatedmaterial> and <separatedmaterial>

In the course of processing a collection, archivists may create lists of materials that have been weeded or sent to another custodial unit (such as a separately administered photography department). In addition, the repository may provide a list of collections that deal with similar topics, contain the same format of materials, or were generated from the same geographic region or during the same political or social era. EAD makes a distinction between materials residing elsewhere that are, or are not, related to the described materials by provenance.

The <relatedmaterial> element encodes information about materials that are neither physically or logically included in the materials described in the finding aid nor are related by provenance, accumulation, or use, but that might nevertheless be of interest to a researcher. A list of related materials might include other collections held by the same repository or by other repositories.

```
<relatedmaterial>
   <head>Related Materials</head>
   <p>Papers of prominent NAACP activists and records of NAACP
   branches and adjuncts are listed below.</p>
   <relatedmaterial>
      <head>Collections of Personal Papers</head>
      <archref>Ella Baker. State Historical Society of Wisconsin,
      Archives Division (Papers, 1959-1965).</archref>
      <archref>Mary McLeod Bethune. Dillard University, Amistad
      Research Center (Papers, 1923-1942).</archref>
      <archref>W.E.B. Du Bois. New York Public Library, Schomburg
      Center for Research in Black Culture (Papers, 1912-1966, bulk
      1942-1948).</archref>
      <archref>William Hastie. Harvard University, Law School
      Library (Papers, 1916-1976, bulk 1937-1976).</archref>
      <archref>Thurgood Marshall. Library of Congress, Manuscript
      Division (Papers, 1949-1991, bulk 1961-1991).</archref>
   </relatedmaterial>
   <relatedmaterial>
      <head>NAACP Branch and Other Records</head>
      <archref>NAACP Legal Defense and Education Fund. Library of
      Congress, Manuscript Division.</archref>
      <archref>NAACP Cleveland Branch. Western Reserve Historical
      Society. (Records, 1924-1967).</archref>
      <archref>NAACP Montgomery Branch. New York Public Library,
      Schomburg Center for Research in Black Culture. (Minutes,
      1954-1955).</archref>
   </relatedmaterial>
</relatedmaterial>
```

The element <separatedmaterial>, on the other hand, encodes information about materials that are associated by provenance to the materials described in the finding aid but that have been physically separated, either by the repository or by some other entity, either before or after the materials were acquired by the repository.

```
<separatedmaterial>
   <head>Material Cataloged Separately</head>
   <list>
      <item>Selected printed materials have been transferred to the
      book collection of The Bancroft Library.</item>
      <item>Photographs have been transferred to Pictorial
      Collections of The Bancroft Library.</item>
      <item>Films and sound recordings have been transferred to the
      Microforms Division of The Bancroft Library.</item>
      <item>Selected maps have been transferred to the Map
      Room.</item>
   </list>
</separatedmaterial>
```

### 3.5.5. Data Fitting No Specific Category: Other Descriptive Data <odd>

The EAD developers could not anticipate or provide a specific element for every type of information that might be found in finding aids created by different types of institutions, particularly in an international context. In addition, inclusion of a generic catchall element seemed a useful technique to help ease the conversion of some legacy finding aids for which it may not be possible without extensive restructuring to tease apart bits of information that would more appropriately be encoded using EAD elements such as <bioghist>, <scopecontent>, or <admininfo>, as in the example below.

The Other Descriptive Data <odd> element was created to accommodate these occasions. It is recommended, however, that you encode information using a more specific element whenever possible, given the potentially negative consequences of the nonspecific retrieval or display results that may result from use of <odd>.

```
<odd>
   <p>Annie Montague Alexander, patroness of the University of
   California, founded and endowed the Museum of Vertebrate Zoology
   in 1908. These papers, which the Museum transferred to the
   Bancroft Library in 1965, consist primarily of letters from
   Joseph Grinnell, the first director of the Museum, discussing
   plans for its establishment, the Museum's collecting policy,
   personnel and expenses, field work, etc. There are also some
   letters from University officials and other members of the Museum
   staff, and miscellaneous letters from government officials,
   collectors and dealers reflecting Miss Alexander's interest in
   collecting zoological specimens. Related material is to be found
   in the official records of the Museum, which were transferred to
   University Archives at the same time.</p>
   <p>Additional papers received Feb. 1967, have been given the call
   number 67/121c.</p>
</odd>
```

## 3.6. Adding Metadata to Describe the Finding Aid

The elements that describe a body of archival materials (the *text* of the finding aid) are bundled in <archdesc>. In an online environment it is also important to include metadata describing the *finding aid itself* at the beginning of the electronic file; it may also be desirable to include a title page and some prefatory information relating to the finding aid. EAD accommodates such needs with <eadheader> and <frontmatter> respectively. The content of both elements relates to the finding aid per se rather than to the archival materials described therein.

### 3.6.1. EAD Header <eadheader>

In the paper environment it has not always been necessary to prepare formal descriptive data *about* the finding aid for inclusion within a finding aid document. Such information is, however, a critical component of an EAD finding aid residing in a machine-readable environment. The <eadheader> comprises a set of metadata about the finding aid that serves to identify unambiguously each particular EAD instance by providing a unique identification code for the document; by stating bibliographic information such as the author, title, and publisher of the finding aid; and by tracking significant revisions to the EAD file. The <eadheader> element and several of its subelements are *required*, and consistent formulation of the information within some of them is essential.

The <eadheader> was modeled on the Text Encoding Initiative (TEI)[69] header element to encourage uniformity in the provision of metadata across document types. The sequence of elements is specified by the EAD DTD, with the expectation that searches by finding aid title, date, language, or repository will be more predictable if all finding aid creators follow a uniform order of metadata elements. Consequently, <eadheader> is a required wrapper element containing four subelements that must appear in the following order: <eadid>, <filedesc>, <profiledesc>, and <revisiondesc>.

[69] The Text Encoding Initiative is an international humanities-based effort to develop a suite of DTDs for encoding literary or other scholarly texts likely to be objects of study. Information is available at: <http://www.uic.edu/orgs/tei>.

In addition, <eadheader> has some important attributes:

- The AUDIENCE attribute should be set to "internal" unless you wish to use the header information to generate a public display, such as in the form of a title page for the finding aid
- The state of completeness of the finding aid may be indicated by using the FINDAIDSTATUS attribute, which can be set to "unverified-partial-draft," "unverified-full-draft," "edited-partial-draft," or "edited-full-draft"
- An ENCODINGANALOG may be specified for the <eadheader> independently of that for <archdesc>, since the header information may more appropriately be mapped to a set of metadata elements designed specifically for electronic resource discovery on the Internet, such as Dublin Core, than to MARC or ISAD(G)
- Language encoding for EAD instances utilizes ISO 639-2 Codes for the Representation of Names of Languages, and the LANGENCODING attribute always should be "ISO 639-2"

An <eadheader> start-tag with full content designation of these attributes might look like this:

```
<eadheader audience="internal" encodinganalog="Dublin Core"
findaidstatus="edited-full-draft" langencoding="ISO 639-2">
```

Since <eadheader> captures a full bibliographic description of the finding aid, it is possible to use it to generate a title page for the finding aid. Keep in mind, however, that there is no flexibility in the order in which the elements are encoded, and stylesheets may or may not be able to reorder the elements for output. If you want a nicely formatted title page with information displayed or printed in a specific order, use the <titlepage> element under <frontmatter> for this purpose (see section 3.6.2).

An example of a complete encoded <eadheader> is given in section 3.6.1.5.

### 3.6.1.1. Unique File Identifier <eadid>

The <eadid> element is a *required* subelement of <eadheader> that designates a *unique* identifier for a given EAD instance. The "uniqueness" aspect of this definition is meant very literally, since the value contained in each individual <eadid> element must be distinct from all other occurrences of <eadid> in other finding aids, so as to differentiate each particular electronic file from all others. This is intended to be true not only within a given institution's naming conventions, but optimally across the entire universe of finding aids that might some day come together in a multi-institutional union catalog.

This one-of-a-kind identifier may be encoded entirely within the text of the <eadid> element, or as a combination of the element text and a value in the SYSTEMID attribute that names the repository. In this way a local designation such as "M32," which may be used by multiple archives, can be modified and rendered unique via the addition of a local designation in the attribute, such as the NUC symbol for a U.S. repository.

Three broad categories of designation may be employed in <eadid>:

- Local identification numbers
- Electronic file names
- SGML catalog entries

Local identification numbers, such as call numbers, are best used in conjunction with a local designation in the SYSTEMID attribute.

Electronic file names may be used, either in the form of a Uniform Resource Identifier (URI, a formal file path name) or a mediated name such as a purl (see section 5.4 for a discussion of issues relating to file naming).

The third option is an SGML catalog entry, which names the EAD instance in the same manner that a general external entity is cited (see section 6.5 for more information on entities). This includes the use of a formal public identifier, which may be thought of as an SGML citation form. The SGML catalog entry approach has two advantages. First, it includes sufficient information in the element text to identify uniquely the collection represented in the finding aid rather than simply giving an ambiguous number or file name. Second, as an SGML entity it may be linked through an entry in an external SGML catalog file to the computer storage location of the document. In this way, an actual computer file name, which may change over time, need not be "hard-wired" or embedded in the EAD instance. This eliminates the need to update individual finding aids when the EAD files change names or locations.[70] Unfortunately, XML does not recognize the SGML catalog concept. As a result, the value of using a catalog entry as a surrogate for a specific file name in the <eadid> (or for any entity reference) does not apply with XML systems.

#### 3.6.1.2. File Description <filedesc>

Bibliographic information about the intellectual content of the encoded finding aid is bundled in the *required* element <filedesc>, in which the finding aid's title, subtitle, author, and publisher are encoded in a series of subelements.

The *required* <titlestmt> sublement may include the title and subtitle of the encoded finding aid, the name of the author, and the name of the sponsor, in that order. The *required* <titleproper> within <titlestmt> should be a formal title for the finding aid itself, such as "An Inventory of the Papers of Tom Stoppard at the Harry Ransom Humanities Research

---

[70] For a description of how formal public identifiers for use in an SGML catalog are constructed for the American Heritage Virtual Library Project and the Online Archive of California, see *Encoded Archival Description Retrospective Conversion Guidelines*, available at: <http://sunsite.berkeley.edu/amher/upguide.html#VI>.

Center," or "The Tom Stoppard Papers, 1944-1995: An Inventory of His Papers at the Harry Ransom Humanities Research Center."[71] The <titleproper> element has several attributes, perhaps the most useful of which are EXTENT and PUBSTATUS. The EXTENT attribute indicates whether the finding aid describes all or part of the materials, while PUBSTATUS indicates whether the finding aid is published or unpublished. A fully-encoded <titlestmt> might look like this:

```
<titlestmt>
   <titleproper pubstatus="pub" extent="all">The Tom Stoppard
   Papers, 1944-1995</titleproper>
   <subtitle>An Inventory of His Papers at the Harry Ransom
   Humanities Research Center</subtitle>
   <author>Finding aid prepared by K. Mosley</author>
</titlestmt>
```

Other bibliographic elements within <filedesc> are <editionstmt>, <publicationstmt>, <seriesstmt>, and <notestmt>, which must be presented in the order just stated if they are used. All are optional and may be used infrequently or never by many repositories.

Institutions seldom have the luxury of producing more than one edition of a finding aid, but in an instance where additional materials are acquired and incorporated into the collection and the finding aid subsequently is expanded and updated, <editionstmt> provides the capability of adding edition information. The ease with which finding aids can be published and edited on the Web may encourage more frequent updates or editions.

In a paper environment, repositories may not have considered their finding aids "published," since they typically resided in file cabinets and binders in the repository. In the Internet environment, however, finding aids are considered publications. The element <publicationstmt> contains information about the publication or distribution of the encoded finding aid and can include the repository's name and address, the date of publication, and other relevant details. The entire text of <publicationstmt> can be stated in <p>, or the information can be more precisely encoded using <publisher>, <address>, and <date>:

```
<publicationstmt>
   <p>Harry Ransom Humanities Research Center, 1996</p>
</publicationstmt>

<publicationstmt>
   <publisher>Harry Ransom Humanities Research Center, </publisher>
   <date type="publication">1996</date>
</publicationstmt>
```

Either method of markup is equally valid, but remember that more specific content designation increases flexibility in manipulation of the data.

---

[71] It is important to note that such a title for the *finding aid* itself varies from the title of the *archival collection* that is encoded in <did><unittitle> (see section 3.5.1.1).

If the encoded finding aid is published as part of a monographic series, this information can be encoded in <seriesstmt>. Like <publicationstmt>, <p> may be used in lieu of specific elements, or you may specifically encode the title of the series using <titleproper> and the series numbering using <num>:

```
<seriesstmt>
   <p>Stuffatoria unite, vol. 65</p>
</seriesstmt>

<seriesstmt>
<titleproper>Stuffatoria unite, </titleproper>
<num>vol. 65</num>
</seriesstmt>
```

The <notestmt> element can contain a series of <note>s, each of which would contain a single piece of descriptive information about the finding aid. This use of <note> would be different from its purpose in <did>, where <note> is intended for explanatory, not descriptive, text concerning the archival materials being described.

### 3.6.1.3. Version of the Encoded Finding Aid <profiledesc>

While <filedesc> provides bibliographic information about the intellectual content of the finding aid, <profiledesc> bundles information about the creation of the *encoded version* of the finding aid, such as the name of the encoder, the place and date of the encoding, and the version of EAD used. The creator of the finding aid and the individual who encodes it may or may not be one and the same, depending on institutional workflow and whether the finding aid is new or contains legacy data that is being converted. It may be important to distinguish these individuals, especially if the encoding is done by a third party and does not reflect the encoding policies of the institution that created the finding aid.

The <profiledesc> element is not required, but its use is recommended, since it establishes initial version control for the finding aid. The <profiledesc> element also can record the language(s) in which the finding aid itself was written within the <langusage> and <language> elements. Including this information may enable search engines to restrict searches to finding aids written in selected languages.

```
<profiledesc>
   <creation>Finding aid encoded in EAD V1.0 by Kris Kiesling
   using Author/Editor V.3.5, <date>November 4,
   1998</date>.</creation> <langusage>Finding aid written in
   <language>English</language> and
   <language>Spanish</language>.</langusage>
</profiledesc>
```

### 3.6.1.4. Revisions of the Encoded Finding Aid <revisiondesc>

Keeping track of various versions of a finding aid and the nature of the changes made has long been a standard need of archives, and maintenance of EAD finding aids is no different. The last <eadheader> element, <revisiondesc>, contains information about changes that have been made to the encoded finding aid.

The <revisiondesc> element is intended to document *substantial changes* made to the finding aid, such as those resulting from the addition of collection material or from updating the finding aid from one version of EAD to another. As with <profiledesc>, use of <revisiondesc> is not required but is recommended. It is not necessary (or recommended), however, that you record minor editorial or typographical changes made after the finding aid has been encoded. As with the other <eadheader> elements, <revisiondesc> is modeled on the TEI DTD, which recommends that changes be numbered and listed in reverse chronological order (the most recent change is listed first):

```
<revisiondesc>
   <change>
      <date>January 23, 2000</date>
      <item>2. Finding aid converted from EAD V1.0 to V2.0 by
      Jackie Dooley</item>
   </change>
   <change>
      <date>March 17, 1999</date>
      <item>1. Finding aid revised to incorporate additional
      materials acquired in December 1998, and re-encoded by
      Bill Landis</item>
   </change>
</revisiondesc>
```

Revision of the finding aid also may require that information in other <eadheader> elements will need to be changed. For example, inclusive dates in <titleproper> may expand, you may consider the finding aid to be a new edition if the revisions are extensive, and the creator and creation date of the encoded finding aid may need to be updated in <profiledesc>. A thorough review of the content of the <eadheader> is advisable whenever <revisiondesc> is utilized.

### 3.6.1.5. Encoded <eadheader> example

The following is an example of a fully-encoded <eadheader> element:

```
<eadheader audience="internal" langencoding="ISO 639-2"
findaidstatus="edited-full-draft">
   <eadid systemid="dlc"
   encodinganalog="856">loc.mss/eadmss.ms996001</eadid>
   <filedesc>
      <titlestmt>
         <titleproper>Shirley Jackson</titleproper>
         <subtitle>A Register of Her Papers in the Library of
         Congress</subtitle>
         <author>Prepared by Grover Batts. Revised and expanded by
         Michael McElderry with the assistance of Scott
         McLemee</author>
      </titlestmt>
      <publicationstmt>
         <date>1993</date>
         <publisher>Manuscript Division, Library of Congress
         </publisher>
         <address>
            <addressline>Washington, D.C. 20540-4860</addressline>
         </address>
      </publicationstmt>
      <notestmt>
         <note>
            <p>Edited full draft</p>
         </note>
      </notestmt>
   </filedesc>
   <profiledesc>
      <creation>Finding aid encoded by Library of Congress
      Manuscript Division,
         <date>1996.</date>
      </creation>
      <langusage>Finding aid written in
         <language>English.</language>
      </langusage>
   </profiledesc>
   <revisiondesc>
      <change>
         <date>1997</date>
         <item>Encoding revised</item>
      </change>
   </revisiondesc>
</eadheader>
```

## 3.6.2. Title Page and Prefatory Matter <frontmatter>

Some repositories formally publish selected finding aids as monographs or other types of publication. Even if your repository does not have this practice, you may want to create a formal title page for your encoded finding aids for online presentation purposes. The element <frontmatter> is a wrapper element containing two subelements that provide publication-type structures, <titlepage> and <div>.

The <titlepage> element serves to group bibliographic details about an encoded finding aid, including <titleproper>, <subtitle>, <author>, <sponsor>, <publisher>, and <date>. Unlike many other <eadheader> elements, these elements can be applied in any order that suits your needs for formatting or order of information. In addition, <titlepage> can incorporate illustrations, institutional logos, or other graphic images. If <frontmatter> is used, the <titleproper> should match the <titleproper> used in the <eadheader> <filedesc> <titlestmt>.

The <div> element is a generic textual element that provides access to textual formatting elements such as <head>, <p>, and <list>; it can be used to encode forewords, acknowledgements, introductions, or any other type of prefatory matter.

Many EAD users have found <frontmatter> to be unnecessary, as they have instead achieved satisfactory online results by displaying to users selected elements from the <eadheader>.

## Chapter Four

# AUTHORING EAD DOCUMENTS

## 4.1. The Authoring Process

The process of applying SGML markup to documents, known as "authoring," involves several steps. These steps are summarized below and are described in greater detail in later sections of chapter 4 or elsewhere in these *Guidelines*.

### 4.1.1. Select Authoring Software

A variety of software choices are available for authoring EAD-encoded finding aids, which means that you must first select a particular application to use. This selection process involves careful evaluation of features, cost, appropriateness for your institution's technical environment, and suitability of the tool for creating new finding aids or for converting those already existing in machine readable form. Available software options are described in section 4.2.

### 4.1.2. Obtain the EAD DTD

Whichever software application you use, a copy of the EAD DTD will be required at some point in the authoring process. Some application vendors include a copy of the DTD with their software, or it may be obtained from the *Encoded Archival Description Official Web Site* at the Library of Congress.[72] Some SGML/XML authoring tools convert the DTD into an internal proprietary structure for more efficient manipulation within the particular product; examples include the rules files for Author/Editor and logic files for WordPerfect. Each software manufacturer supplies the software needed to convert the DTD into its own binary format; the necessary files for these applications are also available at the *EAD Help Pages* Web site[73] and may be downloaded in lieu of the DTD.

### 4.1.3. Encode the Finding Aid

A variety of methods may be employed to mark up a finding aid, depending on existing institutional workflows and software, staffing, cost considerations, and technical sophistication. The status of each particular document also may affect the techniques used: for example, whether the document being encoded is a newly-created finding aid, an existing finding aid that is not yet in machine readable form, or an existing electronic finding aid. Relevant administrative issues are reviewed in section 2.5, and detailed encoding instructions are in chapter 3.

### 4.1.4 Validate the EAD Document

To ensure conformity, proper processing, and data interchange, the encoded document must be compared to the specifications of the DTD to ensure that the markup adheres to the EAD standard. This process involves two steps: parsing and validation. This functionality may

---

[72] The *Encoded Archival Description Official Web Site* is available at: <http://www.loc.gov/ead/>.

[73] The *EAD Help Pages* are available at: <http://jefferson.village.virginia.edu/ead>.

be accomplished either by a parser that is built into the authoring software or by a separate program. Parsing is discussed in greater detail in sections 4.3.3 and 6.2.4.

## 4.2. Options for Authoring Software

A variety of software applications may be used to create EAD documents. This section describes four broad categories of authoring tools by type of application:[74]

- Text editors and word processors
- Native SGML/XML editors
- Text converters
- Databases

The overview of each type explains how that type of software generally functions, cites representative products available at the time these *Guidelines* were written, and characterizes the general advantages and disadvantages of each method. This marketplace currently is very dynamic, with the emergence of XML and XML-compliant software as a potentially significant force in a variety of environments, including office productivity tools, relational database managers, and electronic commerce.[75]

Additional steps will be required to produce an attractive printed version of the finding aid for public use, since the document will include all of the EAD tagging but will lack any formatting or other presentational directions. Several options are available, including the use of stylesheets produced through use of formatting languages such as XSL and DSSSL that can be used to specify the layout of print copies generated from EAD finding aids. See section 5.3.3 for information on stylesheets and section 5.3.4 for a discussion of print output.

### 4.2.1. Text Editors and Word Processors

Because an SGML document exists as a simple text file, it is possible to key an EAD finding aid using any software that can output a document in ASCII format. This includes text editors that come with your operating system, such as the DOS Editor, Windows Notepad or the Macintosh SimpleText programs. Word processors also may be employed, but the files must be exported in ASCII format rather than in the word processor's proprietary native format.

*Advantages*: Low cost, ready availability, and user familiarity are the chief virtues of these products.

*Disadvantages*: Text editors and word processor applications have no built-in knowledge of the rules of the EAD DTD and hence no method of verifying conformance to it. You must

---

[74] Other taxonomies are certainly possible.

[75] Information about many of the software products, both commercial and freeware, and the specific EAD-related files mentioned in this chapter is provided in the *EAD Help Pages*, available at: <http://jefferson.village.virginia.edu/ead>. New information will be added as additional products become available. Detailed information on many products also may be found in Robin Cover's *SGML/XML Web Page*, available at: <http://www.oasis-open.org/cover>.

rely, therefore, on the encoder's knowledge of EAD to ensure that data elements and attributes are correctly applied. You will have to employ a separate application to validate the document. Several are available currently as freeware, including NSGMLS and XML-specific parsers from Microsoft, IBM, and others.

When keying an EAD document using a text processor, you must be particularly careful about the use of certain characters and symbols. For example, the characters &, <, >, ", and ' have special meaning for SGML processors, as they may be either part of the text or part of the markup, and it is necessary to differentiate between the two. It is possible to include these and other "nonstandard" characters, such as letters that carry diacritics in non-English languages or other symbols not found on standard keyboards, in EAD documents by use of entity references (see section 6.5.2.1 for a discussion of character entity references). Extensive manual keying of entity strings may, however, significantly slow the authoring process. When using a word processor to create an EAD instance, particular care must be taken to ensure that an entity reference to the appropriate ISO character is inserted for such non-Latin letters and symbols instead of the proprietary escape codes that word processors typically use to display such characters. You will also have to generate the "prolog" section of the EAD instance manually (see section 6.2.3 for information about the EAD prolog).

### 4.2.2. Native SGML/XML Editors

Many software packages are available that are designed specifically for authoring SGML/XML documents such as EAD instances. These products may be differentiated by the operating systems for which they are available, their capacity to generate documents in SGML or XML (or both), or by their "look and feel."

With regard to look and feel, some software displays the text of the EAD instance in a linear fashion, with both the markup and the content of the finding aid appearing as a continuous block of text. In other software, markup appears in one window in the form of a tree structure that displays the hierarchical and nesting relationships of the elements, and the text of the finding aid appears in a parallel window. Software applications representative of both categories are described below, emphasizing those currently being used by archivists to create EAD documents.

#### 4.2.2.1. Linear Editors

Author/Editor, initially developed by SoftQuad but now distributed by Interleaf, is a widely employed editor typical of this product category. It is available in both Windows and Macintosh versions, performs continuous DTD validation, includes standard cut-and-paste editing features, a spell-checker and thesaurus, and has a built-in macro language. It has limited capabilities, using its internal styles features, to produce print copies from an EAD document, though it can work with the Quark Express desktop publisher to generate finely formatted output. Author/Editor requires a DTD to be compiled into its internal "rules" file format (ead.rls, available via the *EAD Help Pages*[76]).

Corel's WordPerfect word processing software began including SGML authoring capabilities with version 6.0. It too requires that the DTD be converted into its internal structure as a "logic" file (ead.lgc, available via the *EAD Help Pages)* and also incorporates the standard text manipulation features one would expect in a word processor. Printing the finding aid in a format suitable for public use (without tags and with appropriate physical layout on the page) requires application of the "styles" feature in WordPerfect.

#### 4.2.2.2. Tree-structured Editors

Interface Electronics offers Internet Archivist, an authoring package designed specifically for EAD.[77] The structure of the document being encoded displays in one window in a tree or hierarchical view, while the content of each element and its associated attributes appear in text boxes within the principal frame. The package features built-in conversion to HTML and simple printing capabilities.

The ADEPT Editor software from ArborText similarly displays the element structure as a tree in a secondary window and the text of the EAD document in the main window. Like other products in this category, it offers a full range of text processing features and has probably the most complete set of specialized functions for SGML authoring of any available tool. The format of both the screen view and the print output of the SGML instance is governed by two separate stylesheets written according to the FOSI specification (see sections 5.3.1 and 5.3.3 for a discussion of stylesheet languages). ADEPT Editor is available for most operating systems, including Windows, Macintosh, UNIX, and OS2. It was among the first commercial authoring packages to incorporate XML functionality.

Similar products in this group include Adobe's Framemaker + SGML and Vervet's XML Pro. As XML enters the commercial marketplace, software companies such as SoftQuad (with XMetaL) and Macromedia (with Dreamweaver 2) are adding XML editing capabilities to their HTML editors.

*Advantages*: Both types of native editors (linear and tree structured) have many useful features that make them an attractive option. The software "knows" SGML in general and the DTD being used in particular. By directly incorporating the DTD, the software can provide continuous validation of a document during the authoring process. These particular applications include many of the features that you would expect in a full-featured word processor, including a spelling checker, thesaurus, macros, internal styles governing the display of text, and templates. They also will manage entities and generate the document's prolog.

---

[76] The *EAD Help Pages* are available at: <http://jefferson.village.virginia.edu/ead>.

[77] For more information, consult the company's Web site, available at: <http://www.interface.com/ead>.

Although native editors assume that users have a general knowledge of the structure and application of a particular DTD, the software's prompts and pull-down menus aid the user in the selection of elements and the assigning of attributes. They also help encoders to insert and manage character and file entities. In a sense, the effort is done "up front" during the initial data entry phase. Once the document is finished, no further work is required, with the possible exception of printing a user-friendly version of the inventory.

*Disadvantages*: Some knowledge of the DTD is required of the encoder, though mastering the software itself generally is no more complex than for any typical office computer application. You probably will have to learn on your own, however, since local training centers are not likely to feature courses in such specialized tools. In addition, the cost of software may be a factor with some products. All of these applications are priced as specialized rather than commodity products, with prices beginning around $450, though Corel does offer significant educational discounts for WordPerfect.

Generating finely formatted print copies often involves additional steps and skills and sometimes additional software. Native editors are best suited to the keying of new or existing inventories not already in electronic form rather than for conversion of existing electronic files. This is because using such editors to encode existing machine-readable texts requires much cutting and pasting of the file after it has been opened in the editor and therefore may actually prove more time consuming (and therefore more costly) than simply rekeying the text.

### 4.2.3. Text Converters

Text conversion software transforms existing machine-readable text from its original format into an encoded document that conforms to a particular DTD. This category includes tools specific to source documents in a particular file format, such as Microsoft Word Rich Text Format (RTF), or a particular DTD structure; generalized and special purpose SGML-aware programming languages; and word processing macro languages.

Conversion always proceeds from the premise that there is information available in the source document that permits the conversion software to map equivalencies between text or codes in the original document and comparable EAD elements. Such information may include physical formatting data such as punctuation, capitalization, tabbing and indention; word processing styles; or other markup codes such as elements from another SGML DTD or from MARC tags. In general, the greater the consistency in the application of these clues in the source document, the more reliable and complete the conversion. Do not presume that these techniques can be applied successfully to any and all existing electronic texts, absent such consistent conversion "hooks."

Microsoft's SGML Author for Word is a generalized tool for converting documents created in the Windows version of Word into SGML documents. It accomplishes the conversion by using Word styles and templates features. You create styles, one corresponding to each EAD element, in a Word template for your documents, and then you formally create a link in the SGML Author software between each style and the equivalent EAD tag. This map is stored in an association file. As the finding aid is keyed into a Word document, appropriate formatting styles are applied to the text. During the conversion process, the software reads the association file and encodes the text of a particular document with the appropriate SGML tagging. TagPerfect software from the Finnish firm Delta Computers offers comparable functionality for converting Word documents into SGML.

As an alternative to these off-the-shelf solutions, you may choose to create your own program to accomplish the conversion. There are three general categories of tools for doing so, and they are distinguished by the complexity of the effort and power of the languages involved. The simplest languages to learn and apply are the internal macro languages of Word and WordPerfect, and some archival repositories have successfully used them for conversion. The macro programming language in version 8.0 of WordPerfect includes special features that address SGML-specific issues. Beginning with Word97, Microsoft has changed its macro language from WordBasic to Visual Basic for Applications. The macros that can be written using these tools can range in complexity from very simple to highly sophisticated.

A number of special purpose programs have been developed expressly for the task of converting structured text into SGML documents. These include DynaTag from INSO Corporation and Balise from AIS Software. They employ a complex programming syntax and are geared to experienced programmers. Balise is described, for example, as closely resembling the C++ language.

Another conversion option that falls somewhere between these two poles is Perl. A widely employed and well-documented programming language, Perl was designed expressly for the type of text manipulation that is required for conversion of existing finding aids to EAD. It has been used at several repositories by staff with an affinity for such technical undertakings. While one can purchase an introductory Perl manual in order to begin learning this programming language, be forewarned that it will take time to master Perl.

*Advantages*: Converters permit you to leverage existing machine-readable files and familiar software, provided that existing files are structured in a manner that will enable such transformation. By using the same software for creating inventories as you do for other office documents, you avoid the cost of a new suite of software. You also eliminate or substantially reduce the time required to learn a new application, thereby improving the likelihood of staff acceptance. There is an implicit assumption in such an *ex post facto* conversion scenario that the authors of documents will need only minimal, if any, knowledge of the underlying DTD structure. Also, since the original document was probably produced using a word processor, you avoid the need for additional steps to generate print copies for public use. Text conversion may be an effective approach for the encoding of legacy data already in electronic form and may also be suitable as part of your workflow for the production of new inventories.

*Disadvantages*: While staff costs (in terms of the overhead associated with knowing specialized software and the EAD DTD) are assumed up front during the authoring process when you use a native editor, similar overhead costs occur both before and after the fact with converters. First, source documents must be carefully formatted in advance to facilitate subsequent conversions. Development of the conversion routines themselves may involve an extended iterative design process. The conversion itself may prove more or less automatic, but manual intervention or post-conversion manipulation might be required. Some converters may be sensitive to variations occurring in source documents, either because the organizational structure of archival collections themselves vary or because of changes in finding aid formats over time. Programming adjustments may be required. Careful quality control review is necessary to insure that automated processes actually generate the desired output.

### 4.2.4. Databases

Some archives create and store descriptive information using off-the-shelf relational database management (DBMS) software. This approach may be particularly attractive for repositories that wish to link collections management data stored in a DBMS with the associated descriptive metadata typically found in finding aids. In this scenario, EAD encoding may be applied to text stored in the database during the process of generating output from the database system. This assumes both that the field structure of the database corresponds to EAD elements and that the software has the functional capability to generate output in the format of an EAD-compliant document. One feasible scenario may be to use a DBMS to generate container lists and perhaps series descriptions, while keying lengthier narratives such as biographical or scope and content notes in a word processor.

Eloquent Software's Gencat program is a proprietary DBMS that offers output of files in multiple formats, including EAD. Some archives have already written their own applications to export data from a database as EAD documents, but fairly advanced programming skills are required to do so. A potentially complex, yet extremely critical, issue in the design of such a database is the development of an architecture that supports the multilevel hierarchical structure of the components of an archival collection that is at the heart of EAD. Part of the challenge may lie in the fact that many archival database systems are very "flat," allowing only one or two levels of hierarchy to be expressed.

The use of databases may become more widespread and simpler to implement in the future when producers of relational databases such as Oracle, Sybase and others implement XML functionality into their products, as they have promised.

*Advantages*: Use of a DBMS may be advantageous for institutions with substantial investments in such applications. It may also be valuable for those needing to interchange descriptive metadata of the type found in EAD finding aids with other applications, such as collection management or records management systems.

*Disadvantages*: The programming required to implement such a database and export its data to EAD may required highly specialized training or skills. In addition, conversion of a "flat" database structure into EAD will fail to exploit some of EAD's power to express archival hierarchies.

### 4.3. Technical Issues in Authoring

This section provides discussions of the following technical issues as they relate to the authoring of EAD documents:

- The structure of the EAD DTD and its associated files
- EAD as both an SGML and an XML DTD
- Parsing EAD instances to verify conformance with the DTD
- Data interchange between MARC records and EAD finding aids
- The various effects of encoding features on output

#### 4.3.1. Structure of the EAD DTD

The EAD Document Type Definition (DTD) is an essential component of the authoring process. As a document, the DTD is constructed according to a strict syntax specified by the SGML standard. For file management purposes, components of the EAD DTD have been divided in a modular fashion into the ead.dtd file and four other associated files that function together as a unit. Two of these (see below) are not required if the finding aid is encoded using EAD in XML mode. All five files are simple text documents in ASCII format that can be viewed and edited in text or word processing software. The five files are:

- ead.dtd
- eadbase.ent
- eadnotat.ent
- eadchars.ent
- eadsgml.dcl

*ead.dtd*—This is the core EAD DTD file. It is brief, containing a version history of the DTD plus entity references that invoke the other files in the EAD suite. It also contains three *conditional sections* that enable or disable the following features: XML compatibility, XLink functionality, and the specialized features of EAD's array of tabular elements. The use of these features is described in sections 4.3.2.1 (XML compatibility), 4.3.5.4 (tabular layout), and 7.2.4 (XLink functionality).

*eadbase.ent*—This is the largest file of the group and contains the SGML rules for EAD.

*eadnotat.ent*—This file contains references to the various types of notational (nontext) files that might be used within an EAD document. These include common image file formats such as GIF, JPEG, TIFF, and MPEG (see section 6.5.2.4.2 for more information on notational files).

*eadchars.ent*—This file contains references to the various character sets that might be used in an EAD document. All character sets are referenced by their standard ISO identifiers.

This file is not required if the document is created in XML, which uses the Unicode character set (or some subset thereof) by default (see section 6.5.2.1 for more information on character sets).

*eadsgml.dcl*—This is the SGML declaration file, which specifies various features of the DTD that a processing application may need to know. While many DTDs utilize a standard SGML reference declaration, EAD employs its own version. Some software applications incorporate the text of the declaration at the beginning of each SGML instance. All XML documents employ a default declaration and so do not require the use of this file.

### 4.3.2. SGML versus XML

EAD is written so that it can be made to conform to the specifications of either SGML or XML. The form of the DTD and its associated files that is available from the EAD home page at the Library of Congress is SGML compliant. While XML may, in general, be thought of as a subset of SGML, there are five differences in XML that must be accommodated to make an EAD document XML-compliant. You must be particularly aware of these differences when converting existing SGML versions of documents into XML.

#### 4.3.2.1. Changes in the DTD Files

If the DTD is to be used with XML applications such as validating processors, one change must first be made to the "ead.dtd" file. There is a section towards the end of the file headed "SGML EADNOTAT AND EADCHARS INCLUSION/EXCLUSION." At the end of this section, there is an entity reference that reads "<!ENTITY % sgml 'INCLUDE' >". To "switch off" SGML compatibility and "switch on" XML compatibility, change 'INCLUDE' to 'IGNORE'.

When you make this change, observe that the explanatory note in this section of the DTD file points out that "for XML, the eadnotat.ent file should be invoked in the declaration subset of [the] individual instance." This means that the file "eadnotat.ent" must be explicitly declared as an entity in the prolog of each EAD instance that contains links to notational (nontextual) data such as graphics files (see section 6.2.3 for a general discussion of the document prolog). For XML instances, the prolog of EAD-encoded finding aids should therefore read:

```
<!DOCTYPE ead PUBLIC "-//Society of American Archivists//DTD
ead.dtd (Encoded Archival Description (EAD) Version 1.0)//EN"
"ead.dtd"
[
<!ENTITY % eadnotat PUBLIC "-//Society of American
Archivists//DTD eadnotat.ent (Encoded Archival Description
(EAD) Notation Declarations Version 1.0)//EN" "eadnotat.ent">
%eadnotat;
]>
```

While it is not necessary to declare the notation file "eadnotat.ent" if the finding aid does not contain a link to notational data such as graphics files, it is probably safest to add it in all cases as a default. Note that the Uniform Resource Identifiers (URIs), in this case simple file names that refer to the "ead.dtd" and the "eadnotat.ent" files, must point to the exact physical location of these two files on your system. Their content may therefore vary from the above examples in accordance with your local storage practices for the DTD and its associated files.

#### 4.3.2.2. Case Sensitivity

Markup in SGML is not case sensitive for element or attribute names. For compatibility with the Unicode character set specifications, however, XML markup *is* case sensitive for this data. The EAD DTD prescribes that element and attribute names must all be in lower case for XML compliance. Some SGML authoring or parsing software automatically writes out such names in upper case. The resulting files must be edited to change all attribute and element names to lower case if such files are intended for use in an XML-compliant system. A conversion macro written for Microsoft Word is available via the *EAD Help Pages*.[78]

#### 4.3.2.3. The XML Declaration

A declaration that the file is an XML document must appear at the beginning of each XML instance. It has three components: the XML version employed, whether the document uses an external DTD such as EAD, and optionally, the Unicode character encoding scheme utilized (such as UTF-8). A typical XML declaration might read:

```
<?xml version="1.0" standalone="no" encoding="UTF-8"?>
```

#### 4.3.2.4. Empty Elements

Lastly, SGML and XML differ in the markup syntax used for elements declared to be "empty" in the DTD; that is, elements that contain neither other elements nor PCDATA. The relevant EAD elements are <lb>, <extptr>, <extptrloc>, <ptr>, and <ptrloc>. Except for <lb>, which is a formatting device, these are all linking elements that utilize attribute values to point to other locations or files. In SGML, empty elements require only a start-tag (<lb>). XML adds an additional form called the *empty-element tag*, which has the syntax <lb/>. In XML systems either the empty-element tag form (<lb/>) or the use of both start- and end-tags (<lb></lb>) is valid; however, the XML standard declares that the empty-element tag form must be employed "for interoperability." While the meaning of this statement is admittedly vague, it is easiest simply to use the empty-element-tag syntax (<lb/>) as your default in XML documents.

[78] The *EAD Help Pages* are available at: <http://jefferson.village.virginia.edu/ead>.

### 4.3.3. Parsing

It is important to verify the conformity of an EAD document to the specifications of the DTD. This should be done regularly during the authoring process in order to reveal any errors made during encoding, and it also must be done once as a final step prior to publishing an encoded finding aid. This process is known as parsing and may be accomplished in several ways (See section 6.2.4 for additional technical information on parsing). Native SGML and XML editors, as well as programs like WordPerfect and Framemaker + SGML, have built-in parsers that continuously monitor DTD compliance. There are also numerous stand-alone parsers that are freely available. James Clark's SP program is considered to be among the best for SGML; it may be configured for XML as well.[79] Currently other free XML parsers are available from IBM/Lotus, DataChannel, and Microsoft. One must observe a bit of caution with XML parsers, as a number of those currently on the market are validators only; this means that they check for a "well-formed" XML file rather than actually parsing the file against the appropriate DTD.

### 4.3.4. Sharing Data Between MARC Records and EAD Finding Aids

Many archival repositories (particularly in the United States) that create electronic finding aids also produce a MARC catalog record for each collection described in an EAD finding aid, and operational advantages may be possible by sharing data between the two electronic files (see section 1.6 for a discussion of the descriptive relationship between catalog records and finding aids). The migration of data may flow in either direction—from finding aid to MARC record, or vice versa—depending on factors such as the relationship of the data in each, the sequence in which each is created, and institution-specific workflow. Two techniques for data exchange currently are possible.

Both the Windows and Macintosh operating systems permit the transfer of data from one application to another (via the clipboard and scrapbook respectively), and it is therefore a simple matter to cut-and-paste text between a catalog record and a finding aid document. You can simply open your catalog editing software and EAD authoring application simultaneously, in separate windows on the desktop, and transfer the information. This may be particularly useful if the existing legacy finding aid comprises only a container list and can be combined with the contents of a MARC record containing summary contextual information such as a scope and content note.

Some repositories may require a more automated approach in order to transfer large quantities of such data in batch mode. One option would be to write your own conversion program to transform the data from MARC into EAD, or vice versa. Another approach would be to use the MARC DTD developed by the Library of Congress. A simple DOS program from Logos Research[80] converts records from the MARC "transmission format" into the MARC DTD structure, and vice versa. The Library of Congress also offers two free

---

[79] James Clark's SP program is available at: <http://www.jclark.com>.

[80] Logos Research's MARC-related resources are available at: <http://www.logos.com/marc>.

programs, written in the Perl language, to convert records between these two formats.[81] Once a MARC record has been converted into the MARC DTD structure, you can use a transforming application to render the data from the MARC DTD syntax into the appropriate EAD syntax. Such transformations may be accomplished by various tools such as an XSL processor used in conjunction with an XSL stylesheet (see section 5.3.3.2 for a discussion of XSL and stylesheets). Among these tools is PatML, a freeware product from IBM.[82]

Future development of the xml:namespace standard may make it possible to include information encoded in more than one DTD within a single EAD instance. As a result, we may have a third option in the future in which MARC data, in the MARC DTD structure, might be embedded directly in the EAD instance without first necessitating its transformation into EAD.

### 4.3.5. Effects of Various Features on Output

While EAD markup focuses on designating the content and structure of the finding aid, there are certain aspects of encoding that may affect document output, both online display and printouts. Among these are whitespace, punctuation, headers, tabular displays, and certain other elements and attributes.[83] In applying the following guidelines, be aware that the need for consistency in union catalogs of finding aids may require that you make modifications to accommodate system requirements.

#### 4.3.5.1. Whitespace

Areas within an EAD document that do not include text because of a blank space (such as between words), a tab, a carriage return, or a line feed may have meaning. Such areas are known as *whitespace*, which is preserved in SGML within the text of a document, though not necessarily in markup, according to a complex set of specifications. In contrast, an XML processor must pass along all characters, including whitespace, to an application, which may or may not preserve them.

We cannot necessarily anticipate the actions that future processors will take on current text. With both SGML and XML, it is therefore prudent not to attempt to format text by incorporating whitespace in your document, other than between words, but rather to manipulate display completely through a stylesheet. Two examples may help illustrate how SGML and XML handle whitespace.

Keying text in the following manner into an SGML authoring application

```
<p>November 1:       The work of the Commission began ... </p>
```

[81] The Library of Congress' MARC-related programs are available at: <http://www.loc.gov/marc/marcdtd/usermanual.html>.
[82] Information about PatML is available at: <http://alphaworks.ibm.com/tech/patml>.
[83] Section 4.3.5.3 describes how the <head> and <emph> elements and the LABEL and RENDER attributes affect display.

will not ensure that rendering software such as a browser will actually display the text as follows:

> November 1:      The work of the Commission began ...

It is much more likely with current software that the six blank spaces will be compressed into one. There are certain circumstances, however, in which one must be careful to ensure that at least one space does appear between words. This is true for inline elements, especially those that might be nested. Consider the following example:

```
<p>The movie, <title render="italic">Shakespeare in
Love</title>, won the Academy Award for best picture.</p>
```

Without the space before the <title> start-tag and after the </title> end-tag, the text might be rendered as follows:

> The movie,*Shakespeare in Love*,won the Academy Award for best picture.

Where the need for spacing in a prescribed situation can be anticipated (such as when a <unitdate> always follows <unittitle>) and a universally valid style rule can therefore be applied, a stylesheet may be used to supply the whitespace required. Unfortunately, not all situations are so predictable; for example, as shown above, you may not be able to guarantee that a space will be required after every instance of <title> when it occurs within a <p>. In such cases, your markup should include a single space following the inline element. It's better to be safe than sorry! Most processing software will reduce extra whitespace to a single space, but it would be quite problematic to expect your system to supply spacing where none exists.

#### 4.3.5.2. Punctuation

Terminal punctuation that appears at the end of the text within an element may be keyed into the body of the document or supplied by a stylesheet. It is advisable to key in periods at the end of full sentences. Other decisions will be situational.

Punctuation within the body of a paragraph of text must be entered as data. Marks of punctuation such as colons and commas that are used between EAD elements for visual recognition or clarity, however, may be more safely supplied by a stylesheet; this approach enables global changes in such formatting to be accomplished at a later date with a minimum of effort by simple changes to the stylesheet.

The XSL style language provides the ability to reorder the sequence of elements, and such resorting of text may affect output punctuation as well. Elements that are initially keyed in a particular sequence and separated by some mark of punctuation may later be resorted into another sequence. For example, embedded punctuation in the <unittitle> element in the following markup

```
<unittitle>Papers,</unittitle><unitdate>1975-1997</unitdate>
```

might read correctly in one case when displayed as:

Papers, 1975-1997

but would include a superfluous mark of punctuation if this text were presented "out of line," in this manner:

Title: Papers,
Dates: 1975-1997

It is therefore preferable to supply such punctuation for display purposes through your stylesheet. In some circumstances, however, such as the <persname> element in the following example, you should supply the punctuation within the markup; this is because you cannot predict whether a comma will always follow a <persname> element within a <p>. Moreover, this text is unlikely to be reordered for display. Since the text might be extracted for indexing purposes, however, it is advisable to place the second comma outside the <persname> element so that it is not inadvertently treated as a part of the name:

```
<p>The author, <persname altrender="bold">Bill
Smith</persname>, was born in 1912.</p>
```

#### 4.3.5.3. Headings

The <head> element, which is widely available in EAD, and the LABEL attribute, which is available only in the <did> subelements, provide two methods for incorporating text that assigns a name or header to certain sections of a finding aid.[84] The phrase "Scope and Content of the Collection" at the beginning of a <scopecontent> element is one example of such a heading. There may be long-term advantages to generating such display via a stylesheet, however, in lieu of actually encoding the heading phrase into the finding aid by using <head> or LABEL, because the stylesheet approach facilitates global modification of the heading information

On the other hand, the content of a heading may be unique to a particular finding aid in a way that cannot be anticipated by a stylesheet or derived from other text in the document; in such a case, the use of <head> is ideal.[85]

[84] See section 3.5.1.1 for a discussion of the difference between <head> and LABEL.

[85] Note that the same uses and limitations of stylesheets apply in similar fashion in the context of the <emph> element and the RENDER attribute.

#### 4.3.5.4. Tabular Display

Finding aids often present data in a columnar or tabular format. Typical examples are the listing of biographical data by year and event, or the layout of box and folder or microfilm reel and frame numbers in container listings. Such displays may be thought of in the same terms as a spreadsheet: a series of cells containing data in a grid of rows and columns. Elements such as <date> and <event> define the data that constitutes the information in each "cell" that will be included within a tabular display. They are then wrapped up in a <chronlist>, <list>, or <table> element. It is possible for a stylesheet to formulate the desired tabular layout based on this markup by implication, rather than by having to designate explicitly that every <event> is a separate cell.

Within the <dsc> element, EAD includes an optional model of tabular displays that *does* require the deliberate specification of each cell, wrapping <drow> and <dentry> tags around them. Experience with EAD has shown, however, that effective tabular displays can be generated in the <dsc> and other areas of the finding aid by using stylesheets without the need to add this extra layer of tabular markup. Both the Cascading Style Sheets (CSS) language and the Extensible Style Language (XSL) can create tabular layout (see section 5.3.3 on stylesheet languages). Consequently, the <drow> and <dentry> tabular model is not included as a default feature of the EAD DTD, nor is it detailed in these *Guidelines*, though its application is documented in the *Tag Library*.[86]

Should you wish to invoke tabular layout, you must alter the section of the ead.dtd file headed "<!-- TABULAR DSC  INCLUSION/EXCLUSION  -->" in the following two ways:

- Change the value 'IGNORE' in the entity <!ENTITY % tabular  'IGNORE' > to 'INCLUDE'.
- Change the value 'INCLUDE' in the entity <!ENTITY % nontabular 'INCLUDE'> to 'IGNORE'.

[86] *Encoded Archival Description Tag Library, Version 1.0* (Chicago: Society of American Archivists, 1998), 33-35, 108-109, 115-116.

### 4.4. Document Control

As you begin to create EAD documents, the consistency of your data and effective management of the various electronic files will quickly become significant administrative concerns. The issues fall into five major categories:

- Encoding consistency
- DTD conformance
- File names and locations
- Version control
- Security

#### 4.4.1. Encoding Consistency

In addition to mastering the guidance offered in the *EAD Tag Library* and these *Guidelines*, you should develop local "best practice" guidelines to record your decisions regarding the EAD elements and attributes to be used, their relationships to each other, the order in which they will be presented to structure a complete finding aid, depth of tagging of data such as proper names, and other such determinations. Regardless of the software you are using to encode your finding aids, the use of templates will help to enforce consistency.

#### 4.4.2. DTD Conformance

Various types of SGML software can help enforce valid encoding by controlling how and where an encoder may apply particular elements and attributes. In addition, running a complete EAD instance through an SGML parser will determine whether the finished file constitutes valid SGML.

#### 4.4.3. File Names and Locations

As your population of EAD documents grows from a few dozen to hundreds or even thousands in number, the resulting array of computer files will become a problem if not properly managed. You will have EAD document files, entity files of text and images, stylesheet files, and the EAD DTD files themselves, all of which require careful file management.

Section 5.4 discusses the effects that issues such as changing file names, file directory structure schemes, or Web site locations have on the publication process and suggests options—such as an SGML catalog, file handlers and purls—for dealing with them. Good file management, however, begins during the authoring process with the systematic assignment of a standard naming protocol for files and a logical directory structure for organizing files on your computer. You also will need some type of system—a file, an index, or even a database—that tracks the names that have been used and associates them with a unique and meaningful description of the collection represented by the electronic version. This is necessary both to ensure administrative sanity and to enable the proper functioning of systems for user indexing, display, and retrieval.

### 4.4.4. Version Control

Long before EAD was developed, it was routine for repositories to update existing finding aids, either to incorporate additions to collections, to reflect improved physical processing, or to upgrade descriptive information. Archivists therefore are already aware of the importance of maintaining a record of earlier versions of finding aids in order to ensure that queries based in those versions can be successfully answered. As finding aids are encoded in EAD and made more widely available, the frequency of revisions may increase, due both to ease of revision and feedback received from users. It will therefore be important to maintain awareness among repository staff of the importance of such record keeping.

Use of the <revisiondesc> subelement within <eadheader> may be useful in this regard (see section 3.6.1.4 for additional information). Documentation of the processes that you develop for encoding will also be helpful.

### 4.4.5. Security

As with all important computer files, you should perform regular backups of your finding aid files, locate at least one set of backup files offsite, and maintain virus protection software on your system. In addition, you should give users only *read-only* access to copies of finding aid files, not *read-write* access to the original files.

# Chapter Five

# PUBLISHING EAD DOCUMENTS

## 5.1. Overview of the Publishing Process

Encoding a finding aid in EAD is the first important step in making the content of an archival collection electronically available to users; the encoded finding aid may then be "published." Three essential aspect of electronic publication of finding aids are addressed in this chapter:

- Resource discovery—How the public, searching for particular information on the Web, will locate relevant finding aids in your collection
- Resource delivery—How your repository will make use of browsers, file formats (SGML, XML, or HTML), and stylesheets to display EAD files
- File management—How your institution will identify, organize, and manage these electronic documents

## 5.2. Resource Discovery

A principal goal of EAD is to enable users to identify relevant collections and then to locate specific materials therein. As a first step, a repository must of course provide some means by which finding aids can be discovered, searched, and displayed. While there are a variety of techniques for dissemination and access, including compilations on CD-ROM or distribution via a client-server application over a local area network, the most common choice today is through the use of browser technology, either over the World Wide Web or via a local intranet. Three approaches, including combinations of the three, currently are in vogue for providing access to finding aids:

- Listing finding aids on a Web page
- Linking them to MARC records in online catalogs
- Offering direct access to their content via full text search software

### 5.2.1. Listings on a Web Page

For repositories with ready access to a Web site, the simplest publishing solution is to create standard HTML-encoded Web pages that contain references to collections for which EAD finding aids are available. Such citations may be in the form of brief entries (as in a repository guide); may be embedded in a narrative or bibliographic essay on some aspect of the institution's holdings; or may be presented as simple lists of collections arranged by creator, repository, collection area, or subject matter. Current examples of this approach range from simple listings that enumerate the names of collections held by the institution, to groupings of holdings by broad subject areas, to listings that contain brief notes on the scope of each collection in the manner of an annotated bibliography. Finding aids may be accessed, one at a time, by selecting a hyperlink on the Web page that retrieves the EAD document and loads it to the user's browser. This scenario does not provide the capability to search the contents of multiple finding aids simultaneously, but once a user downloads a finding aid onto her computer, she can use the searching features of the browser software to perform keyword queries of the document's contents.

This option requires space on a Web site where a repository can load its files and the technical training necessary to design and create HTML-encoded pages.

*Advantages*: This approach is relatively easy to accomplish and inexpensive to carry forward if you have access to a Web site.

*Disadvantages*: The only information that the user initially has about the contents of the collection is the context that is provided on the page that contains the link to it. This may make the process of selecting relevant finding aids somewhat tedious.

### 5.2.2. MARC Records Linked to Finding Aids

Many U.S. repositories use MARC-based online catalogs as one avenue of access to their collections. A growing number of such catalogs now have Web interfaces and are another vehicle for making finding aids available to researchers.

The USMARC format includes field 856, which is used to record a citation to any external electronic resource, such as an EAD-encoded finding aid that is related to the collection described in that MARC record. Field 856 may include a uniform resource locator (URL) for that resource. Web interfaces to online catalogs render the URL as a hyperlink, which, when selected, displays the associated file, in this case a finding aid, in the user's browser. Repositories that use a Uniform Resource Name (URN) can record their globally unique identifier as a "handle" in the 856 field.

```
856 42  $3 finding aid $d eadpnp $f pp996001 $g
        urn:hdl:loc.pnp/eadpnp.pp996001 $u
        http://hdl.loc.gov/loc.pnp/eadpnp.pp996001

856 42  $3 An electronic version of the inventory for this
        collection may be found at $u
        http://www.mnhs.org/library/findaids/00020.xml
```

**Figure 5.2.2a.** *Two examples of the USMARC 856 field. The first contains a URN ($g) followed by a URL ($u) and the second only a URL ($u).*

*Advantages*: The technical requirements for this approach are relatively modest and inexpensive if your online catalog has a Web interface. You will need to modify the relevant MARC record by adding the appropriate linking data in the MARC 856 field. Additionally, you will need space on a Web-accessible server to mount the EAD files.

This approach leverages existing indexing in the online catalog that captures information about the context and content of each collection. It mimics existing two-step finding aid systems in which the researcher first queries the catalog for broad name, place, or topical indexing of the collection, and is then directed to a finding aid in a separate file for more detailed information. With the introduction of MARC catalogs into many repositories, the first part of this process (consulting the online catalog) was automated. With online access to EAD files, this becomes an all-electronic process as the MARC record is linked dynamically to the online finding aid.

*Disadvantages*: This scenario presumes the availability of both MARC records for collections and a Web-accessible online catalog. The cost of creating the former or installing the latter just to make finding aids accessible may be quite expensive. It also creates an ongoing cost in the maintenance of the electronic links between the catalog entry and the EAD file (see section 5.4 for a discussion of file management issues).

While using the catalog as a gateway to one's finding aids provides many access points into the collection, users still cannot initially search the full text of the finding aid; whether this is a weakness or an advantage is a matter of perspective. One point of view holds that this is less than fully satisfactory, since full searching of the rich content of one or many finding aids is not possible. The other side argues that the summary catalog description, with access terms constructed in standardized forms, performs a useful filtering function, limiting search results to those aspects of the collection deemed sufficiently important to appear in a synopsis. For many reasons, this may be preferable to being bombarded with a large number of irrelevant hits such as a full-text search of large finding aid files may bring. The results of such a query may resemble the consequences of attempting to drink a sip of water from a gushing fire hydrant.

### 5.2.3. Full-Text Search Software

The most sophisticated and technically complex delivery method is to provide simultaneous, full-text querying of multiple finding aids by specialized search software. These tools permit the user to search the entire contents of many finding aids simultaneously, taking advantage of the EAD markup to facilitate requests for specific types of data, such as titles, dates, or names. The growing popularity of the XML standard is increasing the number of such systems that can handle EAD-encoded files.

The applications that fall into this broad group offer so many different features that they are difficult to categorize precisely. They include basic Web authoring and distribution products that offer search and retrieval capabilities, as well as complex, feature-rich document management systems, usually marketed to large corporations, that have numerous files and sophisticated publishing requirements. Many are quite expensive. Nevertheless, such systems may be suitable for large institutions with extensive holdings of electronic texts, or for consortia that share online services. Additionally, several firms offer substantial educational discounts, which can greatly reduce a repository's software costs.

The Enigma search engine from Insight, Inc., the InQuery search engine from the Center for Intelligent Information Retrieval, the BASIS text database from Open Text, and the Dual Prism software suite from AIS Software offer electronic publishing for SGML and XML files. Other applications include document management software such as the Livelink system from Open Text, Live Publish from the Folio Products Division of Open Market; ArborText's Epic system; and INSO's DynaText family of products, which includes DynaTag and a Web publishing component called DynaWeb.

To provide access to collections in this manner, an archives must install the software that will index the files and format them for display on a Web-accessible server (see section 5.3 for information on the use of stylesheets in formatting documents). Each of these products includes a search interface that is partially to fully customizable by the archives. In a typical query, the user enters search terms that are passed to the server. The server executes the request and returns the results to the user's browser, typically listing brief information about each relevant collection. The user may then select and download the desired finding aids one at a time. This process is analogous to the brief listings of book titles that many online catalogs deliver in response to a search that results in multiple hits.

*Advantages*: The chief virtue of this method is that users can search simultaneously the full text of many finding aids, either from a particular repository or from multiple institutions, as in a union catalog. A query may reveal information about some portion of a collection that is significant to a particular researcher, but that does not constitute a sufficiently large part of the collection to have been noted in a summary MARC catalog record; many finding aids contain a wealth of information about subject content that the researcher can mine in this way. The search interface may be structured to permit retrieval based on specific content markup, such as enabling a search for all data encoded in a <corpname> element by prompting users to limit a search to "names of organizations." This approach provides easy, integrated access to many collections.

*Disadvantages*: Search engines are relatively expensive to acquire and require advanced computing skills to program and maintain. As mentioned in section 5.2.2, your ability to perform in-depth queries may increase recall but will certainly decrease the precision of many searches. The nature of the query interface, the type and level of indexing, and the presentation of the results set are additional theoretical and practical concerns that have not been clearly developed at this early stage in the implementation of EAD. More experience with retrieval issues will clarify user understanding of and requirements for both the search interface and the display of results, which will, in turn, help to refine these applications.

## 5.3. Resource Delivery

A key step in the find aid "publication" process is delivery of finding aid files to a user's browser in a form that the browser can display. A repository has several technical options for making this happen; the possibilities are determined by Web technology and involve a complex interplay of three related factors:

- Aspects of how browsers display text
- The file format that is sent to the user's browser
- The stylesheet method employed to control display of the document

### 5.3.1. How Browsers Display Text

EAD markup designates only the structure and content of the document, not how it will appear on the page or computer screen; a specific method must be employed to format the file for display. The solution is a stylesheet, which is a set of instructions that governs how the EAD file will be formatted. This formatting may be applied to the finding aid either at the repository before it is sent to the user, or on the viewer's browser. In the latter instance, the stylesheet (which is simply a text file) is sent along with the EAD document to the browser, which then processes it.

Before learning about various stylesheet formats, we will examine how a browser might process text files encoded in SGML, XML, or HTML in order to display them correctly. In a typical scenario, the browser initially reads the encoding scheme of the document and interprets its structure as a *tree*, in which the *document element* (see figure 6.2.1b), such as <ead> or <html>, is the base of the tree. For example, the tree for an EAD document will have two or three major branches (<eadheader>, the optional <frontmatter>, and <archdesc>). The <archdesc> branch subdivides into <did>, <scopecontent> and other branches, which in turn further subdivide until one finally comes to the "nodes" or leaves at the end of each branch, where the textual content of the finding aid is found. For an example of how such a tree might be graphically represented, examine the Windows Explorer feature of the Windows operating system, which displays the hierarchical and nested relationships of the drives, directories, subdirectories, and files on your computer.

Once the tree has been built, the browser compares the file to its DTD to ensure conformance. A *presentation engine* in the browser then renders the text of each node for display, controlling properties such as screen placement and the size, type, and color of the font. In doing this, it follows certain rules embedded in a stylesheet.

The formatting rules (or stylesheet) for HTML documents are *hardwired* into the browser; in other words, they are included as part of the programming of the browser software. The display of each HTML element in Navigator or Internet Explorer is thus determined in advance by Netscape or Microsoft (each in a slightly different way). This is feasible because there are only about 80 HTML tags whose display must be predefined.

The default display may be overridden, however, by an external stylesheet file that causes the presentation engine in the browser to display the document in a different way. Such external stylesheets are optional for HTML files but are required when the document sent to the browser is encoded in XML or SGML; this is because the formatting of elements in these schemes is not built into the browser. Indeed, this formatting cannot be preordained, since the number of elements that could be defined by current and future DTDs in SGML or XML is virtually unlimited. A stylesheet therefore must be employed.

### 5.3.2. File Format Delivery Options

Just as there are multiple methods for authoring EAD-encoded finding aids, there are several ways in which these documents may be delivered electronically to users. One critical factor that differentiates these methods is the file format in which the document is transmitted, and three possibilities exist: SGML, XML, or HTML. The choice of stylesheet methodology is circumscribed by the file format decision.

#### 5.3.2.1. SGML Format

Inasmuch as EAD began as an SGML-based application, and EAD files are created and stored in SGML format, it would seem reasonable to deliver documents to users in their original EAD encoding. Unfortunately, software developers have chosen not to build SGML functionality directly into their Web browsers, due at least in part to the technical complexity that stems from the standard's great flexibility. Neither Netscape Navigator nor Microsoft Internet Explorer can interpret the structure of an EAD file in SGML syntax. However, a user can install another program, either Panorama Publisher from Interleaf (formerly sold by SoftQuad) or MultiDoc Pro from Citec, that works with the browser to display an SGML file. The reader's browser is configured so that when it receives an SGML file, the helper application is loaded into the browser, interprets the file, builds the document tree, and configures its display.

To deliver SGML manifestations of EAD-encoded finding aids on the Web, you must mount your EAD files on a Web-accessible server, along with the necessary stylesheets[87] and navigators and the EAD DTD files. In turn, users must have loaded either the Panorama or MultiDoc Pro software on their computers and have properly configured their browser to work with it. EAD documents are matched with specific stylesheets either through an association provided by a *catalog file* on the server (see section 6.5.2.4.1) or by a processing instruction embedded in each finding aid that points to the relevant stylesheet file, also stored on the server. Processing instructions (PIs) are an SGML device for inserting into a document information that is intended for processing by a proprietary software application rather than by a parser.

[87] See section 5.3.3.5 for more on Panorama style sheets. Both Panorama Publisher and MultiDoc Pro use the same style language.

*Advantages*: Panorama and MultiDoc provide a very effective presentation of the finding aid, including a useful navigator feature that provides a visual road map of the document, enhances user understanding of the collection, and aids in sophisticated searching that is built into the software. The presence of the entire document, with its full SGML structural encoding, on the user's computer permits fast and powerful searching based on content markup, as well as speedy navigation through the document once it has been downloaded.

*Disadvantages*: Unfortunately, unlike many other Web viewers and plug-ins, neither of these applications is available for free, but must be purchased by the user who wishes to display your finding aids. Since casual users may be unwilling to spend the time or money necessary to acquire the software, the usefulness of this scenario is diminished for general Web distribution. It may be more feasible in closed environments, such as a single archives, library or campus that can supply all users with the viewer (which could then be used not only for viewing finding aids, but also other SGML-encoded documents such as scholarly texts). Additionally, although the stylesheet language employed by each product is accessible through a robust editor, both are proprietary. Style specifications developed for this publishing environment will not be transferable to others.

#### 5.3.2.2. XML Format

XML was developed to provide the power and functionality of SGML on the Web, and EAD documents can be made XML-compliant (see section 4.3.2 for details). In this publishing scenario, the archives stores EAD-encoded finding aids in XML format (rather than in their native SGML format) on a Web-accessible server. Each EAD instance includes a processing instruction that points to the location of the stylesheet that is to be applied to its presentation. After the finding aid has been downloaded to the user's computer, the browser retrieves the referenced style file (written either in the CSS or XSL syntax; see sections 5.3.3.1 and 5.3.3.2 for more information) from the archives' server, and then uses its presentation engine to display the finding aid properly.

*Advantages*: As with SGML, the browser can take full advantage of the structural markup in EAD to effect fast and powerful searches of the document's content. Unlike the SGML scenario, however, no helper application is required because all the required functionality is included in the standard Web browser. The end user needs no special software.

*Disadvantages*: The chief drawback to this approach is that, at the time these *Guidelines* were written, XML functionality was as yet available only in Internet Explorer 5.0, although Netscape is building XML capability into the next release of its Navigator browser. Users with older browsers may use Panorama Publisher or MultiDoc Pro as a helper application to display XML documents in the same way that they process SGML files. It will be a number of years before a critical mass of Web users will be using newer browser versions that can read XML files directly. Until that time, archives will need to provide an alternative delivery method, probably in HTML.

### 5.3.2.3. HTML Format

Given the justification provided in chapter 1 for encoding finding aids in SGML or XML, it may strike you as odd that HTML is suggested as a delivery format for EAD finding aids! But note carefully the use of the phrase "delivery format": HTML is a useful tool for the *distribution and presentation* of text and images, which are its intended purposes and strengths, despite its substantial shortcomings as a data storage format.

The experience of libraries and archives in disseminating MARC-encoded catalog records provides an informative analogy. While such institutions continue to appreciate the many virtues of creating, storing and searching catalog records in MARC format, they have quickly embraced Web interfaces to their online catalogs that deliver records to users in HTML format. No one has seriously suggested, however, that use of MARC be discontinued and that catalog data be created directly in HTML, since the result would be loss of the ability to search by specific types of data such as author, title, and subject. Such a move would seriously cripple user searching of collections, as well as the long-term viability of the catalog records as data rather than as undifferentiated text.

You can achieve the best of two worlds by encoding your finding aids in EAD and then using HTML as the vehicle for publishing them. You accomplish this by converting the markup of the finding aid from the EAD encoding scheme into HTML syntax. This process, technically referred to as "transformation," may happen at the repository in either of two ways.

Several of the publishing systems described earlier, including DynaWeb and Dual Prism, can generate HTML versions of a finding aid in *real time* at the moment that the user requests the file; this is known as *dynamic transformation*. Custom scripting, in programming languages such as Perl, works in conjunction with SGML-aware search engines to generate the HTML version "on the fly," with the script acting as a stylesheet to map data from one tag set to the other. Another software option in this category is Microsoft's Web server software (IIS), which can use a stylesheet written in the XSL language to transform an XML file into HTML, and then send the file out to a reader using its Active Server Page technology. As XML tools mature, such transformation into HTML may occur on both the user's computer and the repository's server.

Alternatively, a finding aid may be rendered into HTML code by the repository and stored on its Web server before any user requests the file. Currently employed conversion techniques include word processing macros, scripts written in Perl, and transforming software such as the Microsoft XSL Processor. The Internet Archivist authoring software has a built-in SGML to HTML converter. The problem with such *a priori* transformation is that one loses some of the functionality of the stylesheet. If a change in the document structure is required, the SGML-encoded master copy is updated, and the HTML version is regenerated. In this scenario, therefore, each finding aid must be individually reprocessed. With dynamic transformation, on the other hand, the results that the user gets on the browser reflect the most up-to-date version of the format without requiring that the individual documents be edited.

*Advantages*: Delivering finding aids as HTML solves the immediate problem that not all users can currently read SGML or XML files. HTML documents are accessible on any browser without additional effort by the researcher. Because standard HTML tags are used, no additional stylesheet need be generated.

*Disadvantages*: Unless the access and retrieval environment permits the user to search the original EAD-encoded document, the value of structured searching is lost. This searching limitation will exist as long as the file on the user's computer contains only the presentation markup of HTML. A less significant potential disadvantage is that staff will have to know both HTML syntax and the transformation language employed in order to implement this delivery option. Storing both an SGML or XML source file and an HTML presentation file for each encoded finding aid will also increase—perhaps double—the file storage space required on your server. Maintaining and updating two versions of each document is an additional expense, one that, complicates both file management and processing workflows.

### 5.3.3. Stylesheet Languages

There are several standardized "languages" for writing stylesheets, including Cascading Style Sheets (CSS), Extensible Style Language (XSL), the Document Style Semantics and Specification Language (DSSSL), and Format Output Specification Instance (FOSI). There also are style languages that are proprietary to particular software products. XSL and DSSSL may be used to transform files from one encoding scheme to another, as described above, in addition to serving as stylesheet languages.

While your repository will have many different finding aids, you probably will need only a few stylesheets, one for each *style* of finding aid that you produce (such as one for small collections and another for more complex finding aids, or one for paper-based collections files and another for microfilms). Considerable potential exists for cross-institutional sharing in the development and use of stylesheets, with repositories adopting, or borrowing and modifying, existing ones from a shared pool of models. The resulting standardization in finding aid appearance, both within and across repositories, might well enhance user comprehension and interpretation of these complex information tools; such sharing also would simplify the finding aid distribution process. Sharing of stylesheets would mandate, however, substantial agreement within and across archives as to the format in which finding aids are to be encoded and displayed. While this obviously involves decisions relating to layout on the screen or page, the inclusion or omission of particular EAD elements also will affect such sharing, especially of legacy data.

### 5.3.3.1. Cascading Style Sheets (CSS)[88]

The CSS specification was originally developed as a way for Web authors to modify the "default" manner in which browsers display HTML files. The first version of CSS, called Level 1, focused on basic presentation issues such as margins, indention, and font characteristics such as size, weight, family, and color. Initial support for CSS was limited and inconsistent in Netscape Navigator and Microsoft Internet Explorer.

In May 1998, the more robust Level 2 version was approved by the World Wide Web Consortium (W3C) as an official Web Recommendation. Microsoft and Netscape both promise full support in their next software releases for Level 2, which features substantially richer formatting capabilities such as tables, as well as specifications for the output of print and screen displays.

Its functionality is straightforward. Once the browser creates the document tree, it applies CSS styles to elements in the order in which they appear in the document. These styles may be applied to either XML or HTML documents, either by embedding the styling specifications directly in the document, or by linking the encoded file to a separate stylesheet file via an HREF link or a processing instruction in the finding aid.

### 5.3.3.2. Extensible Style Language (XSL)[89]

XSL was developed and adopted by the World Wide Web Consortium (W3C) especially for use with XML. It incorporates features of both CSS and DSSSL (see section 5.3.3.3). The first iteration of XSL appeared as a W3C note in November 1997, followed by the first Working Draft release in August 1998. Final approval of XSL as a formal recommendation is not expected until summer 1999.

Supporters of XSL describe it as a more robust styling language than CSS, one that is intended to be employed in more complex presentation situations. Certainly XSL's pattern matching and formatting syntax is more sophisticated than CSS, though with a concomitant penalty in complexity. In addition to its styling functionality, XSL may also function as a transformation agent for the conversion of data from one syntax to another.

XSL also applies styles in a different way than CSS. Once the document tree has been constructed in the processor, XSL creates a second tree, the output tree; hence, the structure of the output can be different than that of the source. For example, you might decide to display the location <physloc> of an item *before* its title <unittitle>, even though <physloc> *follows* <unittitle> in the EAD instance. An XSL stylesheet can simply reorder the elements

---

[88] The World Wide Web Consortium provides further information about Cascading Style Sheets, available at: <http://www.w3.org/Style>.

[89] The World Wide Web Consortium provides further information about Extensible Style Language, available at: <http://www.w3.org/Style>. Information on this topic is also provided in Robin Cover's *SGML/XML Web Page*, available at: <http://www.oasis-open.org/cover/xsl.html>.

in the output tree without any alterations to the source document; styles are then applied to the output tree. This property of XSL also provides the capability to repeat the same data in two different parts of the display, such as by extracting headings to create a separate table of contents while also presenting the headings in situ throughout the finding aid. XSL accomplishes display either by using its own detailed format object specifications or by using the simpler display language of HTML. None of this is possible using CSS, which applies formatting directly to the document tree.

The relatively long approval schedule for XSL has not stifled the development of application software, including incorporation of XSL into Microsoft Internet Explorer 5.0. Several experimental tools are available, including XT and Jade from James Clark, the Koala XSL engine, and Microsoft's MSXSL "technology preview."

#### 5.3.3.3. Document Style Semantics and Specification Language (DSSSL)[90]

DSSSL was developed by the SGML community as an alternative to the existing proprietary, vendor-specific style languages that were once the norm in the SGML publishing industry. Although DSSSL has never been widely adopted, noncommercial applications such as James Clark's Jade program exist that use it to generate output in a variety of formats. Also, DSSSL has been formally adopted as an ISO standard. Like XSL, DSSSL may be used as a transforming language; DSSSL has served as the basis for many other aspects of XSL as well.

#### 5.3.3.4. Format Output Specification Instance (FOSI)[91]

FOSI was developed as a style language for use with the Department of Defense's CALS DTD, but it has not enjoyed wide popularity outside the defense industry environment. It is currently used in the Adept software marketed by ArborText.

#### 5.3.3.5. Proprietary Style Languages

In addition to languages based on open standards, style specifications exist that are proprietary to particular software products. These include the style language developed by Synex Corporation that is used by Interleaf's Panorama Publisher and Citec's MultiDoc Pro software. If a repository delivers SGML files to users of these applications, it must create appropriate stylesheets (and navigator files, which generate "tables of contents" for the browser) using the interactive editor function built into Panorama Publisher and MultiDoc Pro. Proprietary stylesheet-like functions are also built into server software programs such

---

[90] The World Wide Web Consortium provides further information about Document Style Semantics and Specification Language, available at: <http://www.w3.org/Style>. Information on this topic is also available in Robin Cover's *SGML/XML Web Page*, available at: <http://www.oasis-open.org/cover/dsssl.html>.

[91] Robin Cover's *SGML/XML Web Page* provides further information about Format Output Specification Instance, available at: <http://www.oasis-open.org/cover/gov-apps.html#fosi>.

as DynaText, DynaWeb, Livelink, and Balise, which perform transformations of SGML and XML files into HTML.

#### 5.3.3.6. Stylesheet Examples

Stylesheets written in CSS, XSL, or DSSSL syntax are textual documents consisting of a series of two-part rules. The first part of each rule defines the element or elements in the document to which the rule applies. This association may be based on the element's name, its position in the document, or its relationship to parent elements or subelements, attribute values, or other properties. The second component of each rule is an instruction that specifies some aspect of the display of the specified element, such as placement on the screen or page, font size, emphasis (bold or italic), or color.

The following examples show how stylesheet rules would be written in various languages to define the style for the display of the *inclusive dates* of the records in a finding aid. The stylesheet instructions specify that the dates of the archival materials are to appear on a separate line, in 12-point Times New Roman, colored navy, and prefaced by the text "Dates: ".

The first example uses an XSL rule to define display by use of XSL format objects:[92]

```
<xsl:template match="archdesc[@level='collection']/did/
      unitdate[@type='inclusive']"
<fo:block color="navy" font-size="12 pt" font-family="times new
roman">
Dates:
<xsl:apply-templates/>
</fo:block>
</xsl:template>
```

The second example uses an XSL rule to define display through the use of HTML formatting conventions. Technically, this is an XML to HTML transformation, since an XSL processor will generate HTML-encoded output as the result of applying this rule:[93]

```
<xsl:template match="archdesc[@level='collection']/did/
      unitdate[@type='inclusive']"
      <p><font color="navy" face="times new roman" size=
"12 pt">
Dates:
<xsl:apply-templates/>
</font></p>
</xsl:template>
```

[92] The syntax used reflects the XSL Working Draft dated 16 December 1998; this may be modified prior to final adoption of XSL by the World Wide Web Consortium.

[93] The syntax of this example reflects the XSL Working Draft dated 16 December 1998; this may be modified prior to final adoption of XSL by the World Wide Web Consortium.

The third example utilizes the conventions of the Cascading Style Sheets Level 2 specification:

```
archdesc[level="collection"] > did >
unitdate[type="inclusive"]
{color: navy; font-family: times new roman; font-size: 12 pt}

archdesc[level="collection"] > did >
unitdate[type="inclusive"]:before
{content:  "Dates:"}
```

### 5.3.4. Printed Output from EAD Documents

Even though EAD enhances user access to collections by creating electronic versions of finding aids, repositories will still likely need to produce printed copies for local patrons and staff, or for other uses. There are a variety of options for accomplishing this, depending in part on your choice of authoring environments. As noted earlier, native editors either include printing capabilities or require the use of a separate software package to produce finely formatted print copies.

SGML printing applications typically may be used with any SGML instance and are not restricted to files created by related authoring tools from the same vendor, though the two software packages may be closely bundled. Microsoft's SGML Author for Word can convert any SGML document into a Word file, in the same way that it executes a conversion in the opposite direction from Word to SGML. Stylesheet languages and other processors may also be utilized. Current applications include use of the DSSSL standard to generate print output from SGML applications. The capacity to control printing is included in both the CSS and XSL languages, though no implementations of either have yet appeared.

Institutions that create HTML manifestations of their EAD documents might use the HTML file as a source of print copy. This would not be done through the print function of the browser, which typically has limited formatting capabilities, but by importing the HTML file into a word processor (see section 5.3.2.3 for more information on use of HTML files). Current versions of Word, for example, can import HTML documents, remove the tags, and convert the results into a word processing format. Lacking more robust solutions, one can simply remove the tags from the ASCII SGML file and format the document manually. Freeware programs are available in Perl that will strip out the markup from SGML documents.[94] The Internet Archivist authoring software can generate a simply formatted ASCII text output of an EAD file as well. Other authoring tools such as Author/Editor, ADEPT Editor, and XMetaL, as well as the browser plug-in Panorama Publisher, also can produce nicely printed copies of encoded finding aids.

---

[94] For information on freeware Perl programs, consult the Perl Web site, available at: <http://www.perl.com>.

## 5.4. File Management

As was true in the authoring process, effective local management of files is an important feature of a well-run EAD publishing implementation. The use and functionality of stylesheets, catalog files, conversion routines and other programs, and the sequence of internal workflow all must be documented. Version control of documents, including a written audit trail, will be essential as files pass though various manifestations.

Standardized file-naming conventions for internal storage, as well as techniques such as file-handling databases and purl resolvers or handle servers for maintaining persistent file names on the Internet, are critical both to the long-term sanity of the program administrator and to the accessibility of the files over time. Even the novice Web user has encountered the frustrating phenomenon of selecting a hyperlink on a Web page and receiving in return a message that the file could not be found. While there are many potential causes of this problem, one of the most frequent is that the creator has moved the file to another computer location without updating all links, resulting in broken connections.

A single online directory may hold many files, and therefore one promising solution is the creation of an index or other third-party device that stores the server and directory location of multiple files. This limits the information contained in any given hypertext link to a reference to a single persistent location (a server), where the storage details of many files are kept and may be updated simultaneously as filing systems change. This is made possible in SGML via a convention called the *SGML catalog*. Because images, text and other documents may be declared as entities and referred to by name rather than by address in an SGML document, it is possible to store the details about the actual computer location of these entities in an external and centralized catalog file. Unfortunately, XML has not incorporated this feature, but rather requires that all entities include both a relative entity name and a specific address in the form of a Uniform Resource Indicator (URI).

Other solutions might be employed, including purl resolvers and handle servers, both of which work in essentially the same manner.

The purl (persistent uniform resource locator) mechanism utilizes software developed by and freely available from OCLC,[95] and it functions in the following manner. When creating links in Web documents, the author embeds a purl in the document instead of using a conventional uniform resource locator (URL). The purl contains the Internet address of the purl server and a unique name for the document, image or other object that is referenced, instead of the document's absolute Internet address. When selected, the link sends a message to the resolver, which stores a full address for the external object and redirects the query to that location. In this way absolute Internet addresses are maintained on the resolver, where mass updates of information such as server and directory name changes are possible, rather than embedded in individual files, where any alterations in addressing would require the editing of many individual documents.

---

[95] Information regarding the purl strategy is available at: <http://purl.oclc.org>.

This approach does, however, have limitations. The purl software from OCLC runs only on a variety of UNIX platforms. Moreover, the purl naming convention does not effectively support links to specific locations within a document, only to the document as a whole.

Handles are one implementation of Uniform Resource Names (URNs) developed by the Corporation for National Research Initiatives (CNRI).[96] Handles are universally unique identifiers that are registered with a "naming authority," much in the same way that ISBNs are currently distributed and registered for published books. When a handle is used as a resource address in an encoded document, a handle server must resolve the handle, or unique identifier, into an actual address at which the desired resource can be located. Handles and handle servers are a relatively new development, and archivists interested in using this approach may obtain further information on *The Handle System* Web site.

[96] For further information see CNRI's *The Handle System* Web site, available at: <http://www.handle.net/>.

# Chapter Six

## SGML AND XML CONCEPTS

## 6.1. Introduction

This chapter provides an overview of some important concepts in SGML-based information systems in order to give readers of these *Guidelines* a basic understanding of some key technical issues. Differences between SGML and XML are addressed where they are relevant.[97] These issues are examined from the perspective of the EAD DTD itself, with most examples taken directly from the DTD. In addition, this chapter provides the following:

- A jumping off point from which archivists, when they feel ready, can explore the larger world of available information on SGML and XML
- Background on SGML and XML interrelationships and developments that are necessary for readers' understanding of the features of EAD linking elements that are described in chapter 7

Some readers may find chapter 6 overly technical or confusing upon first reading. Chances are that some of its content will not immediately be useful when approaching EAD as a complete novice or with a limited understanding of basic computing technology. It may prove more helpful when revisited later on, after the reader grows more comfortable with the practicalities of EAD encoding. In the same way that you do not need to understand the chemistry of baking in order to make an apple pie provided you can identify the ingredients and follow the proper sequence in mixing them, most archivists will be able to create an EAD-encoded finding aid without a detailed understanding of either SGML or XML.

On the other hand, other readers may find this chapter overly basic if they need even more in-depth information about SGML or XML systems. These *Guidelines* provide ample citations to more comprehensive information resources that are available for those needing more detail than can be provided here (see the footnotes throughout this chapter, as well as the SGML/XML section of the bibliography in appendix G).

[97] Throughout this chapter, an SGML environment is implied unless XML is explicitly mentioned.

## 6.2. SGML Documents

The SGML standard (ISO 8879) is a metalanguage that defines the components of an SGML document.[98] These components are as follows:

- The *Document Type Definition (DTD)*, which specifies the markup that is used with a particular class of documents
- The *SGML Declaration*, which provides technical information to processing software
- The *Document Instance*, which consists of a prolog and the body of the document

### 6.2.1. Document Type Definition (DTD)

A Document Type Definition supplies a formal, human- and machine-readable specification of the elements that can occur in a certain class of document and the markup that can be used to represent those elements. The elements have a logical, hierarchical relationship to one another that is specified in the DTD, which also provides a formal set of rules for the order and frequency of the elements. Figure 6.2.1a illustrates the concept of SGML as a metalanguage.

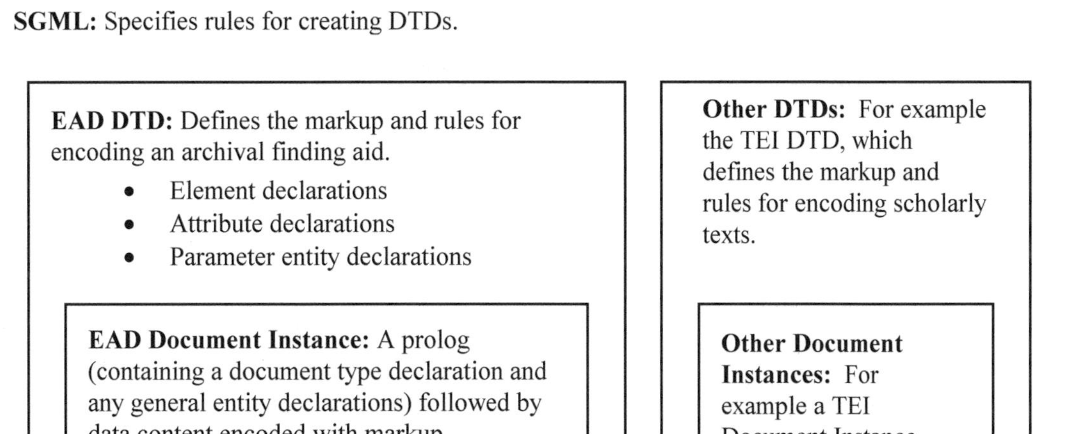


**Figure 6.2.1a.** *The relationship between SGML, individual DTDs, and document instances.*

SGML data structures are based on the premise that the contents of a type of document, such as a finding aid, can be described as a series of hierarchies. For example, a collection may contain series, those series may contain files, and those files may consist of individual

---

[98] For a more detailed overview of SGML, see C. M. Sperberg-McQueen and Lou Burnard, eds., "A Gentle Introduction to SGML" (Chapter 2 of the *Text Encoding Initiative Guidelines*), available at: <http://www-tei.uic.edu/orgs/tei/sgml/teip3sg>.

documents. In SGML, these parent-child relationships are expressed in the DTD. The relationship of elements to one another may be visualized as a tree with a root and central trunk subdividing into smaller and smaller branches with nodes at the furthest extremity of each. Figure 6.2.1b illustrates this concept using the beginnings of EAD's hierarchical structure. The base of this tree structure is referred to in SGML parlance as the *document element*. In an EAD document it is represented by the start-tag <ead>, which signals the beginning of the body of an encoded instance, the base of this tree.

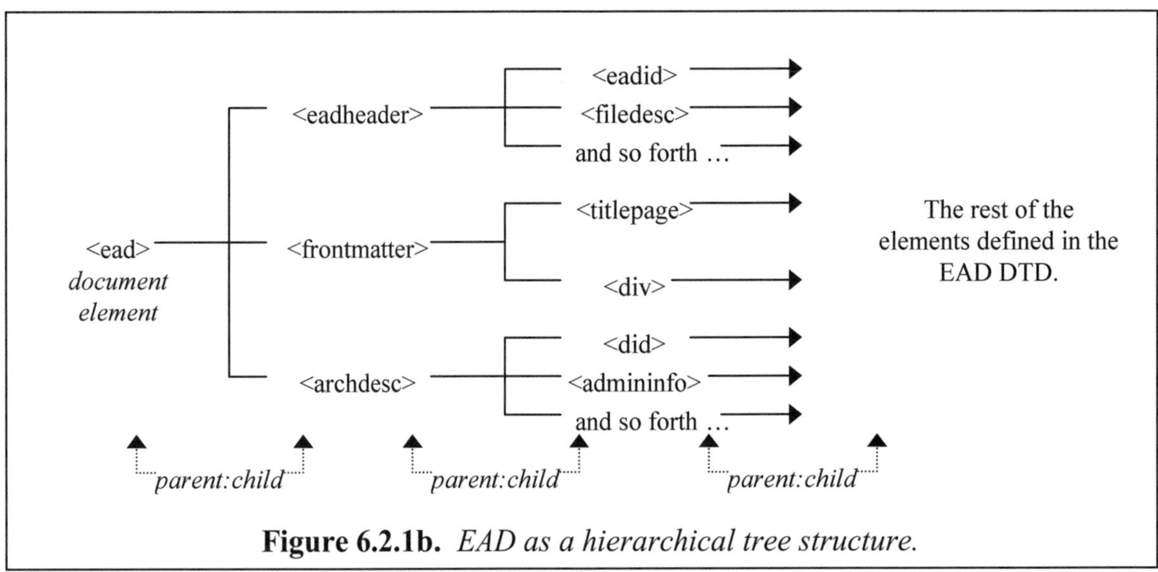


**Figure 6.2.1b.** *EAD as a hierarchical tree structure.*

### 6.2.2. SGML Declaration

The SGML declaration provides technical information to SGML applications, such as authoring and publishing software, about how the DTD and encoded document will use SGML. This includes the base character set employed and the special features of SGML, such as OMITTAG or SHORTREF[99], that are to be permitted. While most SGML applications expect the use of a standard default SGML declaration called the *concrete reference syntax* (CRS), a particular DTD may employ a customized declaration. EAD does employ a customized SGML declaration, which is contained in the file eadsgml.dcl.[100] The XML standard, on the other hand, does not permit such modifications, requiring the use of its own implicit SGML declaration. As a result, as noted in section 4.3.1, EAD documents in XML do not require the use of the eadsgml.dcl file. The eadsgml.dcl file provides an SGML declaration that modifies the CRS in order to come as close to the implicit declaration used in XML as possible. This was necessary in EAD so that a single DTD, with

[99] For further technical information about the SGML declaration, see Charles Goldfarb, *The SGML Handbook* (Oxford: Oxford University Press, 1990), 450-75.

[100] See section 4.3.1 for information regarding the EAD DTD and its associated files.

only the slight modifications noted in section 4.3.2.1, could be used in both SGML and XML systems.

### 6.2.3. Document Instance

Individual document instances must begin with a prolog naming the DTD to which they adhere, which as noted above references the SGML declaration being used, except in XML-compliant files when the SGML declaration is implicit and cannot be modified. Following this prolog, the body of an individual document instance conforming to a particular DTD is composed solely of two types of information:

- *Data* that communicates information to someone (in EAD, this is generally textual data)
- *Markup*, which conveys instructions to a software package that will process or act upon that text in order to index it for searching or to render (e.g., for screen display or print) or transform (e.g., for a voice synthesizer) it for some output device(s)

The prolog of all EAD-encoded document instances must begin with the following document type declaration:

```
<!DOCTYPE  ead  PUBLIC  "-//Society of American Archivists//DTD
ead.dtd (Encoded Archival Description (EAD) Version 1.0)//EN">
```

The string <!DOCTYPE identifies this as a document type declaration, which should not be confused with the similarly named "Document Type Definition." The document type declaration references the DTD that is being used by the document instance. Immediately following the <!DOCTYPE string is the document type name, which is defined by the SGML standard as the minimum literal string that can stand uniquely as a representation of the document type being declared, in this case "ead." In an SGML system, the document type name may be either in upper or lower case. However, since XML is case sensitive and the EAD DTD prescribes that all element and attribute names be in lower case, it may be safest always to render it in lower case to be certain that your files will work in either context.

Having identified the document type, the instance must now make its DTD available to processing applications. This can happen in either of two ways. The entire DTD may be embedded within the DOCTYPE declaration itself in what is called the *declaration subset.* The content of the declaration subset is delimited at the beginning by a left square bracket ([) and by a right square bracket (]) at the end.[101] More frequently, the DTD is stored for efficiency in an external file, which the DOCTYPE declaration references at this point, as in the EAD DOCTYPE declaration shown above. The reference may consist of a formal public identifier whose text is preceded by the keyword PUBLIC. Alternatively, a location-specific system identifier may be given as a reference, signaled by the keyword SYSTEM.

---

[101] Entity declarations are also included in the declaration subset. See section 6.5.2.2 for details.

The relative merits of public identifiers, system identifiers, and a combination of the two are discussed in section 6.5.2.4.1.

### 6.2.4. Enforcing Compliance

Any SGML-aware software application attempting to process an SGML document instance is entitled to expect that the document will do two things:

- Reference an SGML-conformant DTD
- Adhere to that DTD in its markup

A *valid* document instance is one that uses markup in the manner specified by the particular DTD that it references. XML permits *well-formed* document instances that do not reference a DTD, but that must still adhere to the rules in the XML specification. Archivists choosing to use the EAD DTD in XML mode will produce document instances that are both well-formed *and* valid.

In SGML-based systems, the process of testing a document for compliance with the referenced DTD is called "parsing." Parsing is the process of resolving something complex into its component parts. The parsing application in an SGML system goes through several steps to accomplish this. In a typical scenario, it first reads the SGML declaration if there is one and then tests the DTD itself for SGML conformity. Next it reads or parses the markup, expanding text entities and separating text from markup. The document is then transformed into a tree structure so that in the final phase the application can validate the document by comparing its structure to that of the DTD. Simply stated, *parsing* identifies the markup, and *validation* compares that markup against the DTD.

## 6.3. Elements

Elements are the primary building blocks for the markup that is specified by a DTD. Elements—in the form of the tags that represent them—provide the framework for an encoded SGML-compliant document instance. This framework surrounds textual or other data, which is the information content of the document that is intended to be conveyed to an audience.

The element declaration in a DTD is composed of the string <!ELEMENT, followed by an element name, followed by a content model, as in the following example:

```
<!ELEMENT  element_name  content_model>
```

The element name forms the core of each tag that delineates the content of an element in an individual instance of an encoded document. The SGML standard specifies that tags are identified by a left angle bracket (<), followed by the text of the element name and a trailing right angle bracket (>), and that there are two possible tags for each content-bearing element: a start-tag and an end-tag. In their simplest form these tags are identical, with one important exception: the end-tag includes a forward slash (/) between the left angle bracket and the element name.

| Start-tag: | End-tag: |
|---|---|
| `<element_name>` | `</element_name>` |

The start-tag can have a more complex form because it can be qualified by attributes (discussed in section 6.4), while end-tags cannot be so modified.

The following examples contain two fairly simple element declarations from the EAD DTD to illustrate the relationship between element declarations and the tags used in an individual instance of an encoded document. Figure 6.3a contains the EAD DTD declarations for the elements EAD <ead> and Change <change>:

```
<!ELEMENT  ead    (eadheader, frontmatter?, archdesc)>
<!ELEMENT  change  (date, item+)>
```

**Figure 6.3a.** *Element declarations taken from the EAD DTD.*

The element name for each element as declared in the EAD DTD is used to construct tags in individual EAD document instances, as illustrated in this example:

| Start-tag: | End-tag: |
|---|---|
| `<ead>` | `</ead>` |
| `<change>` | `</change>` |

The content model section of an element declaration in an SGML DTD specifies three characteristics of the element:

- What can occur as data inside of the element
- The order, if any, that is to be imposed on that data
- How often subelements contained within the element can or must occur

The order of occurrence in the content model sequence of the element declaration is determined by the following symbols:

| | | |
|---|---|---|
| , | *Comma* | Required order (x then y) |
| \| | *Vertical bar (pipe)* | No required order (x or y) |
| ( ) | *Parentheses* | Content groupings within the broader content model |

The permitted frequency of occurrence of subelements is established by the following frequency indicators, which can appear immediately after the name of a particular element or after a content grouping delineated by a set of parentheses:

| | | |
|---|---|---|
| | *Blank* | Required, may only occur once |
| + | *Plus* | Required, may occur one or more times |
| ? | *Question mark* | Optional, may occur only zero or one times |
| * | *Asterisk* | Optional, may occur zero, one or more times |

Both elements as declared in figure 6.3a are examples of a content model that can only contain other elements, also referred to as *subelements*. The first element declaration in figure 6.3a states that the element Encoded Archival Description <ead> must contain a single required subelement EAD Header <eadheader>, possibly followed by a single optional subelement Front Matter <frontmatter>, followed by a single required subelement Archival Description <archdesc>. The second element declaration states that the element Change <change> must contain a single required subelement Date <date>, followed by one or more required Item <item> subelements (see chapter 3 for a discussion of the use of these and other EAD elements and for examples of their use in encoded finding aids).

The above element declaration examples are illustrative of an *element-only content model*, which means that these elements can have only other elements as content. Obviously all elements declared in the EAD DTD cannot follow this content model, since we must be able to put the textual data that comprises an archival finding aid somewhere within individual EAD-encoded document instances. An SGML-based encoding scheme such as EAD uses the term PCDATA to indicate that "parsed character data" is allowed in the content model for an element. You may not think of the text of your finding aid as "parsed character data," but that is what it is to an SGML-aware software package once your finding aid text is part of an EAD-encoded document. Any text that the content model for an element defines as PCDATA must be parsed by the software in order to determine that it is not markup. The software cannot assume automatically that this element content is or is not markup, and so it must resolve (analyze) its component parts.

SGML-based content models use the term CDATA (character data) to indicate to processing software that data allowed in certain places will *never* contain markup and therefore does not have to be parsed in order to be validated. One common example of the use of CDATA that will be discussed in section 6.4 is supplying attribute values, which can never contain other markup or character entities.

The Abstract <abstract> element provides an illustration of a *mixed content model* that can contain both textual data and other elements or markup. The following example illustrates the content model for <abstract> as established in the EAD DTD:

```
<!ELEMENT  abstract  (#PCDATA | ptr | extptr | emph | lb |
                     abbr | expan| ref | extref | linkgrp |
                     bibref | title | archref)*>
```

This element declaration states that <abstract> has no required content and can contain parsed character data or any of the enumerated elements in any order and as many times as they are needed. In an EAD document, this means that you can put text and the enumerated tags in any combination that you wish between the start-tag <abstract> and the end-tag </abstract> (see section 3.5.1.2.6 for more information on the use of <abstract>).

An SGML-based markup system can define either content-bearing elements, as discussed above, or *empty elements*. The vast majority of elements defined by the EAD DTD contain either other elements or text. Several, in what is known as "mixed content," contain both. A few others, such as the element Pointer <ptr>, are defined as EMPTY. The declaration for this element specifies the following content model:

```
<!ELEMENT  ptr  EMPTY>
```

Empty elements can contain no textual or element content and are tagged using only the start-tag, not the end-tag. SGML processing software knows not to look for an end-tag (see section 4.3.2.4 for information on XML syntax for empty elements). The principal value of the capacity to declare empty elements in an SGML system is to gain access to the attributes available for those elements; this is especially useful for elements that facilitate both internal and external linking from a particular spot in a document. You might use such an element for creating cross references between different points within an encoded finding aid or to create a link to digitized facsimiles of items from the collection described in a finding aid. chapter 7 contains encoded examples and a more in-depth discussion of EAD's linking features.

## 6.4. Attributes

Attributes in an SGML-based encoding system allow information to be added to qualify an element in some way, such as to specify the type of an element, to provide it with a unique identifier, or to provide instructions for how it should be processed or displayed. Attributes are declared in DTDs in much the same way as elements. They are identified by the string <!ATTLIST, and they have values that can either be constrained or unconstrained by the attribute declaration. Possible values for *constrained* attributes are specified within the attribute declaration, forcing the encoder to choose from a closed list of values. *Unconstrained* attribute values are generally specified in the DTD with a CDATA content model, which allows the user to input any value.

Attributes are always related to a previously declared element in a DTD. In other words, the SGML standard does not permit an attribute to stand alone without an element for which it provides some qualification. Attributes provide metainformation about the data content delineated by a particular element and can only appear after the element name within start-tags in an SGML-based encoding system. Attributes are placed into start-tags in the following manner:

```
<element_name  attribute_name="attribute_value">
```

For example: `<c level="series">`

For example, the Component element, delineated by the start-tag <c> and the end-tag </c>, provides, through its subelements and the textual data they contain, a variety of identification and contextual information about a particular component in an archival description. The LEVEL attribute on that component is the means through which the EAD DTD provides for the encoding of metainformation about the level of a particular descriptive component (collection, series, file, item) within the larger encoded archival description.

An attribute declaration in a DTD is composed of the string <!ATTLIST, followed by an element name indicating the element that the attribute will be modifying, followed by the attribute name, followed by the specification of allowable attribute value(s), followed by either a default value or an attribute type.

```
<!ATTLIST  element_name  ATTRIBUTE_NAME  value(s)  type_or_default>
```

Figure 6.4a provides two examples of EAD element and attribute declarations:

```
1.  <!ELEMENT   editionstmt   (edition | p)+>
    <!ATTLIST editionstmt
              id                 ID                       #IMPLIED
              altrender          CDATA                    #IMPLIED
              audience           (external | internal)    #IMPLIED
              encodinganalog     CDATA                    #IMPLIED>

2.  <!ELEMENT   archdesc   (runner*, did, (admininfo | bioghist |
                          controlaccess | odd | scopecontent |
                          organization | arrangement | add | dsc |
                          dao | daogrp | note)*)>
    <!ATTLIST archdesc
              id                 ID                       #IMPLIED
              altrender          CDATA                    #IMPLIED
              audience           (external | internal)    #IMPLIED
              type               (inventory | register
                                  | othertype)            #IMPLIED
              othertype          CDATA                    #IMPLIED
              level              (series | collection
                                  file | fonds | item |
                                  otherlevel | recordgrp
                                  | subgrp | subseries)   #REQUIRED
              otherlevel         CDATA                    #IMPLIED
              langmaterial       CDATA                    #IMPLIED
              legalstatus        (public | private |
                                  otherlegalstatus)       #IMPLIED
              otherlegalstatus   CDATA                    #IMPLIED
              encodinganalog     CDATA                    #IMPLIED
              relatedencoding    CDATA                    #IMPLIED>
```

**Figure 6.4a.** *EAD DTD element and attribute declarations for <editionstmt> and <archdesc>. The three columns in the attribute declarations represent, in order, the name of the attribute, the content model, and the value designation.*

The LEVEL attribute for the Archival Description <archdesc> element provides a good example of both constrained and unconstrained values (see the second attribute declaration example in figure 6.4a). The attribute declaration provides the following *closed list* of possible values for this attribute, thus constraining the choices an archivist can make: collection, file, fonds, item, otherlevel, recordgrp, series, subgrp, subseries. Providing a closed list of values makes inputting those values easier in SGML-aware authoring systems (see chapter 4 for more information on EAD authoring) and ensures consistency of attribute values across repositories for certain important types of information that may be crucial to union databases of encoded finding aids. There are, however, other legitimate names that some repositories may use for levels of archival description. While the list above is closed, one of the choices is OTHERLEVEL, another attribute that is declared in the DTD with a content model of CDATA, meaning that its value is unconstrained (see section 3.5.1 for a discussion of encoding the LEVEL attribute in <archdesc>).

When attribute values are encoded within tags, they are treated by an SGML-aware processing system as *literal values*. This term denotes a string of characters enclosed between either single (') or double (") quotation marks that will not be broken down further for processing. For example, an encoder cannot use an entity reference as the content of an attribute value and expect that the processing software will recognize and resolve that entity (entities are discussed in section 6.5).

Attribute values can be acted upon by SGML-aware processing software in a variety of ways:

- They may be transformed into text for display to end users
- They may control formatting
- They may be used to control indexing of the text
- They may be used to establish internal or external links

In an individual document instance it is important to remember that, unlike the textual data that is the content of many elements, the actual data values of attributes are not immediately available to the end user of that encoded document instance. In order that certain attribute values display to an end user (for example, the LANGMATERIAL attribute value of <archdesc> or the LABEL attribute value of a <did> subelement), you must be using a system or stylesheet that can act upon attribute values and transform them for display (see section 5.3.3 for more on stylesheets).

From a technical perspective, the most striking difference between attributes and elements is the fact that elements, as we have seen, can contain either text or other elements, while attributes can never contain other elements. Attribute values, as previously noted, are expressed in terms of CDATA rather than PCDATA so that an SGML-aware processing software package attempting to validate an encoded document instance will never have to parse those attribute values in search of further markup. Also, as you can see in the attribute declaration examples in figure 6.4a, there is no means in the attribute declaration to control the order in which attributes should occur. In an EAD-encoded document, you may therefore place the declared attributes for any given tag in any order you wish, while elements must be encoded in the order (if any) specified by the element declarations in the DTD.

The examples in figure 6.4a illustrate the variety of attribute values that can be declared in a DTD. The attribute ALTRENDER—which allows an encoder to indicate output rendering preferences to processing software—has a value designation of CDATA, meaning that it is unconstrained and an encoder therefore can assign it whatever value is needed. The attribute AUDIENCE, on the other hand, is constrained to one of two values supplied in a closed list, "internal" or "external." The attribute ID has a value designation of ID, which is an SGML term for a string of characters that begins with an upper- or lower-case letter, contains no whitespace, and is composed only of alphanumeric characters, underscores(_), hyphens(-), colons(:) and full stops(.) A further requirement for attributes with an ID value designation is that their value must be unique within a particular encoded document instance and that there can only be one such attribute per element.

Attribute types are specified at the end of each attribute declaration line in the <!ATTLIST examples in figure 6.4a. The vast majority of the attributes in the EAD DTD are declared as IMPLIED, meaning that individual SGML-based systems may imply values for them if not otherwise declared, but that the DTD will not enforce their occurrence. You will notice in the <!ATTLIST declaration example for <archdesc> that the attribute LEVEL is declared as REQUIRED, which means that a parser will not validate an EAD instance when this attribute is missing.

## 6.5. Entities

Entities allow an encoder to declare an abbreviated name that serves as a substitute for something else. That "something else" can be one of several things:

- A long or short bit of boilerplate text that will be reused frequently throughout the document instance
- A completely different document instance
- A file in a data format that is completely unrecognizable to SGML-aware software (such as image and multimedia files, database objects, and proprietary text-processing file formats)

Once an entity has been declared within a document instance, the encoder can use the abbreviated name as many times as necessary. Processing software, when encountering the abbreviated name, will expand the abbreviation to whatever the entity declaration references. How the entity expansion behaves is chiefly determined by the processing software, but an encoder can often use markup to provide some direction to the software. This is discussed at greater length in chapter 7 on linking elements.

Declaration:

```
<!ENTITY tp-address PUBLIC "-//ABC University::Special
Collections Library//TEXT (titlepage: name and address)//EN"
"tpspcoll.sgm">
```

Expansion:

```
<list type="simple">
<head>Repository Address </head>
<item>Special Collections Library</item>
<item>ABC University</item>
<item>Main Library, 40 Circle Drive</item>
<item>Ourtown, Pennsylvania</item>
<item>17654 USA</item>
</list>
```

**Figure 6.5a.** *An example of an entity declaration followed by the entity expansion.*

Goldfarb and Prescod provide a helpful, if perhaps oversimplified, analogy for entities. They suggest thinking of an entity as a box with a label. The box contains some specified text or data, while the label (the abbreviated name) offers a shorthand way of referring to the box.[102] Entities can range from simple to complex, but they provide powerful ways to increase efficiency, avoid redundancy, and incorporate non-SGML data into encoded document instances.

[102] Charles Goldfarb and Paul Prescod, *The XML Handbook* (Upper Saddle River, N.J.: Prentice Hall, 1998), 478.

Entities can be one of two types: *parameter* or *general.*

### 6.5.1. Parameter Entities

Parameter entities provide a good introduction to some basic entity syntax, but we will not spend much time discussing them, because they can only appear in DTDs (either stand-alone DTDs like EAD, or DTDs that are embedded in the declaration subset of a document instance) and not in the body of individual document instances. Parameter entities are generally used by DTD writers, as they are in the EAD DTD, to bundle commonly used element and attribute declarations into a content model that can be reused easily throughout a DTD, or even shared between DTDs. Parameter entity declarations in DTDs use the following formula:

```
<!ENTITY  %  entity_name  entity_value>
```

Parameter entities must be declared in DTDs before they can be referenced elsewhere in the text of the DTD. A DTD writer would reference a parameter entity as follows:

```
%entity_name;
```

The following example provides an illustration of a parameter entity declaration taken from the EAD DTD:

```
<!ENTITY  %  a.common
        'id           ID                        #IMPLIED
         altrender    CDATA                     #IMPLIED
         audience     (external | internal)     #IMPLIED'>
```

You may notice from prior attribute examples that the literal single-quoted string above looks suspiciously like the contents of an <!ATTLIST declaration, which it is. This entity declaration example basically states that wherever an application reading this DTD encounters the reference "%a.common;" it should substitute the attribute list that appears between the single quotation marks in the above example. This particular parameter entity is referenced frequently throughout the EAD DTD, since the attributes ID, ALTRENDER, and AUDIENCE are available for the modification of the majority of EAD elements. The very first element declared in the "Encoded Archival Description Element Declarations" section of the EAD DTD appears as follows:

```
<!ELEMENT  ead   (eadheader, frontmatter?, archdesc)>
<!ATTLIST  ead
           %a.common;
           relatedencoding   CDATA                  #IMPLIED>
```

At the point at which an SGML-aware software package encounters this parameter entity reference, it will expand the reference so that an encoder utilizing an <ead> tag actually has four available attributes for that tag, RELATEDENCODING plus the three defined by the "a.common" entity declaration. This expansion of the entity reference is one of the steps all SGML-aware software packages must take prior to processing any SGML-compliant encoded text.

There is one final point to make about the above example that illustrates an important property of entities. The example illustrates an *internal* entity declaration, which means that the text for the expansion of the entity reference is declared as part of the entity declaration itself. If that declaration had referenced a text or data file stored outside of the file in which the reference is included (we will see an example of this shortly), it would be an example of an *external* entity declaration.

The percent sign (%) in both the entity declaration and at the beginning of the entity reference in the examples above is what identifies these as parameter, and not general, entities.

### 6.5.2. General Entities

As noted in section 6.5.1, parameter entities can only be used in DTDs. Encoders of individual document instances using an SGML DTD also have entities available to them, called general entities. General entities are more complicated than parameter entities because they can serve a variety of functions within an encoded document instance. The following four sections discuss the types of general entities that are available to EAD users and the way in which some of those entities must be declared in a document instance. Section 6.5.2.1 discusses entities that are not individually declared in the document instance because they are character entities either defined as part of the EAD DTD when it is used in SGML mode, or, in the case of XML, defined as part of the XML specification itself. Section 6.5.2.2 discusses the declaration of entities as part of the prolog to a document instance. Section 6.5.2.3 discusses internal entities, in which the content of the entity expansion is provided as part of the entity declaration. Section 6.5.2.4 discusses external entities that provide addresses for external files required to expand the entity.

#### 6.5.2.1. Character Entities

The simplest form of entities are those that are incorporated through eadchars.ent, one of the files associated with the EAD DTD (see section 4.3.1 for more information on the EAD DTD and associated files). These character entities are defined in standardized ISO (International Standards Organization) character entity sets[103] and are generally for characters and symbols (e.g., a "u" with an umlaut, the copyright symbol, the Greek letter lambda) that are not available on the standard English-language keyboard. The EAD DTD references the following 10 ISO character sets by default:

[103] Robin Cover's *SGML/XML Web Page* provides further information about ISO character entity sets, available at: <http://www.oasis-open.org/cover/topics.html#entities>.

- Added Latin 1
- Added Latin 2
- Greek Symbols
- Alternative Greek Symbols
- Greek Letters
- Monotoniko Greek
- Diacritical Marks
- Numeric and Special Graphics
- Publishing
- General Technical

Note that the character entity set references in the EAD DTD do not by themselves make these character entities available for use in EAD instances. You must have these character sets available in your SGML system in order to make them work in EAD. This is a topic that should be discussed with your system administrator if you plan to use character entities in your encoded finding aids.

In SGML, special typographic and graphic characters are represented with SDATA (specific character data) entity declarations, which provide the abbreviations you will use in character entity references within your encoded documents. These entity declarations appear in the SGML ISO character entity mapping tables that must be a part of your system if you are going to reference nonkeyboard characters. In your EAD instances you can reference individual character entities in the following manner:

```
&#abbreviation;
```

As an alternative to the SDATA abbreviation you can also use the decimal number assigned to the character in the ISO character entity set in use, for example:

| | Character Entity Reference | |
|---|---|---|
| Desired Character or Symbol | ISO SDATA Abbreviation | ISO Decimal Reference |
| © | `&#copy;` | `©` |

XML uses the functionality of Unicode to replace SGML's SDATA-based character entity scheme. Unicode is designed to be all encompassing, incorporating all diacritics, symbols and characters into a single character entity set.

As explained by Goldfarb and Prescod:

> If you are a native English speaker you may only need the fifty-two upper- and lower-case characters, some punctuation, and a few accented characters. The pervasive *7 bit ASCII character set* caters to this market. It has just enough characters (128) for all of the letters, symbols, some accented characters and some other oddments. ASCII is both a character set *and* a character encoding. It defines what set of characters is available and how they are to be encoded in terms of bits and bytes.
>
> XML's character set is Unicode, a sort of ASCII on steroids. Unicode includes thousands of useful characters from languages around the world.

> However, the first 128 characters of Unicode are compatible with ASCII and there is a character encoding of Unicode, *UTF-8*, that is compatible with 7 bit ASCII. This means that at the bits and bytes level, the first 128 characters of UTF-8 Unicode and 7 bit ASCII are the same. This feature of Unicode allows authors to use standard plain-text editors to create XML immediately.[104]

A character or symbol can be referenced using either the decimal number assigned to it in Unicode or its hexadecimal alphanumeric reference in the following manner:

Decimal: **&#***somenumber;*
Hexadecimal: **&#x***somenumber;*

| | Character Entity Reference | |
|---|---|---|
| Desired Character or Symbol | Unicode Decimal Reference | Unicode Hexadecimal Reference |
| © | `©` | `©` |

SGML and SGML systems as they currently exist do not recognize the hexadecimal alphanumeric references, though XML systems do. Furthermore, SGML systems only recognize the Unicode numeric references for the 128 7-bit ASCII characters. Work is currently underway to alter the SGML standard to fully recognize the Unicode character entity set. EAD implementers using SGML software should use the ISO SDATA abbreviations when including character entity references in their EAD instances. When XML-compliant mapping tables become available, it will be easy to swap these for the SGML ISO tables in the system without necessitating any markup changes.

One other point worth mentioning is that although special characters can be included in EAD documents using SDATA abbreviations or decimal and hexadecimal references, many search engines cannot search these entity references, which may cause searches to fail. Until the time when Unicode becomes a standard in use in all of the various software packages utilized in encoding, manipulating, and delivering encoded instances, there will be disparities in how different software expresses special characters. A repository must consider the importance of being able to index and display these special characters in the light of the difficulty in maintaining them through the various stages of the markup and delivery of encoded finding aids.

### 6.5.2.2. Declaring Entities in the Document Prolog

All other general entities to be used in encoded document instances must be declared by placing an entity declaration for each in the declaration subset in the DOCTYPE declaration at the beginning of the EAD instance. As mentioned in section 6.2.3, the declaration subset appears between square brackets ([ and ]) at the end of the DOCTYPE declaration. Because whitespace is not significant within SGML declarations, a popular typographical convention

---

[104] Charles Goldfarb and Paul Prescod, *The XML Handbook* (Upper Saddle River, N.J.: Prentice Hall, 1998), 37.

is to begin a new line just after the opening square bracket and just before the closing square bracket in order to make encoded instance files easier to read. Figure 6.5.2.2a shows a prolog to an EAD instance in which an external general entity is declared:

```
<!DOCTYPE  ead  PUBLIC  "-//Society of American Archivists//DTD
ead.dtd (Encoded Archival Description (EAD) Version 1.0)//EN"  [
<!ENTITY  brblmain  SYSTEM
"http://www.myserver.edu/entities/brblmain.sgm">
]>
```



**Figure 6.5.2.2a** *A general entity declaration within the EAD declaration subset.*

Both the DOCTYPE and ENTITY declarations shown in figure 6.5.2.2a contain quote-delimited *external identifiers*. External identifiers can either be public or system identifiers. Public identifiers provide a form of destination address that is not specific to any one system. Use of a public identifier relies on the SGML system to resolve the nonspecific address to a specific one where the referenced file can be found. Public identifiers are provided for in the SGML standard (ISO 8879), while the syntax for Formal Public Identifiers (FPI)[105], a subset of public identifiers, is specified in the ISO 9070 standard. EAD does not require that all public identifiers be FPIs.

If a public identifier is used (indicated by the keyword PUBLIC), it may be followed by a system identifier in the form of a Uniform Resource Indicator (URI) for the resource. A URI is a broader construct that includes as a subset the more familiar URL (Uniform Resource Locator).[106] URLs, and more broadly URIs, are the addressing mechanisms that facilitate pointing to resources on the World Wide Web. The keyword SYSTEM, instead of PUBLIC, will precede an external identifier when *only* a URI, and no public identifier, is given for the file being referenced. Both keywords are important components in document type declarations and external entity declarations. The relative merits of public identifiers, system identifiers, and a combination of the two are discussed in section 6.5.2.4.1.

Entities like the one shown in figure 6.5.2.2a will be discussed shortly in greater detail. Once an entity has been declared in the declaration subset of a document instance, it can be referenced in the document instance itself at any point where markup is permitted by the DTD (it cannot be used in a place where content has been declared as CDATA). The entity declared in figure 6.5.2.2a would be referenced as follows:

```
&brblmain;
```

---

[105] For a fuller, more technical discussion of Formal Public Identifiers, see Steven J. DeRose, *The SGML FAQ Book* (Dordrecht: Kluwer, 1997), 211-12. See also Charles Goldfarb, *The SGML Handbook* (Oxford: Oxford University Press, 1990), 382-90.

[106] The World Wide Web Consortium maintains an excellent web site that contains definitive information concerning definitions and the ongoing development of URIs, URLs, and FPIs. Available at: <http://www.w3.org/Addressing/>.

#### 6.5.2.3. Internal Entities

As mentioned earlier, general entities that may be used in document instances come in two basic flavors, internal and external. General internal entities are the simplest in that they contain the referenced content expansion directly as a component of the entity declaration. General internal entities contain text and are always included within the instance being parsed. General internal entity declarations in the declaration subset of a document instance begin with the string <!ENTITY, followed by the entity name, followed by the entity content delineated in either single or double quotation marks, as in the following example:

```
<!ENTITY  entity_name  "specification_of_content">
```

Note that the keywords PUBLIC and SYSTEM are *not* necessary in internal entity declarations. Internal entities are only useful for text that is used repetitively within a particular encoded finding aid; they cannot be referenced from other document instances. For example, a repository might utilize a general internal entity in encoding a finding aid in which the name of the organization whose records are described in the finding aid is long, complex, and subject to typographical errors. In such a case, the encoder might declare an entity in the document type declaration as follows:

```
<!DOCTYPE  ead  PUBLIC  "-//Society of American
Archivists//DTD ead.dtd (Encoded Archival Description (EAD)
Version 1.0)//EN"  [
<!ENTITY  stuffsoc  "Society for the Preservation,
Beautification, and General Betterment of the Stufftown
Memorial Stuffatorium">
]>
```

The encoder could then, at multiple points throughout the EAD instance, reference this declared entity as follows:

```
<origination><corpname>&stuffsoc;</corpname></origination>
      [...]
<prefercite><head>Preferred Citation</head><p>[identification
of item], &stuffsoc; Records, Stufftown Memorial Stuffatorium,
Stufftown, NS.</p></prefercite>
      [...]
<bioghist><p>The &stuffsoc; was established in 1872 by the
town council of Stufftown and was endowed initially with a
fund to cover operating and acquisition expenses through the
generous benefaction of … </p></bioghist>
```

Any SGML-aware software encountering these entity references in processing can expand them to the full text provided in the entity declaration prior to processing the encoded instance.

### 6.5.2.4. External Entities

General external entities are intended to be either parsed or unparsed when an SGML-aware software package processes that document instance. In the case of an entity that points to files containing SGML character data, such as a large, oft-repeated markup section, you would want the parsing process to involve both the document instance and the text of the external entity. In other cases, the encoder would not want the externally referenced data files to be validated along with the encoded instance. Examples of the latter include entities that reference external SGML document instances containing other EAD-encoded finding aids or text encoded using a different DTD, or that reference non-SGML data files such as images captured as GIF or JPEG files or MPEG video files.

The next two sections describe the details of the entity declarations that are used to specify parsed or unparsed data.

#### 6.5.2.4.1. Externally Stored Data Intended to be Parsed

First we will consider externally stored EAD-encoded data that is intended to be parsed as part of the document instance in which it is referenced. These external entity references are similar to general internal entity references, except that the literal quoted string must identify the external location of the file to be included in the document instance. This can be done using public identifiers, system identifiers, or a combination of the two.

Using entities in this way can assist a repository in the management of frequently updated information that appears widely across its encoded finding aids. Instead of entering such information as a part of each EAD instance, it can be stored as a separate file and referred to from within each instance using an entity reference. Figure 6.5.2.4.1a below provides an example of contact information that is stored as a separate file, tpncdsp.sgm, so that it can be referenced as an entity in each of the repository's finding aids. Updating this single file when, for example, the repository's area code changes, would change the contact information in all of the repository's encoded finding aids. If the area code information had been hard-coded into each of the individual files, such an update would be much more labor-intensive.

```
<list type="simple">
   <head>Contact Information </head>
   <item>Rare Book, Manuscript, and Special Collections
   Library</item>
   <item>Duke University</item>
   <item>P.O. Box 90185</item>
   <item>Durham, North Carolina</item>
   <item>27708-0185 USA</item>
   <item>Phone: 919/660-5822</item>
   <item>Fax: 919/660-5934</item>
   <item>Email: specoll@mail.lib.duke.edu</item>
   <item>URL: http://scriptorium.lib.duke.edu/</item>
</list>
```

**Figure 6.5.2.4.1a.** *The content of the file* tpncdsp.sgm.

The following is an example of an entity declaration that references the file tpncdsp.sgm using only a public identifier:

```
<!ENTITY tp-ncd-spcoll PUBLIC "-//Duke University::Rare Book,
Manuscript, and Special Collections Library//TEXT (titlepage:
name and address)//EN">
```

This form of entity declaration is valid only in SGML systems. In XML a system identifier must be supplied as well, as illustrated in the following example, in which a relative URI is used:

```
<!ENTITY tp-ncd-spcoll PUBLIC "-//Duke University::Rare Book,
Manuscript, and Special Collections Library//TEXT (titlepage:
name and address)//EN" "tpncdsp.sgm">
```

Finally, the information in figure 6.5.2.4.1a could be declared as an entity using only a system identifier. This approach would also be valid in XML. In the example below the system identifier is given as an absolute URI:

```
<!ENTITY tp-ncd-spcoll SYSTEM
"http://scriptorium.lib.duke.edu/eadfiles/tpncdsp.sgm">
```

The choice of whether to use a system identifier (a relative or absolute URI) or a public identifier (either an FPI or a less formal local public identifier) is largely determined by the system or systems in which you are storing and delivering encoded finding aid data (see section 5.4 for a related discussion of file management). Use of a relative URI, one that does not give the entire address of the referenced file beginning with the transfer protocol used (such as http://), assumes that all referenced files will inhabit a stable directory structure regardless of the server on which they reside. It should be noted here that use of relative URIs may be problematic for managers of union databases of encoded finding aids; archivists planning to submit their finding aids to such collaborative projects should consult the systems manager of the union database prior to deciding to use relative URIs. Using an absolute URI commits you to some file maintenance overhead anytime the files being referenced are moved to a new server, since the entire address of each URI will have to be edited. However, a simple "find and replace" routine will probably alleviate this overhead in most cases.

Use of a public identifier assumes the existence of an SGML catalog file[107] to which a system can turn in order to map, or resolve, that public identifier into a URI. The great strength of a file management system based on public identifiers is that changes in file locations on or among servers can easily be accommodated by changing a single address in the catalog file, rather than changing the entity reference in each individual EAD instance. Planning for future storage and delivery system possibilities requires careful thought as you decide which addressing approach to adopt. A fuller discussion of various options for providing file addresses in external entity declarations is provided in section 7.5.

There is an important difference between referencing files containing encoding excerpts, such as the one illustrated in figure 6.5.2.4.1a, in SGML systems as compared to XML systems. In the former, any chunk of text can be excerpted for reuse provided that it is encoded using the same DTD as the document instance in which the file will be referenced as an entity. XML imposes the additional requirement that the excerpted chunk of encoded text be "well-formed," meaning that it must have a single parent element. The example in figure 6.5.2.4.1a meets this XML requirement, since the tags <list> and </list> enclose all of the other information in the file. If the <list> and </list> tags were removed, however, this file would no longer satisfy the well-formed requirement in XML.

All general external entity declarations, regardless of whether they utilize a public or a system identifier, can be referenced in encoded document instances in the same way that the general internal entity was referenced earlier (see section 6.5.2.3), as shown in the following example:

```
<publisher>Rare Book, Manuscript, and Special Collections
Library<lb>
Duke University<lb>
Durham, North Carolina</publisher>
&tp-ncd-spcoll;
```

#### 6.5.2.4.2. Externally Stored Data Not Intended to be Parsed

The second type of external entity reference points to files containing data that is not intended to be parsed along with the document instance. As noted earlier, there are a variety of reasons why you might not want the parsing software to attempt to resolve the content of the entity that you are referencing. Two prominent reasons are that the referenced file is not composed of textual data that SGML-aware processing software would recognize (such as

[107] Further information regarding the SGML catalog file and the formal FPI structure is available in *Encoded Archival Description Retrospective Conversion Guidelines,* Section VI, "Naming and Declaring Referenced External Entities," available at: <http://sunsite.berkeley.edu/amher/upguide.html#VI>. These guidelines were used in both the American Heritage Virtual Archive Project and the Online Archive of California Project.

GIF-format images), or that the referenced file contains SGML-recognizable character data that is not intended to be a part of your document instance, such as another EAD-encoded finding aid or a literary text encoded using the TEI DTD.

The SGML standard specifies that entity declarations not intended to be parsed use the keyword NDATA followed by a notation name to indicate to application software the type of external file that the entity declaration references. A notation declaration, either in the DTD or in the prolog of an EAD instance, specifies a notation name and a formal public identifier (FPI) for the type of NDATA file used and must occur before you can declare a general external entity. The file endnotat.ent, one of the files affiliated with the EAD DTD, includes a series of standard notation declarations. This provides notations for SGML as well as a number of common non-SGML data types, including JPEG, MPEG, PCX, GIF, and TIFF. Because these notations are declared in the EAD DTD, you can declare external entities in the prolog of your document instance that reference such files. Each notation declaration contains a notation name that you will need to create entity references to that type of file. Notation declarations follow the same format as general external entity declarations. Figure 6.5.2.4.2a illustrates the notation declaration for GIF files from the EAD DTD:

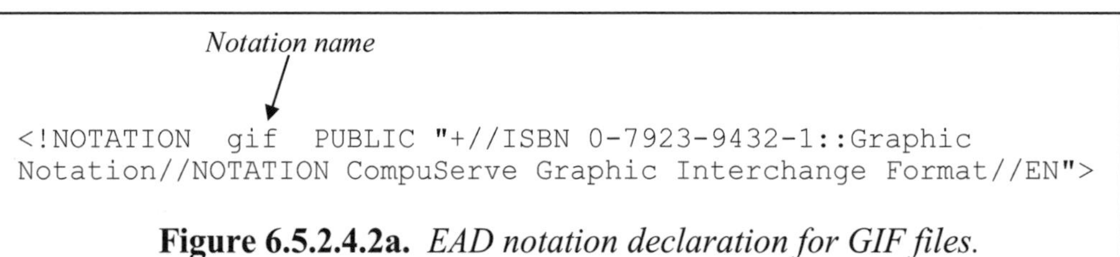


```
<!NOTATION  gif  PUBLIC "+//ISBN 0-7923-9432-1::Graphic
Notation//NOTATION CompuServe Graphic Interchange Format//EN">
```

**Figure 6.5.2.4.2a.** *EAD notation declaration for GIF files.*

When encoding your repository's finding aids, you may wish to include a GIF image of your repository seal or of the repository itself. This can be done by creating a general external entity declaration in the declaration subset of the prolog of each EAD instance. This entity declaration, as previously noted, must provide an address for the image file on your server using a public identifier, a system identifier, or both. A general external entity declaration, using as a system identifier an absolute URI, for the purpose described above might look like this:

```
<!ENTITY lcseal SYSTEM
"http://lcweb2.loc.gov/sgmlstd/panorama/lcseal.gif" NDATA gif>
```

The following is an example of an entity declaration for the same purpose that uses both a public and a system identifier, in this case a relative URI:

```
<!ENTITY dukeseal PUBLIC "-//Duke University::Rare Book, Manuscript,
and Special Collections Library//NONSGML (dukeseal)//EN"
"dukeseal.gif" NDATA gif>
```

By including the NDATA keyword following the URI, you are signaling SGML-aware processing software that the referenced file contains data that should not be processed with your EAD instance. By providing the declared notation name for a data type after the NDATA keyword, you are further giving the processing software a clue about how it might handle this data that it is not supposed to parse.

Because this entity is external to your document instance and not intended to be parsed as part of it, you would not refer to it in your document using the direct entity reference format discussed in section 6.5.2.4.1. Instead, you would use one of EAD's linking elements with an ENTITYREF attribute to provide a reference to the external entity (see section 7.3 for a fuller discussion of EAD's external linking elements and attributes).

# Chapter Seven

## EAD LINKING ELEMENTS

## 7.1. Introduction

Linking elements perform three functions in encoded finding aids:

- They facilitate hypertext capabilities, providing a navigation pathway that end users may use as an alternative to proceeding in a linear fashion through the encoded information in a document instance
- They allow an encoder to add multimedia functionality to a textual document through the incorporation of nontext information such as graphic images or sound files
- They also provide connections to external textual documents

### 7.1.1. The Structure of Links

In an SGML-based encoding scheme like EAD, linking elements and attributes are required in order to effect any link that the encoder wishes to establish. The link itself is really two things: (1) the declaration, through the use of a linking element, that a relationship exists between the information encoded in one element and that available someplace else; and (2) an address, or the name of a resource that can be resolved to an address, for the destination of the link being established, which is supplied as a value of an attribute in the linking element.

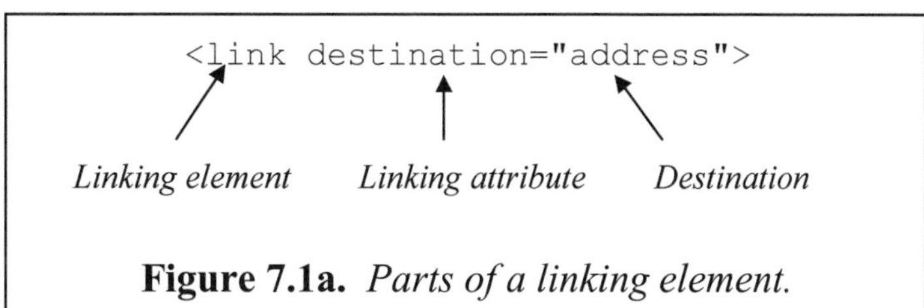


**Figure 7.1a.** *Parts of a linking element.*

Designated elements within encoded documents or entire documents themselves can serve as *resources* in a link, either as *sources* or as *destinations*. When you establish a link by placing a linking element in an encoded finding aid, that element generally serves as the source resource for the link. Each linking element has a group of linking attributes that provide further information regarding the link. Some of these attributes provide addresses for the destination resource for the link, while others provide information about how the link is intended to behave when the document instance is output to some display mechanism. The functionality of various linking attributes will be discussed below in the context of the various EAD linking elements with which they can be used.

It is important to stress that software must interpret the values of linking attributes and stylesheet instructions to actually effect these linking capabilities. Version 1.0 of EAD was designed specifically to support linking as defined in the XLink and XPointer specifications currently in draft format[108]. However, there currently are no commercially available software packages that implement certain linking attributes available in EAD. The discussion in this chapter relates to the broad functionality of the various linking elements and attributes in EAD, and *not* to the specifics of how a particular delivery system will translate or implement these encoded links. The chapter does provide some recommendations regarding attributes that archivists should consider using at a minimum when establishing links in EAD-encoded finding aids.

### 7.1.2. Characteristics of Links

The following 15 elements in EAD can be used to establish links:

- Archival Reference <archref>
- Bibliographic Reference <bibref>
- Digital Archival Object <dao>
- Digital Archival Object Group <daogrp>
- Digital Archival Object Location <daoloc>
- Extended Pointer <extptr>
- Extended Pointer Location <extptrloc>
- Extended Reference <extref>
- Extended Reference Location <extrefloc>
- Linking Group <linkgrp>
- Pointer <ptr>
- Pointer Location <ptrloc>
- Reference <ref>
- Reference Location <refloc>
- Title <title>

Thirteen manage links directly, while two (<daogrp> and <linkgrp>) are wrapper elements that consolidate multiple, related links. These 15 elements have several significant characteristics.

Conceptually, a link has four facets, each of which has only two or three possible values. Different linking elements possess different combinations of these facet values. In any given situation, the encoder of a finding aid will select the proper linking element based on these characteristics and on other considerations that will be described later in this chapter. These are the significant characteristics of links:

- Destination location *Internal* or *External* (See section 7.1.2.1)

[108] Further information on XLink and XPointer, the linking and addressing specifications that are being developed concurrently with XML, is on the World Wide Web Consortium web site, available at: <http://www.w3.org/TR/WD-xlink> for XLink and <http://www.w3.org/TR/WD-xptr> for XPointer.

- Extent — *Simple, Locator* or *Extended* — (See section 7.1.2.2)
- Source location — *Inline* or *Out-of-line* — (See section 7.1.2.3)
- Contents — *Empty* or *With text* — (See section 7.1.2.4)

Attributes play a very important part in linking elements. TARGET, HREF and ENTITYREF are used to provide destination addresses for links. ACTUATE, SHOW and BEHAVIOR work together to govern the way in which processing software presents links to end users. ROLE, TITLE, CONTENT-ROLE, CONTENT-TITLE and other attributes specific to EAD's linking elements provide additional specificity regarding the nature of links or the resources that participate in them.

#### 7.1.2.1. Destination Location

Links can be either *internal* or *external* to an encoded document instance. When encoding a finding aid you might use an *internal link* from an appropriate point within the Description of Subordinate Components <dsc> element to reference the text of an access restriction encoded at the collection level. Within the same finding aid, you might use an *external link* to provide a pointer to the encoded finding aid for a collection of related materials. You might also use an external link to provide a pointer to a digitized facsimile of a photograph or other item contained in the collection being described.

#### 7.1.2.2. Extent

All of the linking examples discussed in the previous paragraph are *single-direction links* that can be traversed only from source to destination, as illustrated in figure 7.1.2.2a.

```
<accessrestrict id="restrict1"><p>Access to some materials
in this collection has been restricted
...</p></accessrestrict>
            [other possible elements and text ...]
<c01 level="series"><did>[...]</did>
<scopecontent>
[...]
<p><ref target="restrict1">Correspondence in this series
between the donor and his son has been restricted as
previously specified.</ref></p>
</scopecontent>
</c01>
```

**Figure 7.1.2.2a.** *A single-direction link.*

An encoder can create a link to and from a destination by establishing two single-direction links that can be traversed in opposite directions, as illustrated in figure 7.1.2.2b.

```
<c02 level="series"><did> <unittitle>Series 4:
Correspondence,
<unitdate>1948-1969</unitdate></unittitle></did>
<c03 level="file"><did id="s04.001"><unittitle>Aardvark
Project, <unitdate>1951-1955</unitdate>
<ptr target="s09.001"></unittitle></did>
</c03></c02>
          [other possible elements and text ...]
<c02 level="series"><did> <unittitle>Series 9: Topical
Files,
<unitdate>1946-1976</unitdate></unittitle></did>
<c03 level="file"><did id="s09.001"><unittitle>Aardvark
Project, <unitdate>1951-1955</unitdate>
<ptr target="s04.001"></unittitle></did>
</c03></c02>
```

**Figure 7.1.2.2b.** *Two single-direction links used to establish links to and from a destination.*

The direction of link traversal in both figures is indicated by arrows. Some software may support the ability to traverse a link from source to destination and back to source without encoding two single-direction links for this purpose.

The focus of this linking discussion will be on *simple links*, since they are universally supported by SGML-aware software applications. Most of the links that an encoder creates in an EAD instance will be simple links. Simple links have these features:

- The source resource for the link is established using a linking element
- One and only one destination for each linking element used is provided by a linking attribute
- Each link is traversable only in a single direction, from source to destination

All other types of links are considered *extended links*. The concept of extended links is currently being clarified and expanded in work on XLink, the linking component of XML, and will be discussed only briefly. EAD has one main category of linking elements that are always extended, the bundling linking elements <linkgrp> and <daogrp>, which will be discussed in greater detail in sections 7.3.5 and 7.3.6. They are considered extended links because they do not themselves contain a destination resource for the established link, but rather bundle multiple *locator elements* (<extrefloc>, <daoloc>) containing addresses for the link's multiple destinations. The attribute XLINK:FORM, which supplies the designation of each linking element as simple, extended or locator, is discussed in section 7.2.4.

### 7.1.2.3. Source Location

An *inline* link is one in which the linking element in the encoded document participates as one of the resources of the link, usually as the source. An *out-of-line* link is one that does *not* participate as a resource in the link being established. This is a new and at this point in time a somewhat theoretical concept that is being developed as part of the XLink specification. Out-of-line links, when systems are developed to support them, will allow you to establish a link between two or more external documents that you do not have the capability of editing directly.[109] This might facilitate, for example, the development of annotation servers to manage "post-it" note commentaries for Web sites. One possible application of this technology for archival information servers could be to provide K-12 teachers with the capability to create a network of links between encoded finding aids—stored and managed externally to the finding aids themselves—that are geared specifically toward student assignments. The concept of out-of-line linking is introduced here so that readers of these *Guidelines* will have a passing familiarity with it as they encounter it in the XML literature, and so that they can understand the choices available for the value of the attribute INLINE (discussed in section 7.2.4). For all practical purposes though, current users of EAD should use the default value of "true" for the INLINE attribute, meaning that the link is inline.

### 7.1.2.4. Contents

Sometimes linking elements are used only as pointers to other locations. No caption or explanation of the link is required. In other scenarios, some explanatory text regarding the link is required. Certain linking elements are designated for each of these situations. Those not intended to include explanatory or descriptive content are defined in the DTD as EMPTY (see section 6.3 for a discussion of empty elements). Often the choice of one element over another will depend on whether a textual description of some sort is required or not.

### 7.1.3. Linking Element Use

Table 7.1.3a lists the 15 linking elements available in EAD arranged according to the characteristics just described.[110]

---

[109] Charles Goldfarb and Paul Prescod, *The XML Handbook* (Upper Saddle River, N.J.: Prentice Hall, 1998), 502-505.

[110] The list in figure 9 on page 12 of the *EAD Tag Library, Version 1.0* contains two errors. It mistakenly identifies <ptrgrp> as a fifteenth EAD linking element. In fact, <ptrgrp> serves as a bundling element for other linking elements but lacks the necessary attributes to function in the same way as the other elements included in the list. Also, the list in figure 9 omits <title>, which *does* function as a linking element in EAD.

| | | Simple Links<br><br>Simple links are *inline.* | Extended Links<br><br>Extended links can either be *inline* or *out-of-line.* These locator links must be bundled using <linkgrp> or <daogrp>. |
|---|---|---|---|
| Internal links | With text | **<ref>** | **<refloc>** |
| | Empty | **<ptr>** | **<ptrloc>** |
| External links | With text | **<archref>, <bibref>, <dao>**[111]**, <extref>, <title>** | **<daoloc>, <extrefloc>** |
| | Empty | **<extptr>** | **<extptrloc>** |

**Table 7.1.3a.** *EAD linking elements categorized by significant characteristics. Since currently available software does not generally support the use of extended links, EAD implementers should consult with their systems expert prior to employing the linking elements shown in the shaded area.*

As mentioned above, the use of any one of these elements[112] signals the establishment of a link between the information being encoded and information available somewhere else. That somewhere else may be within the same finding aid, on the same server, or on some other server available via the Internet.

The following discussion of various linking options will proceed from the simple to the complex. Additionally, it will first describe linking options that any SGML or XML system should be able to support and will then move to an abbreviated discussion of the more complex options that eventually will take advantage of the currently incomplete and unimplemented XLink and XPointer specifications in XML. It bears emphasis here that Version 1.0 of the EAD DTD was designed to support fully XML-compliant encoding when that specification is completely developed and when software is readily available to support its implementation. The degree to which a particular repository will want to take full advantage of many of the more complex linking capabilities in EAD is a decision that will need to be taken in consultation with persons possessing expertise in whatever local delivery system that repository chooses to use for its encoded finding aids. In the current environment, archivists are limited to the simpler linking options discussed below.

It should be noted that for the sake of clarity examples in sections 7.2, 7.3, and 7.4 will only include the linking element attributes being discussed in each particular subsection. Section 7.6, the final section in this chapter, will include several examples of the use of optimally encoded linking elements.

---

[111] Note that <dao> is often used empty but may include <daodesc> if the context needed for a link is not provided by other elements. The <dao> element is not technically an empty element because it is not defined as such in the EAD DTD.

[112] With the exception of <archref>, <bibref>, and <title>, as noted in section 7.3.3.

## 7.2. Internal Linking

Internal linking provides end users with the ability to proceed through the information in an encoded finding aid in a nonlinear way. It also gives you the ability to make explicit connections between related information that appears in different parts of a finding aid. The following sections provide information on the usage of the elements and attributes available in EAD to facilitate internal linking.

### 7.2.1. Pointer <ptr> and Reference <ref> with the TARGET Attribute

Internal linking within a document, the simplest form of EAD linking, is accomplished through use of the TARGET attribute. This attribute, available on only four elements (<ptr>, <ptrloc>, <ref> and <refloc>), allows you to establish a link to a destination somewhere else within the same finding aid. A TARGET attribute must have an "IDREF" value, which means that it must correspond exactly to a value declared as an ID attribute elsewhere in the same encoded document. This one-to-one correspondence is checked by parsing software while validating the document instance; if such correspondence does not exist, the software will report a validation error.

The ID attribute plays a critical role in internal links. The TARGET attribute on the linking element used to establish a source for an internal link contains the value of the ID attribute for the destination element. Virtually all EAD elements have an ID attribute and therefore may be the target of an internal link. As noted in the general discussion of attributes in section 6.4, the ID attribute has a value designation of "ID", which requires that its value be unique within a particular encoded document instance. Any element containing text that an encoder wishes to make the target of an internal link must be given a unique value using the ID attribute within that element. Once a unique value is assigned, this encoded information can serve as a link target.

To create an internal link, you must do the following:

- Use one of the four internal linking elements with an available TARGET attribute to establish a source for the relationship declared by the link
- Provide a destination address (a valid ID value) for the link using the TARGET attribute within that element

In figure 7.2.1a, the text of an access restriction note has been encoded at the collection level, and a unique ID value has been established for that note. In both figures below, some elements have been omitted in order to focus on the link-related points being made.

```
<archdesc level="collection" langmaterial="eng"
type="inventory">
<did>[...]</did>
<admininfo>
<accessrestrict id="restrict1">
<head>Access Restrictions</head>
<p>This collection is open for research to all researchers
with the following exception: Series 2 (Correspondence)
contains 15 folders of student recommendations that are
closed for 75 years under the jurisdiction of the state
Student Records Act (1968:042). The first of these folders
will be available to researchers on 1 January 2035 and the
last on 1 January 2047.</p>
</accessrestrict>
</admininfo>
</archdesc>
```

*Use of ID attribute creates potential for this information to be a link destination*

**Figure 7.2.1a.** *Establishing a unique ID value.*

In figure 7.2.1b, a linking element has been used to establish a relationship between access restriction information within the series-level description and the collection-level note illustrated in figure 7.2.1a. This encoding eliminates the need for repetition at various levels of description of the access restriction information.

```
<dsc type="combined">
<c01 level="series">
<did>[...]</did>
</c01>
<c01 level="series">
<did>
<unittitle>Series 2: Correspondence,
<unitdate type="inclusive">1952-1975</unitdate></unittitle>
<physdesc><extent>4.4 linear ft.</extent></physdesc>
</did>
<scopecontent><p>The Correspondence Series contains ...</p>
<arrangement><p>The bulk of the contents of the series
arrived at the repository in chronological order and this
arrangement has been retained. The single exception is a file
of student recommendations on which access restrictions have
been imposed.<ptr target="restrict1"> These folders have been
temporarily removed to a restricted box in the
collection.</p></arrangement>
</scopecontent>
</c01>
</dsc>
```

*Link source established using <ptr> element; link destination provided using TARGET attribute*

**Figure 7.2.1b.** *Using a linking attribute to establish a link to the ID value encoded in Figure 7.2.1a.*

In order to alert the end user about the availability of a link, the use of the empty element <ptr> might result in the insertion of a link indicator icon in place of <ptr> when this encoded document is displayed. How such an icon is displayed will be determined by the system or display application (a client browser, a stylesheet, or an SGML server).

Alternatively, the link in figure 7.2.1b could have been declared using <ref>, which must contain text or other elements, as shown in the following example with a reencoded excerpt from figure 7.2.1b. The display to an end user would most likely involve highlighting the text contained within the <ref> element to indicate the presence of the link, in the manner of an HTML browser.

```
<arrangement><p>The bulk of the contents of the series arrived
at the repository in chronological order and this arrangement
has been retained. <ref target="restrict1">The single
exception is a file of student recommendations on which access
restrictions have been imposed.</ref> These folders have been
temporarily removed to a restricted box in the
collection.</p></arrangement>
```

### 7.2.2. The Nonlinking Bundling Element Pointer Group <ptrgrp>

In some cases you may wish to create multiple, internal, single-direction links from a particular location in the encoded document; this requires that the pointer elements be *bundled*. EAD includes provisions for both a bundling element for internal links that can be used anywhere in the finding aid (see section 7.2.3), and an element that can be used to bundle internal links only from within the Index Entry <indexentry> tag. Bundling together a group of simple, internal links within an index entry requires the use of a nonlinking element, Pointer Group <ptrgrp>. This might be used in order to provide a name index for a correspondence series that is arranged chronologically. In figure 7.2.2a an encoded container list includes a unique ID value for each <unittitle>. In figure 7.2.2b <ptrgrp> is used within an index of correspondents to bundle multiple internal simple links to the various folders that contain items from each indexed correspondent. The decision regarding which linking element to use in this case would be determined by the need to include the text of the index entry as part of the link indicator in the resulting display (in this case, use <ref>), or *not* to include the text (in this case, use <ptr>).

```
<c02 level="file"><did>
<unittitle id="corresp197306"><unitdate>June-December
1973</unitdate></unittitle>
</did></c02>
<c02 level="file"><did>
<unittitle id="corresp1974"><unitdate>1974</unitdate>
</unittitle>
</did></c02>
<c02 level="file"><did>
<unittitle id="corresp197501"><unitdate>January-August
1975</unitdate></unittitle>
</did></c02>
```

**Figure 7.2.2a.** *Establishing unique* ID *values for several elements.*

```
<add>
<index>
<head>Correspondence Index</head>
[other possible elements and text ...]
<indexentry><persname>Doe, Jane S.:</persname>
<ptrgrp>
<ref target="corresp197306">24 August 1973</ref>
<ref target="corresp1974">28 February and 16 July 1974</ref>
<ref target="corresp197501">15 March 1975</ref>
</ptrgrp></indexentry>
[other possible elements and text ...]
</index>
</add>
```

**Figure 7.2.2b.** *Using a linking attribute to establish a link to the* ID *attribute value encoded in Figure 7.2.2a.*

### 7.2.3. Linking Group <linkgrp> as a Bundling Element for Pointer Location <ptrloc> and Reference Location <refloc>

Outside of the <indexentry> tag, internal links also can be bundled using the Linking Group <linkgrp> element. [113] The linking elements <refloc> and <ptrloc> must be used with <linkgrp> instead of <ref> and <ptr>. Another difference is that <linkgrp>, unlike <ptrgrp>, is a linking element. The link created is considered an extended link. Unlike the example in figure 7.2.2b, in which <ptrgrp> bundles a group of independent simple links, <linkgrp> conceptually creates a single link with the potential for multiple source and destination resources by bundling a group of elements (<ptrloc> or <refloc>) that serve only as locators, providing addresses for the extended link's resources. The <linkgrp> element is used with <ptrloc> and <refloc> to create extended internal links to other information contained in the same encoded finding aid.

Generally the use of <linkgrp> should be reserved for links that themselves have some specific element of commonality, where bundling would enhance the ability of the link destinations to function together. The primary usage of <linkgrp> will likely be for bundling external links (see section 7.3.5). Currently available software may not be capable of implementing <linkgrp> for display to end users, nor are XLink developments, including the concept of extended links, finalized. Archivists interested in the potential use of extended links in their finding aids should follow XLink developments.[114]

---

[113] The description of <linkgrp> on page 172 of the *Encoded Archival Description Tag Library, Version 1.0* states that this element can only be used "to enable a set of multidirectional, out-of-line links." Please note that <linkgrp> also can in fact be used to bundle inline links, both external and internal.

[114] Current information regarding XLink development by the World Wide Web Consortium is available at: <http://www.w3.org/TR/WD-xlink>.

### 7.2.4. The XLINK:FORM and INLINE Attributes

EAD defines two linking attributes that you will not need to include in your document instances at this time. While they may not currently be useful, however, these attributes do introduce concepts that archivists who are interested in XML developments may find helpful. Both of these attributes could be used in either internal or external linking, so this discussion is applicable both here and below in section 7.3 on external links.

The terms "simple," "extended" and "locator" all are values for the attribute XLINK:FORM, which is conditionally available on all EAD linking elements and will in the future allow software to readily recognize a specific link as being of a type defined in the XLink specification. This attribute is specific to XLink functionality in the EAD DTD, and it is characterized as conditionally available because, in order to be used, XML functionality must be "turned on" in the DTD file ead.dtd. In order to do so, you must edit the values of two parameter entity declarations in section "XLINK INCLUSION/EXCLUSION" in the file ead.dtd. These values are encoded as follows when this file is obtained from the official EAD Web site hosted by the Library of Congress:

```
<!ENTITY % xlink          'IGNORE'        >
<!ENTITY % noxlink        'INCLUDE'       >
```

This means that the XLink functionality is "turned off," which is the default for the EAD DTD because most SGML software cannot handle the colon (:) in the attribute name XLINK:FORM. In order to enable XLink functionality when using XML software in the future, you must change these parameter entity declarations in your local copy of the ead.dtd file so that they appear as follows:

```
<!ENTITY % xlink          'INCLUDE'       >
<!ENTITY % noxlink        'IGNORE'        >
```

The value of this attribute is declared as FIXED and is set by the DTD for each linking element. Even when the XLink functionality remains "turned off," familiarity with the role that each linking element plays as designated by this attribute can help encoders understand the proper way to use these linking elements in various situations. Table 7.2.4a categorizes the 15 EAD linking elements by the fixed value of their XLINK:FORM attribute.

| | |
|---|---|
| xlink:form="simple" | <archref>, <bibref>, <dao>, <extptr>, <extref>, <ptr>, <ref>, <title> |
| xlink:form="extended" | <daogrp>, <linkgrp> |
| xlink:form="locator" | <daoloc>, <extptrloc>, <extrefloc>, <ptrloc>, <refloc> |

**Table 7.2.4a.** *Fixed XLINK:FORM attribute values for EAD linking elements.*

The attribute INLINE is not specific to XLink functionality, and so it is not turned "on" or "off" in the file ead.dtd. INLINE has a value of either "true" or "false," with the default value being "true," meaning that a link is inline. Unless an encoder wishes to change the value of this attribute to "false" to indicate that a link is out-of-line, the attribute need not be used in encoding (see section 7.1.2.3 for a discussion of inline and out-of-line linking).

The attribute INLINE is available on all simple and extended linking elements as categorized in table 7.2.4a. In extended links, the INLINE attribute, if used, would appear on the bundling element, since INLINE is not an attribute option on individual locator elements. As stated previously, current EAD users need not explicitly encode this attribute. The default value of "true" is recommended until the XLink specification and software that will support out-of-line linking is closer to completion.

### 7.2.5. The PARENT Attribute on the Container <container> and Physical Location <physloc> Elements

The PARENT attribute is a special case that is only available in the Container <container> and Physical Location <physloc> elements. The PARENT attribute is different from EAD's other linking elements, however, in that no link traversal is involved from a user's perspective. It is intended to make accessible to software information about a "parent" container without having to encode it repeatedly. This attribute is provided so that the ID attribute can be used to create a shortcut when encoding, for example, box and folder information using <container>.

As noted in section 3.5.2.4, archivists may wish to consider encoding the container and/or folder information for each descriptive component (<c> or <c0x>) below the subseries level, in other words for those hierarchical descriptive components for which box and folder numbers are frequently given in print-based finding aids. A computer processing an encoded document cannot intuit the same meaning from the layout of a container list that a human being processing the same information can. Encoding containment information for each component will insure that container list data will be useful computationally as more sophisticated systems develop in the future for the manipulation and repackaging of data from archival finding aids. Not encoding this information for each component may make it difficult for data to be reused in such systems as they develop.

For example, a person would readily understand, in the following excerpt from a container list, that all three folders are in Box 12:

| Box | Folder | Contents |
|---|---|---|
| 12 | 1 | Breakdance, 1989-1991 |
| | 2 | Fosse, Bob, 1980-1984 |
| | 3 | Jitterbug, 1938-1942 |

The problem arises when this same container list is encoded in EAD, as shown in figure 7.2.5a:

```
<c02 level="file"><did>
<container type="box">12</container>
<container type="folder">1></container>
<unittitle>Breakdance, <unitdate type="inclusive">1989-
1991</unitdate></unittitle>
</did></c02>
<c02 level="file"><did>
<container type="folder">2</container>
<unittitle><persname>Fosse, Bob</persname>,
<unitdate type="inclusive">1980-1984</unitdate></unittitle>
</did></c02>
<c02 level="file"><did>
<container type="folder">3</container>
<unittitle>Jitterbug, <unitdate type="inclusive">1938-
1942</unitdate></unittitle>
</did></c02>
      [...]
```

**Figure 7.2.5a.** *Encoding of container information that may be problematic for computer processing and repackaging of the data.*

To a computer processing this file, the descriptive unit "Fosse, Bob" is housed in a folder but not in a box. This is because the closing of the </c02> for the preceding descriptive unit "Breakdance" effectively cuts off the information about Box 12 for use in the processing of succeeding <c02> components. This may not cause a problem if EAD encoding is used only for generating a linear online finding aid. It could, however, become problematic in the future when application software attempts to extract descriptive component information from an encoded finding aid. This might be required in order to present an end user, as the result of a search, with a hit list of folder-level information across multiple collections and multiple repositories. Such a scenario is currently possible for repositories or consortia with access to a good programmer and an SGML-aware search engine. Even in the linear display of finding aids, however, the encoding in the above example has the potential to generate a display that would force the end user constantly to scroll up and down to find the relevant box number for a particular folder, especially in cases in which a box contains a lot of folders.

The PARENT attribute makes it possible, if you are using a delivery system that is technically capable of supporting its use, to drop the <container type="Box"> encoding from all but the first component that falls within each new box and still provide the computer with the necessary information to process unambiguously the containment information for each descriptive component. Figure 7.2.5b is a reencoding of figure 7.2.5a, demonstrating use of the PARENT attribute:

```
<c02 level="file"><did>
<container id="box12" type="box">12</container>
<container type="folder">1</container>
<unittitle>Breakdance, <unitdate type="inclusive">1989-
1991</unitdate></unittitle>
</did></c02>
<c02 level="file"><did>
<container parent="box12" type="folder">2</container>
<unittitle><persname>Fosse, Bob</persname>,
<unitdate type="inclusive">1980-1984</unitdate></unittitle>
</did></c02>
<c02 level="file"><did>
<container parent="box12" type="folder">3</container>
<unittitle>Jitterbug, <unitdate type="inclusive">1938-
1942</unitdate></unittitle>
</did></c02>
      [...]
```

**Figure 7.2.5b.** *Using the PARENT attribute to establish containment relationships unambiguously.*

The PARENT attribute is declared in the EAD DTD with a value of IDREF, the same as the attribute TARGET. Figure 7.2.5b illustrates declaration of a value for an ID attribute on the <container> tag for the first instance of a new box, which can then be referenced using the PARENT attribute on the <container> tag for each successive folder contained within that box. Software processing a document thus encoded would now have access to the box information for every descriptive component in the box. Currently available commercial application software does not have the capability of utilizing the PARENT attribute, but repositories with in-house SGML programming expertise may be able to take advantage of this attribute to avoid repetitive tagging of containment information.

For delivery systems that cannot support the use of the PARENT attribute but that can suppress the delivery of information encoded with the AUDIENCE attribute set to "internal," an alternative encoding of figure 7.2.5a is provided in figure 7.2.5c. This approach supplies the containment information for each descriptive component and does *not* utilize the PARENT attribute; by using the AUDIENCE attribute, a stylesheet could be used to create a linear finding aid display that masks repetitious box numbers from the end user.

```
<c02 level="file"><did>
<container type="box">12</container>
<container type="folder">1</container>
<unittitle>Breakdance, <unitdate type="inclusive">1989-
1991</unitdate></unittitle>
</did></c02>
<c02 level="file"><did>
<container type="box" audience="internal">12</container>
<container type="folder">2</container>
<unittitle><persname>Fosse, Bob</persname>,
<unitdate type="inclusive">1980-1984</unitdate></unittitle>
</did></c02>
<c02 level="file"><did>
<container type="box" audience="internal">12</container>
<container type="folder">3</container>
<unittitle>Jitterbug, <unitdate type="inclusive">1938-
1942</unitdate></unittitle>
</did></c02>
      [...]
```

**Figure 7.2.5c.** *Using the AUDIENCE attribute to mask repetitive box information included to facilitate computer processing.*

## 7.3. External linking

External linking from an encoded document can be accomplished in several ways. The "purest" SGML method for establishing such links is through the use of general entity declarations and entity references (section 6.5 provides a basic overview of both). An alternative approach to external linking is available using the HREF attribute directly in a linking element in order to bypass the need to declare an entity to establish an address for a link. The ideal system may actually be a hybrid one that stores and maintains EAD-encoded finding aids in an SGML system that can take advantage of an SGML catalog to pair persistent entity names with system addresses that may change as files are moved. Delivery of the finding aid data may be in an XML system in which the entity reference information is resolved "on the fly" into an HREF URI that exists only transiently in the file space of the end user's browser.

### 7.3.1. The ENTITYREF Attribute

Unlike the internal links discussed in section 7.2, external links declare a relationship between information within an EAD instance and another file or document that exists outside of the instance in question. The ID attribute that provides the destination address for internal links therefore is not necessary. The provision of a destination address for external links is accomplished by creating a general external entity declaration in the document type declaration of a document instance. This entity declaration contains the specifics detailing how an SGML-aware processing system can find the destination of the external link. The entity declaration also serves to inform the processing system what sort of information format it can expect when the destination file does not consist of text that is recognizable to the system.

Figure 7.3.1a creates two general external entity declarations in the document type declaration of an encoded finding aid instance:

```
<!DOCTYPE  ead  PUBLIC  "-//Society of American
Archivists//DTD ead.dtd (Encoded Archival Description (EAD)
Version 1.0)//EN"  [
<!ENTITY  tedschell  SYSTEM
"http://www.archivesrus.gov/findaids/ead/ms045.sgm" NDATA
sgml>
<!ENTITY  schellpix  SYSTEM "http://www.myserver.edu
/images/ms023_schell.gif"  NDATA  gif>
]>
```

**Figure 7.3.1a.** *Two general entity declarations in a document type declaration.*

The first declaration provides as a system identifier an absolute URI on a server at some fictitious government archives for an EAD-encoded finding aid for the Theodore R. Schellenberg Papers. The second declaration provides an absolute URI for a GIF image housed on the same server as the encoded document instance in which the link will be declared.

Section 6.5.2.4.2 provides information about external entity declarations to files not intended to be parsed with the document instance. The present section will discuss using linking elements to create links within a document instance to those files. Establishing links to declared entities is accomplished with an ENTITYREF attribute in the chosen linking element. The value designation in the EAD DTD for the ENTITYREF attribute is ENTITY, a keyword meaning that the attribute value will be validated when the encoded document instance is parsed, ensuring that an entity declaration exists to match each ENTITYREF attribute used. Figure 7.3.1b provides an example of two linking elements containing destination addresses to the entities declared in figure 7.3.1a:

```
<add>
<relatedmaterial>
<head>Related Collections</head>
<archref entityref="tedschell">
<origination>
<persname source="lcnaf" normal="Schellenberg, T. R., 1903-1970"
role="creator">T. R. Schellenberg</persname></origination>
<unittitle>Theodore R. Schellenberg Papers,
<unitdate type="inclusive">1938-1970</unitdate></unittitle>
<extptr entityref="schellpix">
<unitid type="collection number">MS-045</unitid>
<repository><name>Archives R Us</name></repository>
</archref>
 [other possible elements and text ...]
</relatedmaterial>
</add>
```

**Figure 7.3.1b.** *Using the ENTITYREF attribute to establish links.*

In this example, the Archival Reference <archref> element with an ENTITYREF attribute is used to supply a link to an encoded finding aid for a related collection. The External Pointer <extptr> element with an ENTITYREF attribute is used to supply a link to a picture relevant to the archival collection. The <archref> element is discussed in greater detail in section 7.3.3, and the <extptr> element is explained in section 7.3.4.

### 7.3.2. The HREF Attribute

EAD offers the HREF attribute as an alternative to using ENTITYREF for providing a destination address for external links. For those acquainted with the attributes available in Hypertext Markup Language (HTML), HREF will look very familiar.

Since the development of the SGML standard, the World Wide Web and the HTML encoding scheme that serves as its markup foundation have taken the world of networked communications by storm. The advantages and disadvantages of both HTML and SGML are discussed in chapter 1, so suffice it to say here that the Web introduced some simplifications of SGML that ongoing XML developments aim to incorporate. One of these simplifications is to add to the SGML entity-based linking scheme the capability of using the direct address-referencing capacity of the HREF attribute. Version 1.0 of the EAD DTD fully supports this development.

Use of the HREF attribute is relatively simple; it involves only the single step of providing a URI for the destination resource directly within the linking element itself. Figure 7.3.2a illustrates a reencoding of the ENTITYREF example in figure 7.3.1b above, using instead the HREF attribute; this eliminates the need for the entity declarations shown in figure 7.3.1a. Note that the encoder retains the choice of using an absolute URI or a relative URI to provide the destination address (see section 6.5.2.4.1 regarding the strengths and weaknesses of these options).

```
<add>
<relatedmaterial>
<head>Related Collections</head>
<archref href="http://www.archivesrus.gov/findaids/ead/ms045.sgm">
<origination>
<persname source="lcnaf" normal="Schellenberg, T. R., 1903-1970"
role="creator">T. R. Schellenberg</persname></origination>
<unittitle>Theodore R. Schellenberg Papers,
<unitdate type="inclusive">1938-1970</unitdate></unittitle>
<extptr href="../images/ms023_schell.gif">
<unitid type="collection number">MS-045</unitid>
<repository><name>Archives R Us</name></repository>
</archref>
 [other possible elements and text ...]
</relatedmaterial>
</add>
```

**Figure 7.3.2a.** *Using the HREF attribute to establish links.*

Some of the advantages and disadvantages of choosing to use a linking scheme based on entities or on the HREF attribute will be discussed in section 7.5. Perhaps the most important factor in making a decision about which linking attribute to use in order to provide a destination address for a link is a basic knowledge of how linking is supported in the particular system in which you will deliver your finding aids. Use of the HREF attribute does not allow for provision of the same amount of information concerning the destination resource of the link as does the entity-based scheme. Note, for example, that the entity declaration for the GIF image in figure 7.3.1a provides specific information to the delivery system software about the non-SGML data resource to which a link is being established. Provision of this specific information is not possible using the HREF attribute, so the delivery system will have to attempt to make this determination based on the file type suffix appended to the filename (.gif).

### 7.3.3. Archival Reference, Bibliographic Reference, and Title <archref>, <bibref>, and <title>

The elements <archref>, <bibref>, and <title> can serve multiple functions in an encoded finding aid, only one of which is to provide the capability for external links when needed. Unlike <extptr>, for example, which has no use other than as a linking element, these elements may be used for reasons other than declaring a link (see section 3.5.4 for information on nonlinking uses of these elements). An archivist might use <archref> to encode a citation to separately described archival materials that are related to the collection for which she or he is creating an EAD finding aid. If no electronic finding aid exists for that separately described collection, it would not be necessary to use the linking attributes available in <archref>. In this case <archref> and its subelements would be used to encode only a textual description of the related collection. Similarly, an archivist might use <bibref> to encode a citation to a published work that is related to the archival collection being described. Use of the linking attributes would depend on whether or not a surrogate bibliographic record or an electronic version of the published work was available as the destination for a link.

This section also provides a discussion of an alternative use for <archref>, which has proven useful to some repositories for virtually reuniting large collection descriptions that, for practical purposes, have been broken into smaller components for encoding.

#### 7.3.3.1. General Usage of <archref>, <bibref>, and <title>

Figures 7.3.1b and 7.3.2a illustrate two ways in which attributes available for use in the <archref> tag might be used to establish a link to descriptions of related collections, separated materials, or a citation to another archival collection in a bibliography.

The element <bibref> can be used in a similar manner for creating links either to surrogate descriptions or to the actual text of published materials available online. For example, an encoded finding aid for the papers of the author Paul Laurence Dunbar might include a bibliography of Dunbar's published works. The full text of some of Dunbar's poetry is available online (encoded in SGML using the TEI DTD) through the American Verse Collection of the University of Michigan's Humanities Text Initiative.[115] Figure 7.3.3a illustrates the encoding of bibliographic references to Dunbar's works, the first citation with no link and the second with a link directly to the full online text:

[115] The Humanities Text Initiative is available at: <http://www.hti.umich.edu/>.

```
<add>
<bibliography>
<head>A Bibliography of the Works of Paul Laurence Dunbar</head>
      [other possible elements and text ...]
<bibref>
<persname role="author" source="lcsh">Dunbar, Paul Laurence, 1872-
1906</persname>.
<title pubstatus="pub">The Best Stories of Paul Laurence
Dunbar</title>.
<imprint><geogname>New York</geogname> : <publisher>Dodd, Mead &
Company</publisher>, <date type="publication">[1938]</date>
</imprint>
</bibref>
      [other possible elements and text ...]
<bibref href="http://www.hti.umich.edu/bin/amv-
idx.pl?type=header&id=DunbaLyrLL">
<persname role="author" source="lcsh">Dunbar, Paul Laurence, 1872-
1906</persname>.
<title pubstatus="pub">Lyrics of Lowly Life</title>.
<imprint><geogname>London</geogname> : <publisher>Chapman & Hall,
Ltd.</publisher>, <date type="publication">1897</date></imprint>
</bibref>
      [other possible elements and text ...]
</bibliography>
</add>
```

**Figure 7.3.3a.** *A use of both the nonlinking and linking capabilities of <bibref>.*

Note that while the HREF attribute was used in this example, the encoder could just as easily have created an entity declaration containing the URI to the resource and then used the ENTITYREF attribute on <bibref>.

### 7.3.3.2. Using <archref> to Break Up Large Finding Aids

Some EAD implementers have experienced a problem with the downloading of encoded instances for their finding aids for particularly large, complex collections. The difficulties experienced, mainly technical in nature, have been surmounted by one repository through an innovative use of the <archref> tag to reunite virtually collections or fonds that have been split up for encoding purposes.

The Public Record Office (PRO)—which as the national archives of the United Kingdom holds the records of British government departments, courts of law, and other public records as defined by the Public Records Act of 1958 and its schedules—has this problem with many of its finding aids. Each fonds equates to the entire range of surviving records of a department, made up of perhaps 10 or 20 record-creating divisions, each potentially producing dozens of record series (or in PRO parlance, classes) comprising from one to many thousands of documents that are available to end users. The sheer bulk of each fonds (originally envisaged as a discrete EAD instance) immediately posed difficulties for archivists at the PRO: first, in the parsing of files over 2.5 megabytes in size using some of the software commonly available; and secondly and more fundamentally, in the time required by end users to download files on the Internet.

A decision was made to split the files and to link them using <archref>. A parent file would hold the fonds and subfonds (in PRO parlance, departments and divisions) data; individual files would act as finding aids for each series (in PRO parlance, class) and its components. The <archref> tag is used to virtually unite the fonds and subfonds file with all of the series files that are its intellectual subunits and to link the series files back to the parent.

### 7.3.4. Extended Pointer <extptr> and Extended Reference <extref>[116]

While <archref> and <bibref> are used for external linking in very specific circumstances, the elements <extptr> and <extref> can be used more generically to create external links wherever they are appropriate within an encoded finding aid. These two elements serve exactly the same function, and the difference between them parallels that between <ptr> and <ref>, as discussed in section 7.2.1. An empty element, <extptr> should be used when an encoder desires to insert only a linking icon at the point in the encoded document at which a link is established. The <extref> element must contain text or other elements and should be used when an encoder wishes to have highlighted text serve as an indicator of a link. As with all external linking elements, either the ENTITYREF or the HREF attribute can be used with <extptr> and <extref> to provide a destination address for the link being established.

Figure 7.3.4a illustrates an entity declaration for information at the Nobel Foundation Web site on the 1995 prize in Physics given to Frederick Reines, whose papers are described elsewhere in an EAD instance:

```
<!DOCTYPE  ead  PUBLIC  "-//Society of American
Archivists//DTD ead.dtd (Encoded Archival Description (EAD)
Version 1.0)//EN"  [
<!ENTITY  nobelreines SYSTEM
"http://www.nobel.se/laureates/physics-1995.html" NDATA html>
]>
```

**Figure 7.3.4a.** *An entity declaration for an external web site.*

Within the text of the EAD instance, perhaps in a chronologically arranged Biographical Note, <extptr> and the ENTITYREF attribute are used to create a link to Reines' entry at the Nobel Foundation Web site, as illustrated in figure 7.3.4b:

[116] Do not be mislead by the appearance of the term "extended" in the element names of these two elements. They are used to create *simple* links, not extended, as determined by the fixed value of their XLINK:FORM attribute (see section 7.2.4 for more information on this attribute).

```
<bioghist>
<head>Biographical Note</head>
<chronlist>
      [other possible elements and text ...]
<chronitem>
<date>October 1995</date>
<event><extptr entityref="nobelreines">Awarded Nobel Prize in
Physics by the Royal Swedish Academy of Sciences</event>
</chronitem>
      [other possible elements and text ...]
</chronlist>
</bioghist>
```

**Figure 7.3.4b.** *Using <extptr> to link to a declared external entity.*

Alternatively, the link in figure 7.3.4b could have been declared using <extref>, which must contain text or other elements, as shown in the reencoded example below. Although system-dependent, the most likely implementation of this encoding would involve the highlighting of the text included in the <extref> element to indicate the presence of a link.

```
<chronitem>
<date>October 1995</date>
<event><extref entityref="nobelreines">Awarded Nobel Prize in
Physics by the Royal Swedish Academy of
Sciences</extref></event>
</chronitem>
```

Finally, the above link could have been established by using the HREF attribute, either by itself or paired with an entity declaration, to directly encode the URI for the Nobel Foundation Web site information on Reines:

```
<chronitem>
<date>October 1995</date>
<event><extref href="http://www.nobel.se/laureates/physics-
1995.html">Awarded Nobel Prize in Physics by the Royal Swedish
Academy of Sciences</extref></event>
</chronitem>
```

### 7.3.5. Linking Group <linkgrp> as a Bundling Element for Extended Pointer Location <extptrloc> and Extended Reference Location <extrefloc>

In addition to the use of the <linkgrp> element to create multiple source and destination internal links (see section 7.2.3), <linkgrp> also can serve to create the same kind of external links. As noted in section 7.2.3, the link created using <linkgrp> is considered an extended link with multiple source and destination resources, for which location information is provided using one of the two extended locator elements, <extptrloc> or <extrefloc>. Such a link would be considered inline if the information encoded within the <linkgrp> served as the source resource for the link. At some future point when the XLink specification is more completely developed, it also should be possible to set the value of the attribute INLINE to "false" and create multiple-destination out-of-line <linkgrp> links in which the information encoded within the <linkgrp> does not participate as either a source or destination resource in the link. The primary usage of <linkgrp> will be to bundle pointers to different versions of the same resource or to express a relationship between links that bundling could enhance from a software perspective.

Like <extptr> and <extref>, <extptrloc> and <extrefloc> serve exactly the same function. The difference between them is the encoder's desire to include text as the link indicator (in this case use <extrefloc>) or *not* to include text (in this case use <extptrloc>).

### 7.3.6. Digital Archival Objects <dao>, <daogrp>, and <daoloc>

The <dao> suite of elements (Digital Archival Object <dao>, Digital Archival Object Description <daodesc>, Digital Archival Object Group <daogrp> and Digital Archival Object Location <daoloc>) is included in EAD for the specific purpose of creating links to electronic representations of information resources from archival collections. At present these likely will be digital facsimiles of original materials in another format (such as GIF images of photographs, MPEG files of analog recordings, or TEI-encoded versions of paper-based texts), but in the future more and more archival material will originate in digital formats.

Three of the four elements mentioned above are linking elements. The <daodesc> element, the one exception, is available for use when "the <unittitle> or other descriptive information in a Component <c>" is insufficient to identify the digital object(s); <daodesc> essentially provides for a caption for digital archival objects when one is necessary.[117]

It is important to grasp the distinction between the <dao> suite of elements and other external linking elements that EAD makes available. The <dao> suite is intended for use only where the destination of the link is something that, based on its provenance and custodial history, is part of the collection being described by the encoded finding aid in which the <dao> tags are included. Links to all other materials should be created using the other external linking elements (such as <extref> or <extptr>) discussed in section 7.3.

The element <dao> is available to create a simple link to a digital representation of any material included in an archival collection. The <daogrp> element, which must be used to bundle multiple <daoloc> elements, is available to create an extended link to multiple versions of digital facsimiles of collection materials (see section 7.1 for an overview of these linking concepts).

While it may often appear to be empty, <dao> itself is not declared in the EAD DTD as an empty element. The content model for this element states that it may contain either zero or one <daodesc> elements. Therefore, while it may appear frequently with no content, it is

---

[117] *Encoded Archival Description Tag Library, Version 1.0* (Chicago: Society of American Archivists, 1998), 102.

not technically an empty element in the same way as <ptr>, which is declared in the DTD with the content model EMPTY. As a result it must always appear with both a start-tag and an end-tag, regardless of whether or not it contains a <daodesc>. This is also true of <daoloc>.

An archivist might choose to create links to digital facsimiles for two photographs from the same folder within a collection. Figure 7.3.6a illustrates an entity declaration for each of these two JPEG images:

```
<!DOCTYPE  ead  PUBLIC  "-//Society of American
Archivists//DTD ead.dtd (Encoded Archival Description (EAD)
Version 1.0)//EN"  [
<!ENTITY  f0042_1  SYSTEM
"http://www.myserver.edu/images/fonds0042_image1.jpg" NDATA
jpeg>
<!ENTITY  f0042_2  SYSTEM  "http://www.myserver.edu
/images/fonds0042_image2.jpg" NDATA jpeg>
]>
```

**Figure 7.3.6a.** *Entity declarations for two JPEG images.*

Even though the rest of the collection is described only to the folder level, the archivist chooses to encode the folder containing the two original photographs at the item level and to establish links to the digital facsimiles using a <dao> tag for each item, as illustrated in figure 7.3.6b:

```
<dsc type="combined">
      [other possible elements and text ...]
<c02 level="file"><did><unittitle>Photographs,
<unitdate type="inclusive">1895-1928</unitdate></unittitle>
</did>
<c03 level="item"><did><unittitle>John Smith graduation
portrait,
<unitdate type="single" normal="18950528">May 28,
1895</unitdate></unittitle>
<dao entityref="f0042_1"></dao></did></c03>
<c03 level="item"><did><unittitle>Wedding of John Smith and
Stella Jones, Windsor, Ontario, <unitdate type="single"
normal="18970606">June 6, 1897</unitdate></unittitle>
<dao entityref="f0042_2"></dao></did></c03>
</c02>
      [other possible elements and text ...]
</dsc>
```

**Figure 7.3.6b.** *Using <dao> to establish links to digital image facsimiles.*

The <daogrp> element is used instead of <dao> when it is necessary to bundle together different versions of the same resource. For example, suppose the image links established in figure 7.3.6b included both a thumbnail and a larger reference image for each link. In order to unambiguously encode the relationship between the pair of files for each image, it would be necessary to use <daogrp> to bundle a <daoloc> pointer for each related file, as in the following reencoding:

```
<dsc type="combined">
      [other possible elements and text ...]
<c02 level="file"><did><unittitle>Photographs,
<unitdate type="inclusive">1895-1928</unitdate></unittitle>
</did>
<c03 level="item"><did><unittitle>John Smith graduation
portrait,
<unitdate type="single" normal="18950528">May 28,
1895</unitdate></unittitle>
<daogrp>
<daoloc entityref="f0042_1thumb"></daoloc>
<daoloc entityref="f0042_1"></daoloc>
</daogrp>
</did></c03>
<c03 level="item"><did><unittitle>Wedding of John Smith and
Stella Jones, Windsor, Ontario, <unitdate type="single"
normal="18970606">June 6, 1897</unitdate></unittitle>
<daogrp>
<daoloc entityref="f0042_2thumb"></daoloc>
<daoloc entityref="f0042_2"></daoloc>
</daogrp>
</did></c03>
</c02>
      [other possible elements and text ...]
</dsc>
```

**Figure 7.3.6c.** *Using <daogrp> to establish links to related versions of digital image facsimiles.*

### 7.3.7. The XPOINTER Attribute

XPointer, very generally, refers to a specification for pointing to *specific locations* within an encoded document (as opposed to pointing to the *entire* document) using a URI. This specification is currently under development by the W3C[118] and is based on concepts already in place in the Text Encoding Initiative (TEI) DTD[119] and in HyTime (ISO 10744:1992)[120], an international standard for hypertext features. XPointer creates a standardized syntax for

[118] Current information on XPointer developments is available on the World Wide Web Consortium web site, available at <http://www.w3.org/TR/WD-xptr>.

[119] C. M. Sperberg-McQueen and Lou Burnard, eds., "Linking, Segmentation, and Alignment," Chapter 14 in *Guidelines for Electronic Text Encoding and Interchange. TEI P3*. Available at: <http://www.uic.edu/orgs/tei/p3/doc/p3.html>.

[120] Charles Goldfarb, et al., *A Reader's Guide to the HyTime Standard.* Available at: <http://www.hytime.org/papers/htguide.html>. See also Steven J. DeRose and David G. Durand, *Making Hypermedia Work: A User's Guide to HyTime* (Dordrecht: Kluwer, 1994).

specifying locations within encoded document instances based either on encoded ID attribute values, on directions based on the SGML tree structure of a document instance, or on a combination of the two. This would allow an encoder to create links fairly easily to or from specific points within external documents for which the encoder does not have editing permissions (the documents reside on someone else's Web server). The capabilities provided by XPointer are a necessary precursor to the creation of the out-of-line links (see section 7.1.2.3). Readers of these *Guidelines* who are interested in more general information on the XPointer specification will find discussions of it, though perhaps out of date by the time you read it, in most currently available books on XML.[121]

Within EAD, XPOINTER is an attribute available on all "simple" and "locator" linking elements, as categorized in table 7.2.4a. The inclusion of this attribute is one of the forward-looking aspects of EAD that anticipates the stabilization of XML's XLink and XPointer specifications in the not-too-distant future. In SGML systems that are capable of implementing it, use of the XPOINTER attribute allows an encoder to create—using XPointer syntax to create the value of that attribute—a pathway for a link to a specific point within an external encoded document. An SGML-aware delivery system should be capable of resolving the content of an ENTITYREF destination address and the content of an XPOINTER attribute from a single EAD linking element in order to create, on the fly, an XML-compliant HREF link to the specific point within the document that the encoder intended as the destination for the link. This will give implementers of EAD the ability to take advantage of some of the link management strengths of the entity-based approach in SGML (discussed in section 7.5), while still being able to utilize XPointer capabilities when they are more fully developed and stable.

---

[121] For a useful basic discussion of the underpinnings of XPointer development, see Charles Goldfarb and Paul Prescod, *The XML Handbook* (Upper Saddle River, N.J.: Prentice Hall, 1998), 511-15.

## 7.4. Link Properties

There are several linking attributes that should always be used to provide further information regarding links that have been established within an EAD instance. While not technically required by the DTD, the use of the TARGET, ENTITYREF or HREF attributes as discussed above must occur in order for a link to be operational. Unlike the destination-provision attributes, the use of those attributes discussed in the present section is optional in the sense that a link technically can be established through the provision of just a destination address and nothing else. However, the use of the ACTUATE and SHOW attributes is encouraged in order to provide minimal instructions to processing software about how links within that instance should behave. Many current delivery systems may not be capable of utilizing the information provided by these attributes. It is nonetheless a good idea explicitly to encode links with these minimal instructions about how you intend systems to actualize them.

Use of the remaining attributes discussed herein is recommended only when the type of link being created or the software used to deliver the encoded document requires it. All of the attributes discussed in this section can be used for either internal or external links.

### 7.4.1. The ACTUATE, SHOW, and BEHAVIOR Attributes

The ACTUATE and SHOW attributes should be used together in linking elements to provide some indication to system software of the desired display of the information that is the target of a link. The values for both of these attributes are constrained by the DTD, so an encoder must choose a value from a closed list.

ACTUATE refers to the way in which traversal of a link will be initiated. The value "auto" indicates that the link should be automatically traversed by the system when an end user reaches it, displaying, for example, an image on the screen in an online finding aid without the user having to select or activate any link. This might be useful when linking externally to an image that the encoder intends to display as an illustration in a Biography or History <bioghist> note. The value "user" indicates that the end user must initiate in some way, perhaps with a mouse click or a voice command, the traversal of the link. This might be useful, for example, when the link destination is an internal "see also" reference or an external finding aid for a related collection, which an end user may wish either to explore or to ignore.

SHOW indicates the intended behavior of the link once it has been traversed. It has three possible values. The value "embed" indicates that the destination resource of the link should be embedded in the encoded document in place of the linking element and would generally be used in tandem with the ACTUATE attribute value "auto". The value "replace" indicates that the link's destination resource should replace the text surrounding the link's source resource in the same browser window, while the value "new" indicates that a new browser window should be opened for displaying the destination resource of the link. Either of these values for SHOW generally would be used with the ACTUATE value "user".

In certain cases the constrained values of the attributes ACTUATE and SHOW may not provide enough guidance for particular system software. When this occurs, the attribute BEHAVIOR, whose value is completely unconstrained, may be used to provide whatever instructions the system software needs concerning the desired behavior of the link.

Figure 7.4.1a illustrates the use of the attributes ACTUATE and SHOW in an internal link that alerts the user that other materials on a particular organization exist elsewhere in the collection. Because the <ref> element is used, the text contained between the start-tag and end-tag will probably, depending on the system, be highlighted in some way when this document appears on a display monitor. The end user must initiate traversal of the link by selecting the highlighted link text. The text in the targeted area of the finding aid will replace the text surrounding the link's source in the browser window. Note that an ID attribute value has been assigned at the appropriate component level so that a cross-reference link also can be established in the encoding of Series 4 in this collection.

```
<c01 level="series">
<did><unitid>Series 1: </unitid>
<unittitle>Correspondence, <unitdate type="inclusive">1946-
1970</unitdate></unittitle>
<physdesc><extent>4.4 linear feet</extent></physdesc></did>
<c02 level="file" id="s1:agba">
<did><unittitle>Apple Growers Benevolent Association,
<unitdate type="inclusive">1950-1952</unitdate></unittitle>
<physdesc><extent>12 items</extent></physdesc></did>
<note><p>See also <ref target="s4:agba" actuate="user"
show="replace">AGBA materials</ref> in Series 4: Topical
Files</p></note>
</c02>
      [other possible elements and text ....]
</c01>
```

**Figure 7.4.1a.** *Using the ACTUATE and SHOW attributes to specify link properties.*

In figure 7.4.1b a link is made to an image of the creator of a collection of personal papers that is being used to illustrate the biographical note in the collection-level description. The link is encoded in such a way that the traversal of the link will happen automatically; the picture will always appear when an end user reads the biographical note.

```
<bioghist>
<dao href="http://www.myserver.edu/images/ms452_port1.gif"
actuate="auto" show="embed"></dao>
<p>Sanford J. Archiviste, depicted above in a 1945 portrait
photograph
from his papers, was a significant intellectual force in the North
American archival world during the mid-twentieth century. [...]</p>
      [other possible elements and text ...]
</bioghist>
```

**Figure 7.4.1b.** *Using the* ACTUATE *and* SHOW *attributes with <dao> to specify link properties.*

Note that <dao> was chosen to establish the link because the digital facsimile that is its destination is of an item from the materials being described. If there were no photographs in the collection and the archivist had found an image from some other source for inclusion in the encoded finding aid, the use of <dao> would not have been appropriate. In such a case either <extptr> or <extref> would be the correct tag to use in establishing such a link, depending on whether or not the inclusion of text within the linking element is desired. Figure 7.4.1c is a reencoding of figure 7.4.1b using <extptr> as the linking element:

```
<bioghist>
<p><extptr
href="http://www.archivists.org/famousFolk/sanford.jpg"
actuate="auto" show="embed"></p>
<p>Sanford J. Archiviste, depicted above in a 1945 portrait
photograph available digitally at the Society of American
Archivists' Web site, was a significant intellectual force in
the North American archival world during the mid-twentieth
Century. [...]</p>
      [other possible elements and text ...]
</bioghist>
```

**Figure 7.4.1c.** *Using the* ACTUATE *and* SHOW *attributes with <extptr> to specify link properties.*

### 7.4.2. The ROLE, TITLE, CONTENT-ROLE, and CONTENT-TITLE Attributes

This group of attributes serves to provide additional information to application software and to end users about the role of a resource in a particular link. In most simple links (that is, single-direction links with one source and one destination) the roles are clear, and these attributes are not needed. In extended links, however, roles may need some clarification for either processing software or end users, in which case these attributes are available. In inline extended links (those established using <daogrp> or <linkgrp> to bundle multiple locator elements) it may be necessary to provide further information to clarify the role of the external resource for which each locator element provides an address.

In such cases the attributes ROLE and TITLE are used in the locator elements to encode information about the role that each remote resource plays in the link. The values of these attributes are unconstrained by the DTD, so encoders must be certain that the values supplied will be meaningful in the context of the intended audience. For ROLE, the audience is the application software and for TITLE it is the end user. It is important to understand that you will need to know something about the requirements of the system in which you will deliver your encoded finding aids before utilizing these attributes in your encoding. Most commercially available systems do not yet support the use of these attributes. The following discussion is intended to provide EAD implementers with a basic understanding of the purpose of each attribute so that they can be used properly in the future when systems do readily support their use.

The ROLE attribute is intended to provide clarification regarding the role of a *remote* resource *to application software* that will be processing an EAD instance. Perhaps a stylesheet has been created in a particular delivery system that assigns behavior to image links based on whether they are identified as "thumbnail" or "reference" copies of those images. The encoding for all image links (simple and extended) in files using that stylesheet may be required by the delivery system to specify which of these roles an image will play. Figure 7.4.2a illustrates the encoding of an image sampler that includes both a thumbnail file and a larger reference file for each image. The <daogrp> tag is used to bundle the group of files for each image. The ROLE attribute on each <daoloc> locator tag is used to specify for processing software the relationship between the files within each <daogrp>. Since <daogrp> is not recursive (cannot be nested within itself), the Other Descriptive Data <odd> element is used to bundle the multiple <daogrp> tags that comprise the image sampler. Of course, entity declarations for all of the images would have to be added to the prolog of the EAD instance (see section 6.5) in order to make the encoding in this example valid.

```
<odd>
<head>Image Sampler</head>
<p>The following photographs are illustrative of the types of
images available in this collection.</p>
<daogrp>
<daoloc entityref="s1_img1-th" role="thumbnail" actuate="auto"
show="embed">
<daodesc><p>Oldest extant photograph of the Lassen County
(Calif.) Courthouse, taken in 1897.
<ref target="s1:LCCph">Link to the location of this image
within the collection description</ref></p></daodesc></daoloc>
<daoloc entityref="s1_img1" role="reference" actuate="user"
show="new"></daoloc>
</daogrp>
<daogrp>
<daoloc entityref="s3_img1-th" role="thumbnail" actuate="auto"
show="embed">
<daodesc><p>Placer mine operations along the Feather River,
Plumas County (Calif.), ca. 1870.
<ref target="s3:MINEph">Link to the location of this image
within the collection description</ref></p></daodesc></daoloc>
<daoloc entityref="s3_img1" role="reference" actuate="user"
show="new"></daoloc>
</daogrp>
        [other possible elements and text ...]
</odd>
```

**Figure 7.4.2a.** *Use of the* ROLE *attribute to specify linking roles.*

The TITLE attribute is intended to provide information *to end users* regarding the role of the remote resource. In many cases, as in the encoding in figure 7.4.2a, this additional information will not be needed, because plenty of clues already exist in the contextual information surrounding the link. Also, as the use of thumbnails to serve as the source resource for links to larger reference images has become more prevalent on the World Wide Web, many end users understand and expect this behavior, so additional information would be superfluous. If an encoder decides, however, that additional information regarding the role of a remote resource in a link is needed, the TITLE attribute is available for that purpose. How the information encoded as the value of this attribute displays to end users is something that would most likely be determined by the particular application software being used to deliver the encoded finding aid.

The final two attributes discussed in this section, CONTENT-ROLE and CONTENT-TITLE, are intended for use *only* with extended links. They provide additional information about the role of the local resource in the extended link. As with the attribute ROLE, CONTENT-ROLE is intended to provide information to application software, while CONTENT-TITLE, like TITLE, provides additional information to end users. In all inline links, which the vast majority of EAD implementers will be using for the time being, the role of the local resource as the source of the link is made clear by the establishment of the link itself. This will not be the case in the future when out-of-line links, in which the local resource may not participate as either a source or a destination, may be possible. Goldfarb and Prescod even relate a scenario in which the values of attributes like CONTENT-TITLE and TITLE may be used by sophisticated application software to present end users with popup menus giving them the choice of selecting from among a variety of sources and destinations for out-of-line links.[122]

[122] Charles Goldfarb and Paul Prescod, *The XML Handbook* (Upper Saddle River, N.J.: Prentice Hall, 1998), 509-10.

## 7.5. Managing External Links[123]

Although EAD may seem at first glance to offer a bewildering array of choices for establishing and managing links, you will likely select a standardized method from among these choices, based largely on the constraints or opportunities offered by the particular system or systems in which you will author and publish EAD-encoded finding aids. Once these choices have been made and documented, encoders will not have to wrestle with choices for each link they want to establish. Do not underestimate the importance of establishing guidelines and documentation for linking within your institutional or collaborative project! Establishing such standards early and rigorously enforcing them in the encoding process will make it much easier in the future to move encoded finding aids and to enhance them for new delivery systems as these inevitably increase in functionality and decrease in both cost and implementation difficulty.

Internal links within any document instance are by their nature fairly simple and do not require any conscious management beyond making certain that your ID and TARGET attributes match up, something a final validating parse of the EAD instance will confirm. This section focuses solely on decisions that must be made about encoding destination addresses for external links and, indirectly, implications for managing the files to which they point.

When processing links from your finding aids to external resources such as text or image files like those shown in Figures 7.3.4a and 7.4.1c, your SGML application needs to know the following two things:

- What special software, if any, is required to view the file?
- Where is the file physically located on your local computer, network, or the Web?

The latter is a particularly vexing problem since file locations tend to change as servers are replaced or directory structures reconfigured. Ensuring that such links remain current and accurate over time is a continuing maintenance issue, one that increases as you add more and more of them to your encoded finding aids.

The remainder of this section concentrates on options available for addressing EAD links to external files generally, but emphasizing those residing on your own server(s). There are two broadly categorized options available: use the ENTITYREF attribute or use the HREF attribute.

- The ENTITYREF approach relies on managing explicit external resource addresses indirectly, either outside of the encoded document instance using a public identifier, or at the beginning of each encoded document instance using a system identifier.

[123] The text of this section is loosely based, with his permission, on an unpublished discussion paper on external linking options prepared by Alvin Pollock, Electronic Text Unit, University of California, Berkeley.

- The HREF approach relies on managing explicit external resource addresses directly at the source of each established link within an encoded document instance.

The strengths and weaknesses of each will be considered. Neither of these options is absolutely correct or incorrect, so these *Guidelines* will not make a final recommendation one way or the other. The decision as to which method to use must be made within the context of your own local administrative and technical realities.

### 7.5.1. Using ENTITYREF

Declaring external files as entities using a formal public identifier (FPI)[124] and then using the ENTITYREF attribute to provide the name of a declared entity as a destination for a link, as illustrated in figure 7.5.1a, is perhaps the most widely employed and technically elegant link management strategy used in SGML-based systems.

```
<!ENTITY pageimage1 PUBLIC "-//University of
California, Berkeley::Bancroft Library//TEXT (US::CU-
BANC::BANC MSS 92/894c::The Arequipa Sanatorium
Records::Letter page image 1)" NDATA gif>

<dao entityref="pageimage1"></dao>
```

**Figure 7.5.1a.** *An entity declaration using only a public identifier (in this case, an FPI), followed by an entity reference to the declared entity.*

In this method, the ENTITYREF attribute in the linking element specifies the location of the resource indirectly, through an entity name, rather than by specifying an absolute computer address such as a URL. This approach has distinct advantages. Declaring an entity using an FPI allows you to use a separate file, such as an SGML catalog file or a handle server[125], to provide an appropriate address or location for the resource based on the type of processing application. These tools serve as roadmaps between entity names (which can be referenced easily from any point within an encoded document instance) and the address or physical location of the resources to which those entity names refer. When the physical locations of resources change over time, only the SGML catalog file needs to be modified; the individual EAD instances containing stable entity names that reference the SGML catalog file need not be edited.

[124] See sections 6.5.2.2 and 6.5.2.4.1 for more information on public identifiers.
[125] See section 6.5.2.4.1 for more information on SGML catalog files and section 5.4 for more information on handle servers.

There are technical disadvantages to this approach. Web browsers that support XML and the use of XSL or CSS stylesheets are unable to access and resolve such entity names into explicit resource addresses such as URLs. It would require specialized programming to create workarounds for this problem. In addition, the overhead of supplying a well-formed FPI (as specified by the ISO 9070 standard) for each digital resource is not insignificant.

For systems that do not support the use of FPIs and catalog files, a system identifier may be specified in an entity declaration in addition to or instead of an FPI, as illustrated in figure 7.5.1b. As discussed in sections 6.5.2.2 and 6.5.2.4.1, a system identifier provides a direct address, in the form of a URI, in the entity declaration.

```
<!ENTITY pageimage1 PUBLIC "-//University of
California, Berkeley::Bancroft Library//TEXT (US::CU-
BANC::BANC MSS 92/894c::The Arequipa Sanatorium
Records::Letter page image 1)"
"http://sunsite.berkeley.edu/arequipa/page1.gif"
NDATA gif>

<dao entityref="pageimage1"></dao>
```

**Figure 7.5.1b.** *An entity declaration using both a public identifier and a system identifier (in this case an absolute URL), followed by an entity reference to the declared entity.*

This combined approach provides an explicit resource address in the entity declaration, but still relies on the use of a delivery application that can access that resource address indirectly from its location in an entity declaration at the beginning of a document instance. For this reason, it will not work with current XML applications that are Web browser based and use XSL or CSS stylesheets to render their display, though this may change as XSL and XSL applications mature.

Additionally, the use of system identifiers in entity declarations may require that individual EAD-encoded files be edited whenever the server location of a particular resource changes, obviating the benefits of using entities to provide indirect file addresses in finding aids. This potential drawback may be mitigated through the use of the search-and-replace capabilities of most standard text editors and also by careful planning of the directory structures you create on the server(s) on which your files are stored.

### 7.5.2. Using HREF

Using the HREF attribute directly at the source of each link to establish a destination address, as illustrated in figure 7.5.2a, eliminates the indirection of the ENTITYREF approach that may be problematic for some applications. Currently and freely available Web browser technology can readily deal with links encoded using this option. Encoding is far easier, particularly for those repositories with little technical expertise or limited resources who may be going it alone in their implementation of EAD. No SGML catalog file is required with this option. If the location of any destination resource changes, linking elements throughout individual finding aid instances must be edited, though this may be easily accomplished using a global search-and-replace operation within a repository's encoded finding aids. Finally, encoders who have experience with HTML certainly will find the HREF notation easier to read and use.

```
<dao
href="http://sunsite.berkeley.edu/arequipa/page1.gif">
</dao>
```

**Figure 7.5.2a.** *An external link established without the use of entity declarations by the direct use of the HREF attribute (in this case using an absolute URL).*

While all these plusses may make this seem an obvious choice, there are definite drawbacks. Certainly keeping references to file location current will be a major maintenance issue, as it is with all Web applications. This process can be supported by the use of any of a number of tools currently available to Web managers that search out and report broken links. The maintenance of local files can be expedited further if only the file name itself ("page1.gif") is embedded in the HREF attribute, with the balance of file path ("http://sunsite.berkeley.edu/ arequipa/") being specified in a stylesheet. Finally, it must be noted that this option presents major challenges for finding aid interchangeability and the implementation of union databases of finding aids because of the problems associated with maintaining location information for external resources.

When using HREF, it is not sufficient simply to specify a URL or system identifier. The processing application needs additional direction as to how to display the resource. Is the image to be inserted into the finding aid at the point where the link occurs or is there to be a hyperlink to an external text file, such an entry in an electronic biographical dictionary? Unless a default option applies to all links, the type of display needs to be specified through the use of the SHOW and ACTUATE attributes.

### 7.5.3. Combining Both Approaches

This option combines the entity-based and HREF-based approaches to encoding URLs for external digital resources. Although this approach presents both addressing options and allows a processing application to determine which to use, it should be noted that including both has caused indexing problems for some SGML-based systems. This method creates an obvious redundancy in the duplication of URLs in both the entity declaration and at the point of the link itself, which would certainly increase both the amount of work in encoding each finding aid and the complexity in editing that would be required when URLs change. Nonetheless, in terms of interchange and in view of the current rapid pace of change in information management and delivery technologies, this may be the most flexible option. The provision of a URL in both the entity declaration and the linking element itself should ideally allow most application software to process whichever resource address it can and ignore the others.

```
<!ENTITY pageimage1 PUBLIC "-//University of
California, Berkeley::Bancroft Library//TEXT (US::CU-
BANC::BANC MSS 92/894c::The Arequipa Sanatorium
Records::Letter page image 1)"
"http://sunsite.berkeley.edu/arequipa/page1.gif" NDATA
gif>

<dao entityref="pageimage1"
href="http://sunsite.berkeley.edu/arequipa/page1.gif">
</dao>
```

**Figure 7.5.3a.** *An entity declaration using both a Public Identifier and a System Identifier (in this case an absolute URL), followed by a link that includes an entity reference to the declared entity as well as a hard-coded* HREF *address.*

## 7.6. Examples of Optimally Encoded Linking Elements

The following examples illustrate optimal encoding of EAD links, both internal and external. How do we define the term "optimal?" For the purposes of these *Guidelines* the term "optimal" means the minimum amount of information about a link that would be required for the link to function effectively in most encoded finding aid publishing systems. The requirements for optimal encoding of links in EAD are really quite simple. Each link must be supplied with two things:

- An address for its intended destination(s)
- Basic information regarding how it should behave when processed by application software

Your choices are limited for meeting both of these requirements, which should make it easy to optimally encode links in your EAD documents. For internal links there is only one option for the first requirement: use TARGET. For external links there are three options for the first requirement: use ENTITYREF, use HREF, or use both. Refer to section 7.5 for more information about the issues involved in making this choice. The second requirement is equally easily met by using both the ACTUATE and SHOW attributes in all of your encoded links. Together these two attributes provide a minimum amount of information about how you intend the links to behave in whatever system will be processing them for presentation to an end user. While not recommended in all cases, the ROLE attribute, as demonstrated in figure 7.4.2a, may be useful to indicate unambiguously to application software the role of each link bundled together using one of the extended linking elements <daogrp> or <linkgrp> (in other words, bundling "thumbnail" and "reference" copies of the same image). Although at present most commercially available software cannot utilize the link behavior attributes ACTUATE, SHOW, and ROLE, it is nonetheless a good idea to supply this information when establishing links in your encoded finding aids.

While these *Guidelines* provide information on optimal encoding for linking attributes, they cannot do the same for questions such as when to establish links and how many links to establish. These questions must be answered locally based on the capability of the application software you are using to publish your encoded finding aids and the goals that your repository and funding sources have set for your encoding project. It is important, however, if you are establishing links within your EAD-encoded finding aids, that you *do* create local guidelines that address these questions, that documentation of the guidelines is readily available to all participants in your local project, and that you enforce the guidelines consistently across the body of encoded finding aids that your project creates over time. In the long run, consistency, standardization, and documentation will make the management of your investment in encoded data describing your archival collections simpler and will increase the ease with which you will be able to take advantage of the inevitable advances in hardware and software technology for the manipulation and delivery of that descriptive data in the future.

The examples below are drawn from other illustrations previously used in this chapter. All links established in these examples are inline (see section 7.1.2.3). The INLINE attribute is not used, since its default value is set by the EAD DTD as "true". Use of the INLINE attribute would not make these examples any less illustrative of optimal encoding.

The illustration in figure 7.6a uses a simple internal link to allow users to check the text of an access restriction statement encoded at the collection level from a point in the component description where the restriction is applicable. Note that the use of the value "new" for the attribute SHOW should open a new window for the text of the access restriction rather than disorienting the user by replacing their current location within the finding aid, which would be the result if the value "replace" was used. Because <ref> was used, application software will likely highlight the text included between <ref> and </ref> to indicate to end users that a link is available.

```
<archdesc level="collection" langmaterial="eng"
type="inventory">
<did>[...]</did>
<admininfo>
      [other possible elements and text...]
<accessrestrict id="restrict1">
<head>Access Restrictions</head>
<p>This collection is open for research to all
researchers with the following exception: Series 2
(Correspondence) contains 15 folders of student
recommendations that are closed for 75 years under
the jurisdiction of the state Student Records Act
(1968:042). The first of these folders will be
available to researchers on 1 January 2035 and the
last on 1 January 2047.</p>
</accessrestrict>
      [other possible elements and text...]
</admininfo>
      [other possible elements and text...]
<dsc type="combined">
       [other possible elements and text...]
<c01 level="series">
<did>
<unittitle>Series 2: Correspondence</unittitle>
[...]</did>
<scopecontent><p>The Correspondence Series contains
...</p>
<arrangement><p>The bulk of the contents of the
series arrived at the repository in chronological
order and this arrangement has been retained. <ref
target="restrict1" actuate="user" show="new">The
single exception is a file of student recommendations
on which access restrictions have been imposed.</ref>
These folders have been temporarily removed to a
restricted box in the collection.</p></arrangement>
</scopecontent>
      [other possible elements and text...]
</c01>
      [other possible elements and text...]
</dsc>
</archdesc>
```

**Figure 7.6a.**

The illustration in figure 7.6b uses an external linking element specifically intended to create links to other archival collections in order to give users access to the finding aid for a related collection of personal papers available at another repository. It also uses a simple external link to insert an illustrative image of the creator of that external set of papers. Because of the attribute values assigned, the text of the reference should be highlighted to alert the end user of the existence of a link, while the image should appear automatically in the text of the reference after the title of the related collection.

```
<!DOCTYPE  ead  PUBLIC  "-//Society of American
Archivists//DTD ead.dtd (Encoded Archival Description
(EAD) Version 1.0)//EN"  [
<!ENTITY  tedschell  SYSTEM
"http://www.archivesrus.gov/findaids/ead/ms045.sgm"
NDATA sgml>
<!ENTITY  schellpix  SYSTEM
"http://www.myserver.org/images/ms023_schell.gif"
NDATA  gif>
]>
<ead audience="external">
      [other possible elements and text ...]
<add>
<relatedmaterial>
<head>Related Collections</head>
<archref entityref="tedschell" actuate="user"
show="replace">
<origination label="Creator:">
<persname source="lcnaf" role="creator">Schellenberg,
T. R., 1903-1970</persname>
</origination>
<unittitle>Theodore R. Schellenberg Papers,
<unitdate type="inclusive">1938-
1970</unitdate></unittitle>
<extptr entityref="schellpix" actuate="auto"
show="embed">
<unitid type="collection number">MS-045</unitid>
<repository><name>Archives R Us</name></repository>
</archref>
       [other possible elements and text ...]
</relatedmaterial>
</add>
</ead>
```

**Figure 7.6b.**

Figure 7.6c illustrates the use of <daogrp> to bundle pairs of thumbnail and reference images for each item. The encoding of the attributes ACTUATE and SHOW in this example would most likely result in the thumbnail image being automatically embedded in the text of the finding aid after the <unittitle> for each item, while the larger reference image would appear in a new browser window when the user activated the link traversal.

```
<!DOCTYPE  ead  PUBLIC  "-//Society of American
Archivists//DTD ead.dtd (Encoded Archival Description (EAD)
Version 1.0)//EN"  [
<!ENTITY  f0042_1  SYSTEM  "../images/fonds0042_image1.jpg"
NDATA jpeg>
<!ENTITY  f0042_2  SYSTEM  "../images/fonds0042_image2.jpg"
NDATA jpeg>
<!ENTITY  f0042_1tmb  SYSTEM
"../images/fonds0042_image1_thumb.jpg" NDATA jpeg>
<!ENTITY  f0042_2tmb  SYSTEM
"../images/fonds0042_image2_thumb.jpg" NDATA jpeg>
]>
<ead audience="external">
       [other possible elements and text ...]
<dsc type="combined">
       [other possible elements and text ...]
<c01 level="series"><did> <unittitle>Series 3: Biographical
Information </unittitle>
       [other possible elements and text...]
</did>
<c02 level="file"><did><unittitle>Photographs,
<unitdate type="inclusive">1895-1928</unitdate></unittitle>
<physdesc><extent>5 items</extent></physdesc></did>
<c03 level="item"><did><unittitle>John Smith graduation
portrait,
<unitdate type="single" normal="18950528">May 28,
1895</unitdate></unittitle>
<daogrp>
<daoloc entityref="f0042_1tmb" actuate="auto" show="embed"
role="thumbnail"></daoloc>
<daoloc entityref="f0042_1" actuate="user" show="new"
role="reference"></daoloc></daogrp></did></c03>
<c03 level="item"><did><unittitle>Wedding of John Smith and
Stella Jones, Windsor, Ontario, <unitdate type="single"
normal="18970606">June 6, 1897</unitdate></unittitle>
<daogrp>
<daoloc entityref="f0042_2tmb" actuate="auto" show="embed"
role="thumbnail"></daoloc>
<daoloc entityref="f0042_2" actuate="user" show="new"
role="reference"></daoloc>
</daogrp></did></c03>
       [other possible elements and text ...]
</c02>
       [other possible elements and text ...]
</c01></dsc>
       [other possible elements and text ...]
</ead>
```

**Figure 7.6c.**

# APPENDICES

# Appendix A

## MINIMUM RECOMMENDED FINDING AID ELEMENTS

The EAD elements listed on the next page comprise the minimum elements recommended for creation of a very basic EAD-encoded finding aid. This list includes both the elements required by the EAD DTD for validation (shown in **bold** type) and additional important structural elements; together these comprise "best practice" for a basic archival description. The list of elements assumes that the archival description begins at the collection, fonds, or series level, but many of the elements listed are applicable at any level of description.

As the brief list of bolded element names reveals, only a handful of elements are *required* to enable an EAD-encoded finding aid to be validated against the specifications of the DTD. Note, however, that an EAD document consisting only of these elements would barely be a finding aid! The list is extremely brief in part due to reasons related to the SGML rules for writing DTDs, and in part because the EAD developers recognized that many "legacy" finding aids do not contain a full or consistent set of data elements, and they did not wish to eliminate such finding aids' potential for conversion to EAD.

Nesting of elements is shown only where it is required, such as for <titleproper> within <titlestmt> within <filedesc>. The <unitdate> element, on the other hand, is shown outside of <unittitle>, even though it is perfectly valid to encode <unitdate> within <unittitle>.

Only those attributes required for validation (LEVEL on <archdesc> and TYPE on <dsc>) and those representing ISAD(G) equivalencies (LANGMATERIAL and LEGALSTATUS on <archdesc>, COUNTRYCODE and REPOSITORYCODE on <unitid>, LEVEL on <c>) are included in the list. It is recommended, however, that you consistently utilize the ENCODINGANALOG, PARENT, and ID attributes if your system can make effective use of them.

The list also illustrates the required *order* for the following sections of an encoded finding aid, as dictated by the EAD DTD:

- The <eadheader> subelements
- The high-level <did> within <archdesc>
- The <did> within <c> or <c0x>

In all other cases, the DTD does not specify a particular order of elements. For example, both the <did> subelements and all elements at the same level as the high-level <did> can be encoded in any order (e.g., <scopecontent> can precede <bioghist> and <admininfo>). Keep the needs of your audience in mind when determining a consistent order of elements for your finding aids.

<**ead**>
<**eadheader**>
<**eadid**>
<**filedesc**>
<**titlestmt**>
<**titleproper**>
<author>
<publicationstmt>
<publisher>
<date>
<profiledesc>
<creation>
<langusage>
<language>
<**archdesc**> with **LEVEL**, LANGMATERIAL, and LEGALSTATUS attributes
<**did**>
<repository>
<corpname>
<origination>
<persname>, <corpname>, <famname> as appropriate
<unittitle>
<unitdate>
<physdesc>
<unitid> with COUNTRYCODE and REPOSITORYCODE attributes
<abstract>
<admininfo>
subelements as appropriate
<bioghist>
<scopecontent>
<controlaccess>
subelements as appropriate
<dsc> with **TYPE** attribute
<c0x> or <c> with LEVEL attribute in as many levels as appropriate
<did>
<container>
<unittitle>
other subelements as appropriate

# Appendix B

## EAD CROSSWALKS

This appendix includes four "crosswalks" intended to enable comparison of EAD elements with the data elements defined in three related metadata standards or frameworks: ISAD(G), Dublin Core, and USMARC. Use of these crosswalks may facilitate mapping of data between and among these metadata tools, such as for exporting data from EAD-encoded finding aids to create USMARC records. Further information about the relationship between EAD and these other standards is contained in various sections of these *Guidelines.*

The four crosswalks are these:

- B.1. ISAD(G) to EAD
- B.2. EAD to ISAD(G)
- B.3. Dublin Core to EAD
- B.4. USMARC to EAD

A conservative approach was taken in compiling these crosswalks. In other words, only clear equivalencies between data elements were included. Other roughly compatible elements that may be identifiable by users were omitted because the match was felt to be ambiguous or uncertain.

Listing of two EAD elements side by side indicates that the second element is a subelement of the first. For example, "<controlaccess><persname>" indicates that the <persname> element should be nested within <controlaccess>.

Listing of different EAD elements on separate lines within a table cell indicates that all of the listed elements can be mapped to the matching data element from the corresponding metadata tool.

## B.1. ISAD(G) to EAD

| ISAD(G) | EAD |
|---|---|
| 3.1.1 Reference code(s) | <unitid> COUNTRYCODE and REPOSITORYCODE attributes |
| 3.1.2 Title | <unittitle> |
| 3.1.3 Dates of creation | <unitdate> |
| 3.1.4 Level of description | <archdesc> and <c> LEVEL attribute |
| 3.1.5 Extent of the unit | <physdesc>, <extent> |
| 3.2.1 Name of creator | <origination> |
| 3.2.2 Administrative/Biographical history | <bioghist> |
| 3.2.3 Dates of accumulation | <custodhist><date type="accumulation"> |
| 3.2.4 Custodial history | <custodhist> |
| 3.2.5 Immediate source of acquisition | <acqinfo> |
| 3.3.1 Scope and content | <scopecontent> |
| 3.3.2 Appraisal, destruction and scheduling | <appraisal> |
| 3.3.3 Accruals | <accruals> |
| 3.3.4 System of arrangement | <arrangement> |
| 3.4.1 Legal status | <archdesc> LEGALSTATUS attribute |
| 3.4.2 Access conditions | <accessrestrict> |
| 3.4.3 Copyright/Reproduction | <userestrict> |
| 3.4.4 Language of material | <archdesc> LANGMATERIAL attribute |
| 3.4.5 Physical characteristics | <physdesc> <physfacet> |
| 3.4.6 Finding aids | <otherfindaid> |
| 3.5.1 Location of originals | <odd> |
| 3.5.2 Existence of copies | <altformavail> |
| 3.5.3 Related units of description | <relatedmaterial> |
| 3.5.4 Associated material | <separatedmaterial> |
| 3.5.5 Publication note | <bibliography> |
| 3.6.1 Note | <odd> |

## B.2. EAD to ISAD(G)

| EAD | ISAD (G) |
|---|---|
| <accessrestrict> | 3.4.2 Access conditions |
| <accruals> | 3.3.3 Accruals |
| <acqinfo> | 3.2.5 Immediate source of acquisition |
| <altformavail> | 3.5.2 Existence of copies |
| <appraisal> | 3.3.2 Appraisal, destruction and scheduling |
| <archdesc> and <c> LEVEL attribute | 3.1.4 Level of description |
| <archdesc> LANGMATERIAL attribute | 3.4.4 Language of material |
| <archdesc> LEGALSTATUS attribute | 3.4.1 Legal status |
| <arrangement> | 3.3.4 System of arrangement |
| <bibliography> | 3.5.5 Publication note |
| <bioghist> | 3.2.2 Administrative/Biographical history |
| <custodhist> | 3.2.4 Custodial history |
| <custodhist><date type="accumulation"> | 3.2.3 Dates of accumulation |
| <odd> | 3.6.1 Note |
| <odd> | 3.5.1 Location of originals |
| <origination> | 3.2.1 Name of creator |
| <otherfindaid> | 3.4.6 Finding aids |
| <physdesc><br><extent> | 3.1.5 Extent of the unit |
| <physdesc><br><physfacet> | 3.4.5 Physical characteristics |
| <relatedmaterial> | 3.5.3 Related units of description |
| <scopecontent> | 3.3.1 Scope and content |
| <separatedmaterial> | 3.5.4 Associated material |
| <unitdate> | 3.1.3 Dates of creation |
| <unitid> COUNTRYCODE and REPOSITORYCODE attributes | 3.1.1 Reference code(s) |
| <unittitle> | 3.1.2 Title |
| <userestrict> | 3.4.3 Copyright/Reproduction |

## B.3. Dublin Core to EAD

Table B.3 maps the 15 elements in the Dublin Core (DC) Element Set to EAD elements within <eadheader> and <archdesc>. DC remains a "work in progress" as of early 1999, and so it is possible that this mapping will change in future.

In mapping DC to EAD, it is first necessary to consider which "resource" the metadata is describing: the finding aid per se, or the collection of archival material. If the described resource is the finding aid, it is most appropriate to map DC elements to subelements of <eadheader>. If, on the other hand, a DC record is being created for an archival collection itself, the DC elements should be mapped to <archdesc> subelements, most of which are found in the high-level <did>.

All DC elements are listed in this table, but some DC elements have no clear corollary in EAD. Where the boxes have been left blank, no clear equivalent exists.

| DUBLIN CORE | EAD <eadheader> | EAD <archdesc> |
|---|---|---|
| CONTENT | | |
| Coverage | | <geogname> (spatial)<br><unitdate> (temporal) |
| Description | <notestmt><note> | <abstract> |
| Type | [126] | <archdesc> with LEVEL attribute |
| Relation | | |
| Source | | |
| Subject | <notestmt><subject> | <controlaccess><subject> |
| Title | <titleproper> | <unittitle> |
| INTELLECTUAL PROPERTY | | |
| Creator | <author> | <origination><persname><br><origination><corpname><br><origination><famname> |
| Contributor | <author> | |
| Publisher | <publisher> | <repository> |
| Rights | | |
| INSTANTIATION | | |
| Date | <publicationstmt><date> | <unitdate> |
| Format | [127] | |
| Identifier | <eadid> | <unitid> with COUNTRYCODE and REPOSITORYCODE attributes |
| Language | <language> | <archdesc> with LANGMATERIAL attribute |

[126] It would be appropriate to establish "archival finding aid" as a resource type if an enumerated list of types is established for Dublin Core.

[127] The data format of an EAD finding aid is SGML or XML.

## B.4. USMARC to EAD

Table B.4 does not include all possible USMARC fields to which EAD elements might be mapped to generate a partial USMARC record for the collection; it instead focuses on the most significant and useful fields. In addition, USMARC fields that contain coded data, such as Leader and Directory fields, are not included, because it is unlikely that such information would be provided in a finding aid in a format that could be directly ported into a USMARC record (or vice versa).

Note that this mapping is between an EAD finding aid and a USMARC record describing that same collection, not to a USMARC record describing the finding aid per se.

The table only includes MARC fields for which there is a direct, logical analog to an EAD element. Where an EAD element has a more specific subelement that can accurately be mapped (such as <acqinfo> within <admininfo>), the subelement is mapped.

The right-hand column listing EAD elements specifies the use of a subelement within another element in some situations. In other cases, this column provides a list of optional elements, leaving it to the archivist to determine which one best fits the data being encoded.

It is most useful to map to USMARC the EAD data that is encoded in the high-level <did> or in other <did>-level elements such as <bioghist>, <scopecontent>, and <controlaccess> to their field equivalencies in USMARC records. Since most repositories create USMARC records only at the "collection level," mapping from more detailed components of EAD finding aids, while theoretically feasible, is less likely to be useful in practical terms.

Note that EAD data being mapped to USMARC fields that require authority-controlled data must be in controlled access form in order to be imported into a valid USMARC record.

| MARC | EAD |
|---|---|
| 041 Language | <archdesc> LANGMATERIAL attribute |
| 100 Main entry--personal name | <origination><persname><br><origination><famname> |
| 110 Main entry--corporate name | <origination><corpname> |
| 111 Main entry--meeting name | <origination><corpname> |
| 130 Main entry--uniform title | <unittitle> |
| 240 Uniform title | <controlaccess><title> |
| 245 Title statement | <unittitle> |
| 300 Physical description | <physdesc><br><extent><br><physfacet> |
| 340 Physical medium | <physdesc><br><physfacet><br><dimensions> |
| 351 Organization and arrangement | <organization><br><arrangement><br><archdesc> LEVEL attribute |
| 500 General note | <odd> |
| 506 Restrictions on access note | <accessrestrict> |
| 510 Citation/references | <bibliography> |
| 520 Summary, etc. | <scopecontent><br><abstract> |
| 524 Preferred citation of described materials | <prefercite> |
| 530 Additional physical form available | <altformavail> |
| 536 Funding information | <sponsor> |
| 540 Terms governing use and reproduction | <userestrict> |
| 541 Immediate source of acquisition | <acqinfo> |
| 544 Location of other archival materials | <separatedmaterial> |
| 545 Biographical or historical data | <bioghist><br><abstract> |
| 555 Cumulative index/finding aids | [128] |
| 561 Ownership and custodial history | <custodhist> |
| 581 Publications about described materials | <bibliography> |
| 583 Action | <processinfo> |
| 584 Accumulation and frequency of use | <accruals> |
| 600 Subject--personal name | <controlaccess><persname role="subject"><br><controlaccess><famname role="subject"> |
| 610 Subject--corporate name | <controlaccess><corpname role="subject"> |

[128] In a USMARC record a note in the 555 field would mention the existence of the EAD-encoded finding aid, but no specific EAD element maps to this field.

| | |
|---|---|
| 611 Subject--meeting | <controlaccess><corpname role="subject"> |
| 630 Subject--uniform title | <controlaccess><title role="subject"> |
| 650 Subject--topical | <controlaccess><subject> |
| 651 Subject--geographic name | <controlaccess><geogname role="subject"> |
| 655 Genre/form | <controlaccess><genreform> |
| 656 Occupation | <controlaccess><occupation> |
| 657 Function | <controlaccess><function> |
| 69x Local subject access | <controlaccess><subject source="local"> |
| 700 Added entry--personal name | <controlaccess><persname><br><controlaccess><famname> |
| 710 Added entry--corporate name | <controlaccess><corpname> |
| 711 Added entry--meeting name | <controlaccess><corpname> |
| 720 Added entry--uncontrolled | <name> |
| 730 Added entry--uniform title | <controlaccess><title> |
| 740 Added entry--uncont./related anal. title | <title> |
| 752 Added entry--hierarchical place name | <geogname> |
| 852 Location | <repository><br><physloc> |

# Appendix C

# FREQUENTLY ASKED QUESTIONS (FAQs)

The answers to these FAQs are intentionally brief, since additional information on all of these topics is contained throughout the *Application Guidelines*. Please refer to the sections cited for further details.

**1. Why was EAD written in SGML, and why should archives use it rather than HTML for making finding aids available via the World Wide Web?**

As explained in section 1.4, SGML provides the capability to encode the full structure and intellectual content of documents in a nonproprietary software environment; as an SGML Document Type Definition, EAD shares these characteristics. Further, SGML's inherently hierarchical approach to data structure mirrors the information hierarchies that have long been a fundamental part of archival description. Thus, use of EAD, which was written specifically for encoding archival finding aids following the rules of SGML, represents an important investment in a repository's finding aid data by capturing the full *meaning* of its structure and content, in addition to enabling sophisticated retrieval, display, and navigational techniques.

HTML, on the other hand, provides only the capability to encode visual presentation characteristics such as font size, bolding, italics, and line breaks. The structure and content of a finding aid cannot be exploited when the encoding is in HTML. Future data migration is not facilitated because the meaning of data elements and their structural relationships are not retained; this increases the likelihood that data will have to be reformatted or reconfigured manually when migration to a new software environment is necessary. See section 1.3 for additional information.

**2. What is the advantage of using EAD to encode a finding aid over creating a local database structure for that finding aid?**

EAD provides a standardized set of data elements for finding aids that was devised by archivists who are experts in archival description. Its developers have refined EAD in response to widespread input received from colleagues from throughout the United States and several other countries. EAD already is in widespread use, and as the archival community gains experience in its use, consistency of practice is likely to improve and software products will be developed to make implementation easier and cheaper. Perhaps most importantly, user comprehension of archival descriptive data can be expected to improve as more and more repositories share the same encoding structure and rules to create finding aids for their collections and disseminate them internationally via the World Wide Web.

Prior to the development of EAD, many repositories already were using in-house relational database software to create finding aids for complex collections in order to take advantage of powerful searching capabilities and the ease of indexing and updating data. Regardless of how well they have served their individual repositories, however, such internal databases lack the standardized data structure and the platform independence that is assured by use of EAD and that is essential for searching across finding aids from multiple repositories.

Use of EAD does not, however, preclude use of database software for local data input and storage. Repositories that already create finding aids using software such as Access or dBase may wish to determine the extent to which their database fields are analogous to EAD elements, make any necessary changes to ensure compatibility, and then call upon the expertise of a programmer to develop a conversion script that will map the database fields into EAD (see section 4.2.4). EAD can then be used as the basis for making the finding aids available to users, as described in chapter 5.

**3. Why was EAD necessary, given that the TEI (Text Encoding Initiative) encoding scheme was already available?**

As discussed in section 1.4, the TEI data structure is designed for encoding literary and other scholarly texts, and it has gained widespread acceptance within the humanities community. TEI does not include many of the specific elements that appear in archival finding aids, however, and thus would not have served the archival community's needs effectively. On the other hand, TEI is an excellent encoding scheme for use by an archives that wishes to encode digitized versions of actual scholarly texts, which can then be linked to EAD-encoded finding aids in appropriate situations.

**4. If we use EAD, do we still need to do MARC cataloging?**

Section 1.6 sets MARC cataloging into context with EAD. At this point in the development of EAD, MARC catalog records constitute important navigational metadata that makes it both easier and more efficient to get to encoded finding aids from existing bibliographic and other systems. Many users begin their searching for research resources in an online library catalog, and it is crucial to maintain summary archival information within such integrated bibliographic systems in order to lead those users to EAD-encoded finding aids and the archival materials they describe.

**5. What is the relationship between EAD and ISAD(G)?**

ISAD(G) is an international standard that provides a framework for multilevel archival descriptions and that can serve as a strong basis for establishing "best practice" for EAD-encoded finding aids. EAD is a much more detailed and specific data structure standard that was developed with ISAD(G) in mind and thus is compatible with ISAD(G). See section 1.2 for additional information.

### 6. How do we get started using EAD?

Chapter 2 outlines a variety of administrative issues that are important to consider at the outset when contemplating use of EAD. As a supplement to chapter 2, the *Implementation Checklist* in appendix D will help you ponder the many organizational variables that must be taken into account in your planning.

Most repositories that decide to go ahead and adopt EAD will face two distinct types of implementation work: creating new finding aids and converting existing finding aids. Each type presents its own challenges, and although this may seem counterintuitive, creating new finding aids is likely to be easier than converting existing finding aids. This is because it will be possible to think afresh about how to structure the content of new finding aids after getting a sense of EAD's data structure. See sections 2.5.3 and 2.5.4 for more information.

### 7. What computer hardware and software does my repository need in order to use EAD?

Due to EAD's basis in the platform-independent metalanguage SGML, users have a wide variety of hardware and software choices; no single environment is required. To be able to encode its own finding aids, a repository will need a minimum of a desktop computer and some sort of software for applying EAD tags to finding aid documents. If a repository wishes to disseminate encoded finding aids on the World Wide Web, or to upload its finding aids into a shared or union database, it also will need a network connection and the ability to serve data to the Internet. As with most hardware and software, the more money you can spend, the more sophisticated the functionality you will be able to afford, but a basic implementation of EAD is feasible with minimal investments in hardware and software. Chapter 4 describes a variety of scenarios for selecting authoring software, and chapter 5 details various methods for serving finding aids to the Web.

### 8. What local EAD conventions is my repository likely to have to develop?

As discussed in section 3.3, it is recommended that each repository examine its existing descriptive practices for both overall consistency and for compatibility with EAD prior to beginning any encoding. Following such analysis, a repository will be able to identify the array of EAD elements and attributes that best fit its descriptive needs, the order in which the elements will be presented for overall presentation of a finding aid, and the visual layout characteristics that will be written into a stylesheet to effect the display of clear and consistent finding aids to users. It is particularly important that such conventions be developed in the context of multi-institutional cooperative projects.

In addition, those repositories that create MARC catalog records may have some decisions to make about how to effect compatibility between MARC records and EAD finding aids, as well as how to alter existing workflow in order to avoid duplication of effort. More information is provided in section 1.6.

**9. What training does archival staff need in order to use EAD, and where is the training available?**

The necessary training will vary depending on the particular tasks that a staff member will be expected to perform. Those who will determine which EAD tags are to be applied to finding aids will need thorough familiarity with both the *EAD Tag Library* and chapter 3 of these *Guidelines.* As of 1998, the Society of American Archivists offers EAD workshops, as does the University of Virginia's summer Rare Book School program. Consortia (including the Research Libraries Group) often sponsor workshops to train participants at the outset of an EAD project.

Those who will use particular software packages to apply EAD tags will of course need training in the repository's chosen software. Systems specialists will need more sophisticated understanding of SGML files and systems; some of this information is provided in chapters 6 and 7 of these *Guidelines.*

For additional information, see sections 1.7.3 and 2.5.2.

**10. What is the easiest way to create EAD-encoded finding aids from scratch?**

The answer to this question depends on a variety of factors, including the realities of a particular repository's staff expertise, the methods currently used for producing finding aids, existing computer resources, and budget for acquisition of software. A variety of options for "authoring" of EAD finding aids (that is, for using computer software to apply EAD encoding to finding aids) are presented in section 4.2.

**11. What are the major considerations associated with converting existing finding aids to EAD?**

Section 2.5.4 discusses conversion of existing finding aids, often referred to as "legacy data." The discussion is organized around three major topics: prioritization of existing finding aids, revision strategies, and conversion techniques.

**12. How should repositories prioritize existing finding aids for conversion?**

As described in section 2.5.4.1, each repository must examine a number of variables and make its own decisions about prioritization. Your decision making may focus on striking a balance between two major issues: which finding aids are considered the most important, and which will be the easiest and quickest to convert.

**13. Can EAD be used to describe three-dimensional materials such as museum artifacts?**

It certainly can. As discussed in section 3.5.2.3, EAD provides the capability to describe materials at the item level at whatever level of detail a repository feels is necessary, and this has been accomplished successfully by a variety of early implementers.

**14. How should repositories ensure the integrity of their encoded finding aids?**

Section 4.4 details five relevant types of "integrity" that must be considered: encoding consistency, DTD conformance, file names and locations, version control, and security. Most will be familiar from your experience with descriptive standards and management of online systems.

**15. In what ways can repositories make encoded finding aids available to users?**

Chapter 5 describes a variety of scenarios for "publishing" EAD finding aids, or in other words, for making them available to users. These scenarios range from the simple and affordable to the complex and costly. In addition to online delivery, EAD finding aids can of course simply be printed.

**16. How does EAD relate to efforts to build digital archives and libraries?**

The development of large databases of EAD-encoded finding aids documenting collections from numerous repositories, and the dissemination of these finding aids on networked systems such as the World Wide Web, can be expected gradually to result in a critical mass of widely available descriptive data about archival materials. Within such a context, the encoded finding aids will provide a viable intellectual infrastructure through which digital copies of original historical materials, or "digital archival objects," can be linked to the finding aids that describe them. In some environments, links will also be made from encoded finding aids to MARC records describing archival collections at a summary level. Thus, users will be able to navigate from MARC records to encoded finding aids to digital representations of actual archival materials. See chapter 5 for additional scenarios by which users may be able to access encoded finding aids.

**17. Where can archivists locate the most up-to-date information about EAD software, tools, projects, and other new developments?**

There are three essential online sources of such information:

The *Encoded Archival Description Official Web Site,* maintained by the Network Development and MARC Standards Office of the Library of Congress, is the official source of the EAD Document Type Definition files. The site also includes background information on the development of EAD, instructions for subscribing to the EAD Listserv, and descriptions (with links) of numerous EAD implementation sites, including some of the most significant cooperative projects. URL: <http://www.loc.gov/ead/>.

The *EAD Help Pages,* maintained by the EAD Roundtable of the Society of American Archivists, contains a wide variety of useful information and links to helpful sites. Items include links to tools and helper files (both those available from commercial vendors and others made available for free by EAD implementers), descriptions of the authoring and publishing software used by individual EAD implementation sites, links to useful readings on SGML and XML, and an "I need help!" feature in which users can write for assistance with a specific question. Archivists are invited to participate in the EAD Roundtable and contribute to the Web site. URL: <http://jefferson.village.virginia.edu/ead>.

The EAD Listserv is an interactive forum for learning the latest EAD news and asking questions of experts. Subscription information is available online at <http://www.loc.gov/ead/eadlist.html>.

In addition, other well-maintained Web sites focusing on EAD, SGML, and XML applications are listed in the *Bibliography* in appendix G.

# Appendix D

## IMPLEMENTATION CHECKLIST

Most repositories will face a multistep process when implementing EAD:

- Converting old finding aids
- Creating new finding aids
- Publishing finding aids on the Web

Each step presents its own challenges, and, as explained more fully in chapters 2, 4, and 5, a broad range of options is available. The following checklist will assist you in thinking about the framework in which EAD can function in your repository.[129]

1. Evaluate the role that finding aids play in your current access or reference services environment.

   a. How are your finding aids currently used?
      - Who uses them?
      - What is the range of circumstances under which they are used?
      - Which of these circumstances reflects the highest level(s) of use?
      - What kind of data is most often sought in your finding aids?
      - Which kinds of queries can be answered effectively using your finding aids, and which cannot?
      - Would online finding aids maintain the current level of effectiveness and also possibly address some of the areas in which finding aids are not so effective?
      - Would online finding aids create new audiences for your materials?

   b. What is the current state of your finding aids?
      - In what physical format are your finding aids?
      - How complete are they? How much confidence do you have in the accuracy of the information they contain?
      - How consistent are the structural components of your finding aids and the data they contain? How clearly are the components labeled?
      - What guidelines have you followed for the construction of your finding aids?
      - How many finding aids do you have that you would immediately or eventually wish to convert to EAD? How many pages of text do they represent?
      - At what rate are you currently producing new finding aids?

---

[129] This checklist is based on an earlier version prepared by Helena Zinkham for use at the Library of Congress Prints and Photographs Division, May 1996.

c. Does your repository currently create MARC records, and, if so, what is the relationship of those records to your finding aids?

2. How will you handle the conversion of existing finding aids?

   a. How will you prioritize conversion of existing finding aids?
      - Your most prominent collections
      - Your most heavily used collections (alternately, your least used collections)
      - Finding aids that are "easiest" to convert (that require the least massaging)
      - Finding aids that might be used more effectively if available online
      - Collections that are split between multiple repositories for which a "virtual finding aid" might be created
      - Collections relating to digital materials that are available online

   b. Which method(s) will you use for conversion?
      - Convert in-house
      - Outsource to a vendor
      - Participate in a cooperative project that provides a conversion service

3. By which method(s) do you hope to provide user access to your finding aids?

   a. By links from a Web-based online catalog
   b. By searching on the Internet via a Web crawler such as Alta Vista or Yahoo!
   c. By going directly to your institution's Web site and browsing the finding aids
   d. By using a search engine at your Web site

4. Determine what resources you will need in order to be able to create EAD-encoded finding aids and publish them on the Web.

   a. What staffing will you need?

   b. What training for that staff will be needed?

   c. What technical support will you need? If not available within your repository, is there another unit within the larger institution that can lend expertise, or can you join a consortium that is already using SGML/XML applications? Is there a possibility of joint systems development or of sharing resources and expertise?

   d. What documentation will you need to acquire, and how many copies?
      - EAD DTD files or recompiled versions of the DTD for specific software applications (.rls file for Author/Editor, .lgc file for WordPerfect)
      - *EAD Tag Library*
      - *EAD Application Guidelines*

- Encoding guidelines for consortial activity

e. What local conventions will you need to develop?
   - Standard format that all your finding aids will follow
   - Standard ways of entering data into specific elements
   - Stylesheets to control display of your finding aids
   - Authoritative forms for search terms not covered by standard authority sources

f. What software might you need to create and publish new encoded finding aids? (No one site will need all of these.)
   - SGML/XML authoring package
   - Word processing software with SGML/XML capabilities or add-on conversion programs
   - Database
   - SGML to HTML converter or HTML authoring tool
   - Conversion tools such as perl scripts, macros
   - SGML/XML parser
   - SGML/XML browser
   - Stylesheet authoring software
   - Search engine

g. What hardware will you need to create and publish your finding aids?
   - Computer workstation
   - Local network connection
   - Internet connection
   - Backup mechanism
   - Server
   - Printer

h. How will you handle quality control?

i. How will encoded finding aids be maintained and updated?

j. How will you handle server maintenance and troubleshooting?

5. Analyze the costs associated with each of the processes above.

   a. Which costs can be covered under your existing budgetary structure?
   b. Which costs represent new areas of expenditure? Which are one-time costs, and which will be ongoing?
   c. Which costs are likely to diminish over time, and which will increase?
   d. Which costs might be covered by external funding, such as from grants?

e. Are there any hidden costs that need to be examined further?
f. Are there likely to be any cost savings in other areas as a result of EAD implementation?

# Appendix E

# EXAMPLES

Each repository implementing EAD must determine how it will use the variety of available EAD elements to encode descriptive data about its collections. You will make these decisions based on a variety of factors, such as your existing descriptive practices and the type of information you typically record about collections; national or format-based standards (such as RAD, APPM, or *Graphic Materials*); and international standards such as ISAD(G).

These *Guidelines* stress the need for *consistency* both in the selection of the minimum set of EAD tags you will include in your finding aids and in the creation of descriptive data content for those tags. All three of the finding aids in this appendix incorporate the minimum finding aid elements recommended in appendix A. You will find it beneficial to make decisions regarding minimum data components and content consistency early in your encoding project, both to increase ease of future data modification and give yourself greater flexibility in how you can present data to end users.

## Example 1

Example 1 describes a collection of personal papers at the collection, series/subseries, file, and (in some cases) item levels, using the "combined" <dsc> approach to emphasize the hierarchical nature of this descriptive information. It uses nested components at the file level for economy of keying, and it utilizes the LEVEL attribute throughout in order to record unambiguously how nested components "belong" to each other at each level. It also encodes containment information (box and folder numbering) within each individual <c0x> component below the series/subseries level. Most repositories will make decisions about how to encode containment information based on the parameters of the system within which they will deliver their encoded finding aids to end users.

In the provision of LABEL attribute values and <head> tags, as well as in all <eadheader> and <frontmatter> data, this example from the University of California at Irvine adheres to the *Encoded Archival Description Retrospective Conversion Guidelines*[130] used by the Online Archive of California. Repositories will be guided in their decisions regarding the use of LABEL attributes and <head> elements by local or union database capabilities of systems or stylesheets to supply this information.

The <?filetitle> processing instruction immediately preceeding the <ead> start-tag in this example is used to provide standardized alphabetized results lists in both the Online Archive of California and the California Digital Library user interfaces.

---

[130] Available at: <http://sunsite.berkeley.edu/amher/upguide.html>.

```
<!DOCTYPE ead PUBLIC "-//Society of American Archivists//DTD ead.dtd
(Encoded Archival Description (EAD) Version 1.0)//EN" [
<!ENTITY hdr-cu-i-spcoll PUBLIC "-//University of California,
Irvine::Library::Dept. of Special Collections//TEXT (eadheader: name
and address)//EN" "hdrcuisp.sgm" --hdrcuisp.sgm-->
<!ENTITY tp-cu-i-spcoll PUBLIC "-//University of California,
Irvine::Library::Dept. of Special Collections//TEXT (titlepage: name
and address)//EN" "tpcuisp.sgm" --tpcuisp.sgm-->
<!ENTITY ucseal PUBLIC "-//University of California,
Berkeley::Library//NONSGML (University of California seal)//EN" ""
NDATA gif>
]>
<?filetitle Phelps (Edna) Collection>
<ead>
<eadheader langencoding="ISO 639-2" audience="internal">
<eadid type="SGML catalog">PUBLIC "-//University of California,
Irvine::Library::Dept. of Special Collections//TEXT (US::CU-I::MS-
R43::Edna Phelps Collection)//EN" "r43.sgm"</eadid>
<filedesc>
<titlestmt>
<titleproper>Guide to the Edna Phelps Collection,
<date>ca. 1810-1981 (bulk ca.1880-ca. 1910)</date></titleproper>
<author>Processed by Lynette Stoudt; machine-readable finding aid
created by
William Landis</author></titlestmt>
<publicationstmt>
&hdr-cu-i-spcoll;
<date>&copy; 1999</date>
<p>The Regents of the University of California. All rights
reserved.</p>
</publicationstmt>
</filedesc>
<profiledesc>
<creation>Machine-readable finding aid derived from MS Word. Date of
source:
<date>February 1999.</date></creation>
<langusage>Description is in
<language>English.</language></langusage>
</profiledesc>
</eadheader>
<frontmatter>
<titlepage>
<titleproper>Guide to the Edna Phelps Collection</titleproper>
<num>Collection number: MS-R43</num>
<publisher>Department of Special Collections
<lb>The UCI Libraries
<lb>University of California
<lb>Irvine, California</publisher>
&tp-cu-i-spcoll;
<list type="deflist">
<defitem>
<label>Processed by: </label>
<item>Lynette Stoudt</item></defitem>
<defitem>
<label>Date Completed: </label>
<item>February 1999</item></defitem>
<defitem>
<label>Encoded by: </label>
<item>William Landis</item></defitem>
</list>
```

```
<p>&copy; 1999 The Regents of the University of California. All
rights reserved.</p>
</titlepage>
</frontmatter>
<archdesc level="collection" langmaterial="eng">
<did>
<head>Descriptive Summary</head>
<unittitle label="Title">Edna Phelps collection,
<unitdate type="inclusive">ca. 1810-1981 </unitdate>
<unitdate type="bulk">(bulk ca.1880-ca. 1910)</unitdate></unittitle>
<unitid label="Collection number" countrycode="US"
repositorycode="CUI">MS-R43</unitid>
<origination label="Creator">
<persname>Phelps, Edna W.</persname></origination>
<physdesc label="Extent">
<extent>Number of containers: 5 document boxes, 1 oversize
folder.</extent>
<extent>Linear feet: 2.1</extent></physdesc>
<repository label="Repository">
<corpname>University of California, Irvine. Library. Dept. of
Special Collections.</corpname>
<address>
<addressline>Irvine, California 92623-
9557</addressline></address></repository>
<abstract label="Abstract">
This collection contains photographs, correspondence, diaries, and
family documents representing the history of at least four
generations of the Phelps, Gulick, Davidson, Humiston, Gooch,
Huntley, Schultz, Willson, and Turner families from 1847-1978. The
bulk of the collection represents the Gulick family, ca. 1880-ca.
1920. Also included are topical files and biographical/subject
research files on various other families and
locations in Tustin and the vicinity, ca. 1810-ca. 1981.
</abstract>
</did>
<admininfo>
<head>Administrative Information</head>
<accessrestrict>
<head>Access</head>
<p>Collection is open for research.</p></accessrestrict>
<userestrict>
<head>Publication Rights</head>
<p>Property rights reside with the University of California.
Literary rights are retained by the creators of the records and
their heirs. For permissions to reproduce or to publish, please
contact the Head of Special Collections and University
Archives.</p></userestrict>
<prefercite>
<head>Preferred Citation</head>
<p>Edna Phelps Collection. MS-R43. Department of Special
Collections, The UCI Libraries, Irvine, California.</p></prefercite>
<acqinfo>
<head>Acquisition Information</head>
<p>Gift of Edna Phelps in 1971, 1981 and 1984.</p></acqinfo>
<processinfo>
<head>Processing History</head>
<p>Preliminary arrangement by Laura Clark Brown in 1997 included
preservation photocopying and discarding of original documents
(photocopies and newspaper clippings). Processed by Lynette Stoudt,
February 1999.</p></processinfo>
</admininfo>
```

<bioghist>
<head>Biography</head>

<p>Edna Phelps collected family photographs, correspondence, diaries, and family documents dating back four generations to her ancestors in Plainview, Illinois. She also collected materials relating to the history of Tustin and the surrounding vicinity from ca. 1810-1981.</p>

<p>In addition to these collecting activities, Edna Phelps edited family diaries and writings and wrote a short document, which is included in this collection, entitled, "One by One the Gulicks Came West." Edna also conducted interviews on early Southern California history with William Huntley (her distant cousin) and George Bartley, whose family settled in El Modena, California in 1882. In 1968-1969 she edited an unpublished work by Helen Gulick Huntley and William M. Huntley (distant cousins of hers) entitled "Tustin Scrapbook," which is located at the California State Library.</p>

<p>Aside from her fascination with family and Orange County history, little else is known about Edna Phelps. She is the great granddaughter of Martin Nickolas Gulick, who is the earliest member of her family represented in this collection.</p>

<p>Martin Nickolas Gulick (1815-1900) was married three times. His first marriage was in 1841 to Eleanor Welch (Edna Phelps' great grandmother) and resulted in three children: Mary Jane (Edna Phelps' grandmother), James Harvey and Eleanor Matilda. This brief marriage ended in 1848 with the death of Eleanor Welch Gulick. Family names of Edna Phelps' aunts, uncles and cousins by this marriage include: Barrett, Crouch, Davidson, Hewitt, Huntley, Munger, Page, Palmer, Reid, Ruggles, Schultz, Scovil, Thompson, Wichersham and Willson.
</p>

<p>Martin N. Gulick's second marriage took place in 1850 to Jane Vanarsdall. They had no children, and she died in 1857.</p>

<p>His third marriage to Annis C. Phelps occurred in 1860 and resulted in the birth of five daughters: Sadie, Alice, Olive, Hattie and another who died in early childhood. Only two of their daughters married, and as far as the information in this collection recounts, no grandchildren survived early childhood. Annis and her daughters, who corresponded through much of the latter part of the 19th century, generated much of the Gulick correspondence in this collection, with topics ranging from describing dress patterns to discussions of living conditions.</p>

<p>The marriage of Martin and Annis Gulick resulted in the meeting and courtship of Mary Jane Gulick (Edna Phelps' grandmother) and Louis Ransom Phelps (half-brother of Annis C. Phelps). Ultimately Mary and Louis were married, at which time Mary was disowned by her father for unknown reasons. The banished couple lived in Jerseyville, Illinois for many years with very few ties to the Gulick family. Their first born (of twelve children) was Ernest Phelps, Edna Phelps' father. Edna may have spent a portion of her childhood in Southern California, as documents in this collection indicate that her grandparents followed her parents there in 1904, settling in Pasadena. Many photographs of the Phelps family are included in this collection.</p>

<p>Most of the Gulick family began moving West during the railroad rate wars that prompted a boom in ca. 1880, sending many Midwesterners to California. Work opportunities and a reduced cost of living were just two of the attractions that appealed to the Gulicks. However, the most attractive aspect of the West seems to have been the weather. As Eleanor Davidson (Edna Phelps' aunt) said in early 1888 as she arrived in San Bernardino, California, by train from Illinois, "I could hardly believe we were in the land of summer

```
till the girls went out and seen flowers and oranges in abundance
and it was so warm."</p>
<p>Many of the Gulicks settled in Orange County and the surrounding
vicinities. Their occupations included orchard fumigation, walnut
production, and preaching. One cousin was known as the jack-of-all-
trades, moving his family around as work became available in various
cities.</p>
<p>By the 1920s, the point at which the bulk of the material in this
collection ends, a network of Edna Phelps' relatives, all
descendents of the Gulicks, were well established in many areas of
Southern California.</p>
</bioghist>
<scopecontent>
<head>Scope and Content</head>
<p>This collection contains photographs, correspondence, diaries,
and family documents representing the history of at least four
generations of the Phelps, Gulick, Davidson, Humiston, Gooch,
Huntley, Schultz, Willson, and Turner families from 1847-1978. The
bulk of the collection represents the Gulick family, ca. 1880-ca.
1920. Also included are topical files and biographical/subject
research files on other various families and locations in Tustin and
the vicinity, ca. 1810-ca. 1981.</p>
<p>Because some of this collection's original material resides at
other institutions (e.g., Bowers Museum, Tustin Area Museum, Western
Association for the Advancement of Local History) or was obtained
from outside research sources, many items are photocopies of
originals. Where the location of an original is known, it has been
noted on the photocopies.</p>
<p>According to the Special Collections collection file, the
Research Files were created by Helen Gulick Huntley. They are made
up of both handwritten and typed notes, many of which were generated
in ca. 1960. Also included in this collection is a typescript
biography on Columbus Tustin by Helen Gulick Huntley.</p>
</scopecontent>
<controlaccess>
<head>Indexing Terms</head>
<p>The following terms are used in the indexing for this collection
in the University of California, Irvine's ANTPAC public access
catalog.</p>
<controlaccess>
<head>Subjects</head>
<persname source="lcnaf">Phelps, Edna W.--Archives.</persname>
<geogname source="lcnaf">Orange County (Calif.)--Archival
resources.</geogname>
<famname source="lcsh">Gulick family--Archival resources.</famname>
<famname source="lcsh">Phelps family--Archival resources.</famname>
<geogname source="lcnaf">Tustin (Calif.)--Archival
resources.</geogname>
</controlaccess>
<controlaccess>
<head>Additional Contributors</head>
<persname source="lcnaf">Huntley, Helen Gulick.</persname>
</controlaccess>
</controlaccess>
<add>
<relatedmaterial>
<head>Related Collections</head>
<p>The following collections in Special Collections at the UCI
Libraries contain related materials:
<list>
<item>
```

```
<archref>
<unitid>MS-R24</unitid>,
<unittitle>Alice Gulick Gooch Photographs</unittitle>
<note><p>(Step-great aunt of Edna Phelps by Martin N. Gulick's third
marriage)</p></note>
</archref></item>
<item>
<archref>
<unitid>MS-R26</unitid>,
<unittitle>Quinn and Jesse Gulick Photographs</unittitle>
<note><p>(Second cousins of Edna Phelps by Martin N. Gulick's first
marriage)</p></note>
</archref></item>
</list></p></relatedmaterial>
</add>
<dsc type="combined">
<head>Container List</head>
<c01 level="series">
<did>
<unittitle>Series 1. Photographs, <unitdate type="inclusive">1855-
1967.</unitdate></unittitle>
<physdesc>
<extent>0.6 linear ft.</extent></physdesc>
</did>
<scopecontent>
<p>This series includes black and white photographs only, unless
otherwise noted on the container list, and is organized in two
subseries.</p></scopecontent>
<c02 level="subseries">
<did>
<unittitle>Subseries 1.1. People, <unitdate type="inclusive">1855-
1967.</unitdate></unittitle>
<physdesc>
<extent>0.4 linear ft.</extent></physdesc>
</did>
<scopecontent>
<p>This subseries includes photographs of family members, both
individual and groups, school classes and friends of the family. It
is composed primarily of Phelps and Gulick family material and is
arranged alphabetically by surname or the name of the place or
institution documented.</p></scopecontent>
<c03 level="file">
<did>
<container type="box">1</container>
<container type="folder">1</container>
<unittitle><famname>Bartley Family</famname>, <unitdate
type="inclusive">1882-1905 </unitdate></unittitle>
</did>
</c03>
<c03 level="file">
<did>
<container type="box">1</container>
<container type="folder">2</container>
<unittitle><persname>Burston, Selina</persname>, <unitdate
type="single">1891</unitdate></unittitle>
</did>
</c03>
<c03 level="file">
<did>
<container type="box">1</container>
<container type="folder">3</container>
```

```
<unittitle><famname>Carson Family</famname>, <unitdate
type="single">1897</unitdate></unittitle>
</did>
</c03>
<c03 level="file">
<did>
<container type="box">1</container>
<container type="folder">4</container>
<unittitle><persname>Chestnutwood, Mrs. A. J.</persname>, <unitdate
type="single">1870</unitdate></unittitle>
</did>
</c03>
<c03 level="file">
<did>
<container type="box">1</container>
<container type="folder">5</container>
<unittitle><famname>Davidson Family</famname>, <unitdate
type="single">1910</unitdate></unittitle>
</did>
</c03>
<c03 level="file">
<did>
<container type="box">1</container>
<container type="folder">6</container>
<unittitle><corpname>El Modena Elementary School</corpname>,
<unitdate type="single">ca. 1892</unitdate>, <unitdate
type="single">1893</unitdate>, <unitdate
type="single">1921</unitdate></unittitle>
</did>
</c03>
<c03 level="file">
<did>
<container type="box">1</container>
<container type="folder">7</container>
<unittitle><famname>Gooch Family</famname>, <unitdate
type="inclusive">1898-1908</unitdate></unittitle>
</did>
</c03>
<c03 level="file">
<did>
<container type="box">1</container>
<container type="folder">8-12</container>
<unittitle><famname>Gulick Family</famname>, <unitdate
type="inclusive">ca. 1875-1915</unitdate>, <unitdate
type="single">1967</unitdate></unittitle>
<physdesc>
<extent>(5 folders)</extent></physdesc>
</did>
</c03>

... [and so forth]

<c03 level="file">
<did>
<container type="box">1</container>
<container type="folder">33</container>
<unittitle>Unidentified, <unitdate>undated</unitdate></unittitle>
</did>
<note>
<p>(Includes 2 <genreform>tintypes</genreform>)</p>
</note>
```

```xml
</c03>
</c02>
<c02 level="subseries">
<did>
<unittitle>Subseries 1.2. Places, <unitdate type="inclusive">1890-
1920.</unitdate></unittitle>
<physdesc>
<extent>0.2 linear ft.</extent></physdesc>
</did>
<scopecontent>
<p>This subseries includes photographs of places in Orange County
and other California locations, as well as images of Kansas,
Oklahoma and Illinois. It is arranged alphabetically by place name
within Orange County, then California, then the rest of the United
States.</p></scopecontent>
<c03 level="file">
<did>
<container type="box">2</container>
<container type="folder">1-5</container>
<unittitle><geogname>Orange County</geogname></unittitle>
</did>
<c04 level="file">
<did>
<container type="box">2</container>
<container type="folder">1</container>
<unittitle><corpname>Irvine Ranch</corpname>, <unitdate
type="single">ca. 1895</unitdate></unittitle>
</did>
</c04>
<c04 level="file">
<did>
<container type="box">2</container>
<container type="folder">2</container>
<unittitle><geogname>Laguna Beach</geogname> and <geogname>San Juan
Capistrano</geogname> Mission,
<unitdate>undated</unitdate></unittitle>
</did>
</c04>
<c04 level="file">
<did>
<container type="box">2</container>
<container type="folder">3</container>
<unittitle><geogname>Orange</geogname>, <unitdate type="single">ca.
1905</unitdate>, <unitdate type="single">1912</unitdate></unittitle>
</did>
</c04>
<c04 level="file">
<did>
<container type="box">2</container>
<container type="folder">4</container>
<unittitle><geogname>Santa Ana</geogname>, <unitdate
type="single">ca. 1910</unitdate></unittitle>
</did>
</c04>
<c04 level="file">
<did>
<container type="box">2</container>
<container type="folder">5</container>
<unittitle><geogname>Tustin</geogname>, <unitdate
type="inclusive">ca. 1890-1920</unitdate></unittitle>
</did>
```

```
</c04>
</c03>
<c03 level="file">
<did>
<container type="box">2</container>
<container type="folder">6</container>
<unittitle>California locations</unittitle>
</did>
<c04 level="item">
<did>
<container type="box">2</container>
<container type="folder">6</container>
<unittitle><corpname>Buena Vista Rancho</corpname>,
<unitdate>undated</unitdate></unittitle>
</did>
</c04>
<c04 level="item">
<did>
<container type="box">2</container>
<container type="folder">6</container>
<unittitle><geogname>Corona</geogname>, <unitdate type="single">ca.
1906</unitdate></unittitle>
</did>
</c04>

... [and so forth]

<c04 level="item">
<did>
<container type="box">2</container>
<container type="folder">6</container>
<unittitle><geogname>Ukiah</geogname>,
<unitdate>undated</unitdate></unittitle>
</did>
</c04>
</c03>
<c03 level="file">
<did>
<container type="box">2</container>
<container type="folder">7</container>
<unittitle>United States</unittitle>
</did>
<c04 level="item">
<did>
<container type="box">2</container>
<container type="folder">7</container>
<unittitle><geogname>Kansas</geogname>,
<unitdate>undated</unitdate></unittitle>
</did>
</c04>
<c04 level="item">
<did>
<container type="box">2</container>
<container type="folder">7</container>
<unittitle><geogname>Plainview, Illinois</geogname>, <unitdate
type="single">ca. 1890</unitdate></unittitle>
</did>
</c04>
<c04 level="item">
<did>
<container type="box">2</container>
```

```
<container type="folder">7</container>
<unittitle><geogname>Tulsa, Oklahoma</geogname>,
<unitdate>undated</unitdate></unittitle>
</did>
</c04>
</c03>
<c03 level="file">
<did>
<container type="box">2</container>
<container type="folder">8</container>
<unittitle>Unidentified, <unitdate>undated</unitdate></unittitle>
</did>
</c03>
</c02>
</c01>
<c01 level="series">
<did>
<unittitle>Series 2. Correspondence, <unitdate
type="inclusive">1852-1978. </unitdate></unittitle>
<physdesc>
<extent>0.7 linear ft.</extent></physdesc>
</did>
<scopecontent>
<p>This series consists of both handwritten original letters and
photocopies of originals. Some files also contain typescript
transcriptions of original correspondence with notes by Edna Phelps
that describe relations of people and places mentioned in the
correspondence. The series is arranged alphabetically by surname of
the author.</p></scopecontent>
<c02 level="file">
<did>
<container type="box">3</container>
<container type="folder">1</container>
<unittitle><persname>Alexander, M.A.</persname>, <unitdate
type="single">1877</unitdate></unittitle>
</did>
</c02>
<c02 level="file">
<did>
<container type="box">3</container>
<container type="folder">2</container>
<unittitle><persname>Barr, Maria</persname>, <unitdate
type="single">1885</unitdate>, <unitdate
type="single">1902</unitdate></unittitle>
</did>
</c02>
<c02 level="file">
<did>
<container type="box">3</container>
<container type="folder">3</container>
<unittitle><persname>Bartlett, Lanier</persname>, <unitdate
type="single">1958</unitdate></unittitle>
</did>
</c02>
<c02 level="file">
<did>
<container type="box">3</container>
<container type="folder">4</container>
<unittitle><persname>Carson, Harlan Page</persname>, <unitdate
type="inclusive">1886-1932</unitdate></unittitle>
</did>
```

```
</c02>
<c02 level="file">
<did>
<container type="box">3</container>
<container type="folder">5</container>
<unittitle><persname>Cochran, Winona Barr</persname>, <unitdate
type="single">1902</unitdate></unittitle>
</did>
</c02>

... [and so forth]

<c02 level="file">
<did>
<container type="box">4</container>
<container type="folder">16</container>
<unittitle><persname>Utt, C.E.</persname>Grower and Shipper, Tustin,
California, <unitdate type="single">1904</unitdate></unittitle>
</did>
</c02>
<c02 level="file">
<did>
<container type="box">4</container>
<container type="folder">17</container>
<unittitle>Unidentified authors, <unitdate type="inclusive">1888-
1892</unitdate></unittitle>
</did>
</c02>
</c01>
<c01 level="series">
<did>
<unittitle>Series 3. Topical material, <unitdate
type="inclusive">1847-1972. </unitdate></unittitle>
<physdesc>
<extent>0.3 linear ft.</extent></physdesc>
</did>
<scopecontent>
<p>This series contains diaries of various family members,
historical writings about the Gulick and Tustin families, and
ephemera. Much of this material consists of photocopies of
originals; in some instances the legibility of these reproductions
is quite poor. The series is arranged alphabetically by surname of
the author when available, otherwise by title or genre of
materials.</p></scopecontent>
<c02 level="file">
<did>
<container type="box">4</container>
<container type="folder">18</container>
<unittitle><persname>Bartley, George</persname>. Transcripts of
interviews by Edna Phelps, <unitdate type="inclusive">1971-
1972</unitdate></unittitle>
</did>
</c02>
<c02 level="file">
<did>
<container type="box">4</container>
<container type="folder">19</container>
<unittitle><persname>Davidson, Eleanor Gulick</persname>. "Short
diary of a journey from Plainview, Illinois to Santa Ana, California
1887-1888," transcript by Edna Phelps, <unitdate
type="single">October 1971</unitdate></unittitle>
```

```
</did>
</c02>
<c02 level="file">
<did>
<container type="box">4</container>
<container type="folder">20</container>
<unittitle><persname>Davidson, Sue and Laura</persname>. "Letters of
Sue and Laura Davidson to Aunt Ollie and Aunt Hattie (Gulick),"
selected and edited by Edna Phelps and Ellen Lee, <unitdate
type="single">1981</unitdate></unittitle>
</did>
</c02>
<c02 level="file">
<did>
<container type="box">4</container>
<container type="folder">21</container>
<unittitle>Deeds and assessment for taxes, Orange County, <unitdate
type="inclusive">1866-1875</unitdate></unittitle>
</did>
</c02>

... [and so forth]

<c02 level="file">
<did>
<container type="box">5</container>
<container type="folder">11</container>
<unittitle>World's Columbian Commission Citrus Fruit Award,
International Exposition, Chicago, <unitdate
type="single">1893</unitdate>. Awarded to <persname>Martin N.
Gulick</persname>. </unittitle>
<note>
<p>ORIGINAL AWARD REMOVED TO XOS FOLDER</p>
</note>
</did>
</c02>
<c02 level="file">
<did>
<container type="box">5</container>
<container type="folder">12</container>
<unittitle>Writings, unidentified,
<unitdate>undated</unitdate></unittitle>
</did>
</c02>
</c01>
<c01 level="series">
<did>
<unittitle>Series 4. Research files, <unitdate type="inclusive">ca.
1810-1981.</unitdate></unittitle>
<physdesc>
<extent>0.3 linear ft.</extent></physdesc>
</did>
<scopecontent>
<p>This series includes historical notes on residents, locations,
and living conditions in Tustin and the vicinity. It is organized in
two subseries.</p></scopecontent>
<c02 level="subseries">
<did>
<unittitle>Subseries 4.1. Biographical notes, <unitdate
type="inclusive">ca. 1810-ca. 1960.</unitdate></unittitle>
<physdesc>
```

```
<extent>0.2 linear ft.</extent></physdesc>
</did>
<scopecontent>
<p>This subseries contains brief historical notes including birth,
death and marriage dates, occupations and other information on past
Tustin residents. The majority of the notes are by Helen Gulick
Huntley; other miscellaneous biographical notes located throughout
this collection have been filed here as well. The subseries is
arranged in alphabetical order by surname of the subject
individual.</p></scopecontent>
<c03 level="file">
<did>
<container type="box">5</container>
<container type="folder">13</container>
<unittitle>Adams-Artz</unittitle>
</did>
</c03>
<c03 level="file">
<did>
<container type="box">5</container>
<container type="folder">14</container>
<unittitle>Ballard-Butterfield</unittitle>
</did>
</c03>

... [and so forth]

<c03 level="file">
<did>
<container type="box">5</container>
<container type="folder">34</container>
<unittitle>Wall-Zeilian</unittitle>
</did>
</c03>
</c02>
<c02 level="subseries">
<did>
<unittitle>Subseries 4.2. Subject notes, <unitdate
type="inclusive">ca. 1850-1981.</unitdate></unittitle>
<physdesc>
<extent>0.1 linear ft.</extent></physdesc>
</did>
<scopecontent>
<p>This subseries includes brief historical notes on locations
(e.g., banks, churches,
houses, etc.) and living conditions (e.g., wages, recreation, real
estate, irrigation,
etc.) in Tustin and vicinity and is arranged alphabetically by
subject.</p></scopecontent>
<c03 level="file">
<did>
<container type="box">5</container>
<container type="folder">35</container>
<unittitle>African-American residents</unittitle>
</did>
</c03>
<c03 level="file">
<did>
<container type="box">5</container>
<container type="folder">35</container>
<unittitle>Banks</unittitle>
```

```
</did>
</c03>
<c03 level="file">
<did>
<container type="box">5</container>
<container type="folder">35</container>
<unittitle>Buildings</unittitle>
</did>
</c03>

... [and so forth]

<c03 level="file">
<did>
<container type="box">5</container>
<container type="folder">37</container>
<unittitle>Water works</unittitle>
</did>
</c03>
<c03 level="file">
<did>
<container type="box">5</container>
<container type="folder">37</container>
<unittitle>Wood Canyon cave</unittitle>
</did>
</c03>
</c02>
</c01>
</dsc>
</archdesc>
</ead>
```

## Example 2

This brief inventory illustrates a finding aid structure and an encoding scheme that was strongly influenced by the repository's analysis of user needs and presentation requirements.[131] A core set of the basic <archdesc> data elements, in a standard order, is included in each of the repository's finding aids: <did>, including an <abstract>, <bioghist>, <scopecontent>, <organization>, <controlaccess>, and <admininfo>. These elements are presented in a sequence that researchers will find useful when determining the relevance of a particular collection to their needs.

Extensive use of <head> and <thead> elements and LABEL attributes provides strong visual marking of the data elements when presented on the screen or on paper, serving both as a navigation aid for the user and as an education device for the new researcher. In the same vein, explanatory notes for users are included in <physloc>, <controlaccess>, and <dsc>. This repository has incorporated into its EAD finding aids its longstanding practice of including all access points used in the collection's online catalog record. Finally, the use of the "combined" <dsc> model emphasizes the hierarchical nature of the archival materials.

This example is XML compliant and uses the EAD DTD in XML mode, incorporating the DTD modifications described in section 4.3.2.

```
<?xml  version="1.0" standalone="no"?>
<!DOCTYPE ead PUBLIC "-//Society of American Archivists//DTD ead.dtd
(Encoded Archival Description (EAD) Version 1.0)//EN" "ead.dtd"
[
<!ENTITY % eadnotat PUBLIC "-//Society of American Archivists//DTD
eadnotat.ent (Encoded Archival Description (EAD) Notation
Declarations Version 1.0)//EN" "eadnotat.ent">
%eadnotat;
<!ENTITY mhslogo SYSTEM "mhslogo.gif" NDATA gif>
]>
<ead audience="external">
<eadheader audience="internal" langencoding="ISO 639-2">
<eadid systemid="MnHi" source="DLC" type="url">39213.xml</eadid>
<filedesc>
<titlestmt>
<titleproper>An Inventory of the Game Laws Violation Records of the
Minnesota Game and Fish Department at the Minnesota Historical
Society</titleproper>
<author>Written by Lydia Lucas.</author>
</titlestmt>
<publicationstmt>
<publisher>Minnesota Historical Society, St. Paul, MN</publisher>
<date>1996</date>
</publicationstmt>
</filedesc>
<profiledesc>
<creation>Finding aid encoded by Kris Kiesling,
```

[131] For a more detailed description of the process used to develop an encoding template at the Minnesota Historical Society, see Dennis Meissner, "First Things First: Reengineering Finding Aids for Implementation of EAD," *American Archivist* 60 (fall 1997): 372-387.

```xml
<date>January, 1998.</date>
</creation>
<langusage>
<language>Finding written in English.</language>
</langusage>
</profiledesc>
</eadheader>
<archdesc type="inventory" level="subgrp" langmaterial="eng">
<did>
<head>OVERVIEW OF THE RECORDS</head>
<repository label="Repository:">
<corpname>Minnesota Historical Society</corpname>
</repository>
<origination label="Creator:">
<corpname>Minnesota. Game and Fish Department</corpname>
</origination>
<unitid label="Collection Number:" countrycode="US"
repositorycode="MnHi">39213</unitid>
<unittitle label="Title:">Game laws violation records,
<unitdate label="Dates:" type="inclusive">1908-1928</unitdate>
</unittitle>
<abstract label="Abstract:">Records of prosecutions for and seizures
of property resulting from violation of the state's hunting
laws.</abstract>
<physdesc label="Quantity:">2.25 cu. ft. (7 v. and 1 folder in 3
boxes)</physdesc>
<physloc label="Location:">See Detailed Description section for box
location</physloc>
</did>
<bioghist>
<head>ADMINISTRATIVE HISTORY OF THE DEPARTMENT</head>
<p>These records were created by two successive agencies:  the Board
of Game and Fish Commissioners of Minnesota (1891-1915) and the Game
and Fish Department (1915-1931). Both had common responsibilities:
protection, propagation, and breeding of game and fish species;
gathering statistics; and enforcing game and fish laws.  They also
operated the state fish hatcheries.  The Department became the
Division of Game and Fish in the newly organized Conservation
Department in 1931.</p>
</bioghist>
<scopecontent>
<head>SCOPE AND CONTENTS OF THE RECORDS</head>
<p>Records of prosecutions for violations of state game and fish
laws; and registers of items (game, fish, firearms, and/or
equipment) confiscated in the field from people caught violating the
laws.</p>
</scopecontent>
<organization>
<head>ORGANIZATION OF THE RECORDS</head>
<p>These records are organized into the following sections:</p>
<p>Record of Prosecutions, 1916-1927.</p>
<p>Seizure Records, 1908-1928.</p>
</organization>
<odd>
<head>FINDING AIDS</head>
<p>A printed version of this inventory is available in the
repository; filed under Game and Fish Commission.</p>
</odd>
<controlaccess>
<head>INDEX TERMS</head>
```

```
<note><p>These records are indexed under the following headings in
the catalog of the Minnesota Historical Society.  Researchers
wishing to find related materials should search the catalog under
these index terms.</p></note>
<controlaccess>
<head>Organizations:</head>
<corpname>Board of Game and Fish Commissioners of
Minnesota.</corpname>
</controlaccess>
<controlaccess>
<head>Topics:</head>
<subject>Fishery law and legislation--Minnesota.</subject>
<subject>Game-law--Minnesota.</subject>
<subject>Law enforcement--Minnesota.</subject>
</controlaccess>
</controlaccess>
<admininfo>
<head>ADMINISTRATIVE INFORMATION</head>
<accessrestrict>
<head>Restrictions:</head>
<p>Unrestricted access.</p>
</accessrestrict>
<acqinfo>
<head>Accession Information:</head>
<p>These records were acquired from the Dept. of Natural Resources
in 1976 as accession 1976.32.</p>
</acqinfo>
<processinfo>
<head>Processing Information:</head>
<p>These records were organized and cataloged in 1977 by Lydia
Lucas.</p>
</processinfo>
</admininfo>
<dsc type="combined">
<head>DETAILED DESCRIPTION OF THE RECORDS</head>
<c01 level="series" id="s01">
<did>
<unittitle>Record of Prosecutions,<unitdate>1916-
1927.</unitdate></unittitle>
<physdesc>3 volumes.</physdesc>
</did>
<scopecontent>
<p>Information provided in each entry:  date of report, name and
address of person arrested, location where offense was committed,
date of arrest, nature of offense, name of judge or justice, result
of trial, amounts of fine and court costs, number of days served if
jailed, name of warden, and occasional added remarks.  Types of
offenses included hunting or fishing out of season or in
unauthorized places, exceeding catch or bag limits, taking
undersized fish, illegal fishing practices such as gill-netting or
dynamiting, illegal hunting practices such as night-lighting,
killing non-game birds, fishing or hunting without a license, and
hunting-related offenses against persons such as fraud and
assault.</p>
</scopecontent>
<thead>
<row>
<entry>Location</entry>
<entry>Box</entry>
<entry>Contents</entry>
</row>
```

```
</thead>
<c02>
<did>
<physloc>112.I.8.1B-1</physloc>
<container type="box">1</container>
<unittitle>August 1916-June 1922</unittitle>
</did>
</c02>
<c02>
<did>
<unittitle>July 1922-December 1926</unittitle>
</did>
</c02>
<c02>
<did>
<unittitle>January-December 1927</unittitle>
</did>
</c02>
</c01>
<c01 level="series" id="s02">
<did>
<unittitle>Seizure Records,
<unitdate>December 1908-January 1928.</unitdate>
</unittitle>
<physdesc>4 volumes and 1 folder.</physdesc>
</did>
<scopecontent>
<p>Information in each entry:  number (sequential for each year),
date, warden's name, location, from whom seized, reason for seizure,
consignor and consignee when illegal shipments if meat were
involved, itemization of articles seized (fish, meat, firearms,
and/or equipment), disposition of seized materials, purchaser if
sold, amount received, and occasional other remarks.</p>
</scopecontent>
<thead>
<row>
<entry>Location</entry>
<entry>Box</entry>
<entry>Contents</entry>
</row>
</thead>
<c02>
<did>
<physloc>112.I.8.1B-2</physloc>
<container type="box">2</container>
<unittitle>December 1908-July 1917</unittitle>
</did>
</c02>
<c02>
<did><unittitle>August 1917-October
1923</unittitle>
</did>
</c02>
<c02>
<did>
<physloc>112.I.8.2F-1</physloc>
<container type="box">3</container>
<unittitle>October 1923-June 1925</unittitle>
</did>
</c02>
<c02>
```

```
<did>
<unittitle>July 1925-June 1927</unittitle>
</did>
<note>
<p>Includes an unexplained recapitulation of selected  seizures for
Oct. 1923 to 1925.  May have been people delinquent in paying
fines.</p>
</note>
</c02>
<c02>
<did>
<unittitle>July 1927-January 1928.</unittitle>
<physdesc>1 folder.</physdesc>
</did>
<note>
<p>pp. 1-37, removed from an otherwise empty volume.</p>
</note>
</c02>
</c01>
</dsc>
</archdesc>
</ead>
```

## Example 3

Example 3 represents the descriptive practices used by the Public Record Office of the United Kingdom for governmental records. It describes a fonds and one of its subordinate series. The standard followed in determining the EAD elements that would be used in this description was the *PROCAT Cataloguing Guidelines* (1998), which are based on ISAD(G) and are internal to the Public Record Office. This example incorporates at both the fonds and series levels the minimum five descriptive elements recommended by ISAD(G). It also provides, at both levels, a selection of information in <admininfo> elements based on the kinds of information the repository normally captures.

```
<!DOCTYPE ead PUBLIC "-//Society of American Archivists//DTD ead.dtd
(Encoded Archival Description (EAD) Version 1.0)//EN" "ead.dtd" [
<!ENTITY prologo SYSTEM "prologo.gif" NDATA gif>
]>
<ead>
<eadheader>
<eadid>es.sgm</eadid>
<filedesc>
<titlestmt>
<titleproper>Records of the Atomic Weapons Research
Establishment</titleproper>
</titlestmt>
<editionstmt>
<edition>Edition 1</edition>
</editionstmt>
<publicationstmt>
<publisher>Public Record Office, Kew</publisher>
<date>1998</date>
</publicationstmt>
</filedesc>
<profiledesc>
<creation>Finding aid created by PRO editorial staff, December
1998.</creation>
<langusage>
<language>English</language>
</langusage>
</profiledesc>
</eadheader>
<frontmatter>
<titlepage>
<titleproper>Records of the Atomic Weapons Research
Establishment</titleproper>
<publisher>
<extptr entityref="prologo">
</publisher>
<publisher>Public Record Office</publisher>
<date>1998</date>
<p>&copy; This Finding Aid is Crown Copyright</p>
</titlepage>
</frontmatter>
<archdesc level="fonds" legalstatus="public" langmaterial="eng"
id="ES">
<did>
<unitid label="Reference" countrycode="GBR"
repositorycode="067">ES</unitid>
```

```
<unittitle>Records of the Atomic Weapons Research
Establishment</unittitle>
<origination label="Creator(s)">
<corpname>Atomic Weapons Research Establishment, 1954-
1973</corpname>
</origination>
<unitdate label="Covering Dates">1944-1986</unitdate>
<physdesc>
<extent>5</extent>
<genreform>series</genreform>
</physdesc>
<repository label="Held at">
<corpname>Public Record Office, Kew</corpname>
</repository>
<abstract>Records of the Atomic Weapons Research Establishment set
up in 1954 to carry out research into, and the testing of, Britain's
atomic weapons.</abstract>
</did>
<admininfo>
<accessrestrict>
<head>Access Conditions</head>
<p>Subject to 30 year closure unless otherwise stated</p>
</accessrestrict>
<acqinfo>
<head>Immediate Source of Acquisition</head>
<p>
<corpname>Ministry of Defence, 1947-, from 1994</corpname>
</p></acqinfo>
</admininfo>
<scopecontent>
<head>Scope and Content</head>
<p>Records of the Atomic Weapons Research Establishment set up in
1954 to carry out research into, and the testing of, Britain's
atomic weapons.</p>
<p>Files relating to the development of Aldermaston and to early
work there (Rowley Collection) are in ES 1. Reports on bombs (Bombs
(B) series) are in ES 2, reports on the structural effects of atomic
weapons (Effects (E) series) are in ES 3, reports on bomb trails
(Trials (T) series) are in ES 5, and Ordinary Reports are in ES
4.</p>
</scopecontent>
<bioghist>
<head>Administrative History</head>
<p>The Atomic Weapons Research Establishment was set up in the late
1940s by the Ministry of Supply. In 1950, the ministry took over the
site at Aldermaston for atomic weapons work. Other research on the
British atomic weapons programme, carried out at the Armament
Research Establishment in Kent, was transferred to Aldermaston in
the same year. In 1954, the Aldermaston site was constituted as the
headquarters of the Weapons Group of the  United Kingdom Atomic
Energy Authority by the UK Atomic Energy Authority Act 1954.
Outstations to the Aldermaston HQ were at Woolwich Common, Foulness
and Orfordness.</p>
<p>The functions of the Atomic Weapons Research Establishment were
scientific and technical research into atomic weapons and the
testing of Britain's atomic bombs.</p>
<p>Early tests were carried out in Australia and the Pacific, and
after 1958, in accordance with the 1958 US/UK Agreement for Co-
operation in the use of Atomic Energy for Mutual Defence Purposes,
at the underground test site in Nevada USA</p>
```

```
<p> Under the Atomic Energy Authority (Weapons Group) Act 1973, the
Weapons Group became the responsibility of the Ministry of
Defence.</p>
</bioghist>
<add>
<relatedmaterial>
<head>Related Material</head>
<p>Records relating to atomic weapons testing can be found in ADM 1,
ADM 116, AIR 2, AIR20,  AIR 27, AVIA 65, DEFE 7 and WO 32.</p>
<p>Photocopies of evidence given to the Australian  Royal Commission
into United Kingdom Nuclear Weapons Testing in Australia are in DEFE
16.</p>
<p>Other material on UK Atomic Energy Research is in AB.</p>
</relatedmaterial>
</add>
<controlaccess>
<head>Index Terms</head>
<geogname>Aldermaston, Berkshire  SU 5965</geogname>
<geogname>United States of America</geogname>
<subject>Nuclear weapons</subject>
<subject>UK Atomic Energy Authority Act 1954 c32</subject>
<subject>Atomic Energy Authority (Weapons Group)  Act 1973
c4</subject>
<subject>US/UK Agreement for Co-operation in the use of Atomic
Energy for  Mutual Defence Purposes 1958</subject>
</controlaccess>
<dsc type="combined">
<c level="series" id="ES-c4">
<did>
<unitid label="Reference">ES 4</unitid>
<unitid label="Former Reference">Ordinary (O) Reports</unitid>
<unittitle>Atomic Weapons Research Establishment: Ordinary (O)
Reports</unittitle>
<unitdate label="Covering Dates">1953-1970</unitdate>
<physdesc>
<extent>1258</extent>
<genreform>reports, volumes</genreform>
</physdesc>
</did>
<admininfo>
<appraisal>
<head>Appraisal Information</head>
<p>The full set of reports has been preserved; where report numbers
are not present it is because reports were not issued.</p>
</appraisal>
<accruals>
<head>Accruals Information</head>
<p>Series is accruing.</p>
</accruals>
</admininfo>
<scopecontent>
<head>Scope and Content</head>
<p>The Ordinary (O) report series cover the research of most
divisions at AWRE and give an overall picture of work undertaken
each year.  They include fundamental research and instrumentation
except for weapons effects trials (ES 3) and overseas trials work
reported in the Trials (T) reports (ES 5).  Many pieces contain
photographs and plans.  The use of brackets in piece descriptions
denotes the area from which sensitive words have been removed.</p>
</scopecontent>
<arrangement><head>Arrangement</head>
```

```
<p>Numerical report series within each year.</p>
</arrangement>
<controlaccess>
<head>Index Terms</head>
<subject>Nuclear weapons</subject>
</controlaccess>
</c>
</dsc>
</archdesc>
</ead>
```

# Appendix F

# GLOSSARY

**Attribute:** Named properties of an element that may carry different values depending upon the context in which they occur. Attributes modify the meaning of the elements to which they apply. Examples of some EAD attributes include STATUS, LEVEL, and TYPE. Several attributes are available to effect character rendering, such as RENDER. Most EAD attributes are optional.

**Authoring Software:** Computer programs that assist in inserting, reading, and editing SGML tags. Sophisticated authoring software also can enforce the rules of a DTD. *See also* **Parser**.

**Cascading Style Sheets (CSS):** A style language that can control the appearance of HTML and XML documents by defining display features such as font types, color and size, as well as text formatting features such as indentions, margins, and tabular presentation. *See also* **Stylesheet.**

**Case Sensitivity:** A characteristic of computer software that considers the case of alphabetic characters to be significant. For example, a case sensitive search engine would not retrieve the character string "Encoding" if the search was entered as "encoding". In XML, tags are case-sensitive, and so all EAD tag names must be entered in lower case.

**CDATA:** *See* **Character Data (CDATA).**

**Character Data (CDATA):** Characters that appear in a part of an SGML document in which text is not parsed and markup is not recognized. This includes the values of an attribute whose content has been defined in a DTD as being character data, or the contents of a marked CDATA section of a document—one that has been delimited and identified as character data. CDATA is useful when it is desirable to pass data to an application without having to deal with the character set issues that would be introduced by parsing, such as when computer code is included within the text of a document. The XML specification uses the expression "character data" in a more general and slightly different way than SGML when it states that "All text that is not markup constitutes the character data of the document." *See also* **Parsable Character Data (PCDATA).**

**Computing Platform:** The type of computer hardware and software (the operating system and applications) being used, e.g., DOS/Windows, Macintosh, UNIX.

**Content Model:** In SGML, defines the structure of and types of elements and subelements contained within a DTD.

**Convention:** An agreed-upon usage, for example, of a term.

**Default Values:** Values that are supplied automatically by the system if the encoder of the finding aid does not specify an alternative value.

**Document Element:** The highest-level element in a DTD. In EAD, <ead> is the document element. (The term "root element" is sometimes used to refer to the document element, but this is incorrect SGML usage.)

**Document Instance:** *See* **Instance.**

**Document Style Semantics and Specification Language (DSSSL):** A language for preparing stylesheets that may be used to specify the formatting of SGML documents or transform them into other formats. An international standard (ISO/IEC 10179:1996). *See also* **Stylesheet**.

**Document Type Declaration:** Provides technical information to SGML authoring and publishing software about how the DTD and encoded document will use SGML.

**Document Type Definition (DTD):** The formal specifications and definitions of the structural elements and markup to be used in encoding specific types of documents in SGML.

**DSSSL:** *See* **Document Style Semantics and Specification Language (DSSSL).**

**EAD Instance:** *See* **Instance.**

**Editing Software:** *See* **Authoring Software.**

**Element:** A component of the structure defined by a Document Type Definition, identified in a document instance by descriptive markup, usually a start-tag <...> and an end-tag </...>.

**Element Name:** The full descriptive name given to each SGML element, e.g. Date of the Unit. *See also* **Tag Name.**

**Empty Element:** An element that contains neither PCDATA nor other elements.

**Entity:** An SGML convention that allows an encoder to specify in a Document Type Definition or in the Declaration Subset of an SGML instance an abbreviated name that serves as a substitute in the instance for something else, such as a block of boilerplate text, another document, or an image file.

**Extensible Markup Language (XML):** A simplified subset of SGML designed so that generic SGML might be served, received, and processed on the World Wide Web in the same way as HTML. XML retains the sophisticated data structuring and validation of SGML, while eliminating many of the options that complicate the development of SGML viewers.

**Extensible Style Language (XSL):** A language for expressing stylesheets which may be used to transform XML documents into other formats or to display XML documents in XML-capable browsers. *See also* **Stylesheet.**

**Formal Public Identifier (FPI):** A text string that serves as a structured citation to an SGML object such as an entity, a DTD, or an element. An FPI includes the name of its owner, the class of objects to which the associated item belongs (e.g., DTD, entity), an arbitrary description of the object, its language, and, optionally, its version. Public identifiers contrast with system identifiers that identify an SGML object by citing a system-specific characteristic, such as a URL or a file name that physically locates the object in a file storage system.

**Formatting Elements:** Generic elements that affect a document's appearance, such as Paragraph <p>, Emphasis (which carries the RENDER attribute for specifying display characteristics such as boldface or italics) <emph>, and Line Break <lb>.

**Header:** A set of SGML elements, such as the EAD Header <eadheader>, which record documentation (or "metadata") about the text itself and its encoding. May also refer to text encoded to appear at the top of each page of a document. Do not confuse with the EAD element Heading <head>, which is used to supply a heading for a block of text.

**HTML:** *See* **HyperText Markup Language (HTML).**

**Hyperlink:** Linking elements that provide nonlinear ways to move around and between digital documents, or to link to related objects such as image or audio files. *See also* **Linking Elements.**

**HyperText Markup Language (HTML):** An SGML-derived markup language used to create documents for World Wide Web applications. HTML encoding effects principally layout and visual representation, not intellectual or hierarchical aspects of document structure, such as those in EAD.

**Instance:** The text and tags (excluding the DTD and related files) of an individual SGML-encoded document, such as a single EAD-encoded finding aid. *See also* **SGML Document.**

**International Standards Organization (ISO):** The preeminent international standards-setting body, made up of representatives from countries worldwide, that oversees the development and ratification of many telecommunications and information-related standards.

**Internet:** A global "network of networks" originally developed by the U.S. Department of Defense and used predominantly for academic and research activities. Today it is also used for commerce, entertainment, and social and community interaction, much of which takes place on the World Wide Web, a service that is delivered via the Internet.

**Legacy Data:** Finding aids created prior to implementation of EAD. Such finding aids often must be restructured to some degree in order to fit within EAD's hierarchical structure and set of data elements.

**Linking Elements:** Elements that enable the creation of hypertext links within an SGML instance or from SGML instances to other digital objects. *See also* **Hyperlink.**

**Markup Language:** A formal way of annotating a document or collection of digital data in order to indicate the structure of the document or datafile and the contents of its data elements. This markup also serves to provide a computer with information about how to process and display marked-up documents.

**Metalanguage:** A set of rules that formally describes the syntax of a markup scheme. SGML is an example of a metalanguage, or in other words, it is a set of rules for establishing markup languages.

**Multimedia:** Digital materials, documents, or products, such as World Wide Web pages or CD-ROMs, that utilize any combination of text, numeric data, still and moving images, animation, sound, and graphics.

**Nesting:** The way in which SGML subelements may be contained within other elements to create a multilevel document. *See also* **Recursion.**

**Paragraph:** The basic unit of text within an SGML document.

**Parent Element:** An element that may contain other elements, referred to as subelements of the parent element. *See also* **Subelement.**

**Parser:** A computer program that checks any encoded document that begins with an SGML declaration to determine whether the SGML tagging being used by the document conforms with the tagging allowed by the DTD that has been declared. Sometimes referred to as a conforming or validating SGML parser. In XML, applications that provide this functionality are referred to as XML validators.

**Parsable Character Data (PCDATA):** Characters that appear in a part of an SGML document in which text is parsed and markup is recognized and which, having been parsed, are determined not to be markup.

In virtually all cases, the text of an encoded finding aid consists of PCDATA. *See also* **Character Data (CDATA).**

**PCDATA:** *See* **Parsable Character Data (PCDATA).**

**Perl:** An interpreted programming language that is supported on many computer platforms and that commonly is used for developing special scripts for manipulating text for World Wide Web applications.

**Plain Text:** Text encoded in the ASCII format. As such, it is software independent and can be imported, read, and exported by virtually every software application.

**Platform:** *See* **Computing Platform.**

**Prolog:** The document prolog precedes the markup of an SGML instance and consists of the SGML declaration, (optional for SGML), an XML declaration (required if the instance is encoded in XML), and the document type (DOCTYPE) declaration, which may contain a DTD represented by a formal public identifier, or by a system identifier, or both.

**Public Identifier:** *See* **Formal Public Identifier (FPI).**

**Recursion:** Recursion refers to SGML elements that may contain one or more instances of themselves. *See also* **Nesting.**

**Render:** To reproduce or display encoded data in a specified manner.

**Root Element:** *See* **Document Element.**

**Script:** A program written in an interpreted programming language such as Perl. Also a term for a macro or batch file, in which a list of commands can be executed without user interaction.

**SGML Declaration:** A formal, standardized set of constructs that informs a computer as to which character set, delimiters and SGML features are being used in an SGML instance.

**SGML Document:** A sequence of data and markup characters that contains an optional SGML declaration, followed by the DTD that is being used, followed by an encoded document instance that conforms to the specifications of that DTD. *See also* **Instance.**

**Standard Generalized Markup Language (SGML):** An ISO standard (ISO 8879), first used by the publishing industry, for defining, specifying, and creating digital documents that can be delivered, displayed, linked, and manipulated in a system-independent manner.

**Stylesheet:** An ASCII text document that is attached to an SGML or XML encoded document and that contains instructions to specify the formatting and display of the encoded document, or to transform it into another format. *See also* **Cascading Style Sheets (CSS); Document Style Semantics and Specification Language (DSSSL); Extensible Style Language (XSL).**

**Subelement:** An element that is available within one or more other elements. In EAD, every element except the document element <ead> is a subelement of one or more parent elements. *See also* **Parent Element.**

**System identifier:** A character string that identifies an SGML object by citing a system-specific characteristic, such as a URL or a file name that physically locates the object in a file storage system.

**Tag Name:** A short, informal, mnemonic name used for an SGML element. An element's tag name appears within angle brackets to specify the start-tag and end-tag. For example, <unitdate> is the tag name for the element Date of the Unit. *See also* **Element Name.**

**Template:** A preestablished layout model using word processing or SGML authoring software that ensures that data entered into it will adhere to a consistent format and content scheme.

**Text Encoding Initiative (TEI):** An international cooperative effort to develop generic guidelines for a standard encoding scheme for scholarly texts.

**Uniform Resource Identifier (URI):** A string, structured according to the syntax of Internet Engineering Task Force RFC 2396, that identifies a resource on the Internet such as a file, a downloadable document, or an image. There are two classes of URIs: those that identify by specifying location (Uniform Resource Locators) and those that do so by naming the resource (Uniform Resource Names), such as purls (persistent URLs). *See also* **Uniform Resource Locator.**

**Uniform Resource Locator (URL):** A string, structured according to the syntax of Internet Engineering Task Force RFC 1738, that specifies the location of a resource on the Internet such as a file, an image or a downloadable document. A URL includes the type of naming scheme employed (http, ftp, telnet, news, file, etc.), a separating colon, the location of the host, and a path to the resource. URLs may be either absolute (containing the entire address of the resource) or relative (containing only a part of the address). Partial addresses may be used as long as the processing agent is able to resolve the full locations based on their context. Relative URLs enable terseness in documentation and the dynamic generation of links; they also minimize referential problems that may occur when hierarchical naming systems or file locations are modified.

**Wrapper Element:** An element designed only as a container for other elements. Wrapper elements may have attributes but must contain one or more subelements in order to include text.

**XLink (XML Linking Language):** Specifies constructs that may be inserted into XML resources to describe links between objects. XLink uses XML syntax to create structures that can describe the simple unidirectional hyperlinks of HTML as well as more sophisticated multidirectional links.

**XML:** *See* **Extensible Markup Language (XML).**

**XML Linking Language:** *See* **XLink (XML Linking Language).**

**XSL:** *See* **Extensible Style Language (XSL).**

# Appendix G

# BIBLIOGRAPHY

## Encoded Archival Description (EAD)

"American Heritage Project." (http://sunsite.berkeley.edu/amher/)

Bouché, Nicole L. "Implementing EAD in the Yale University Library." *American Archivist* 60 (fall 1997): 408-19.

DeRose, Stephen J. "Navigation, Access, and Control Using Structured Information." *American Archivist* 60 (summer 1997): 298-309.

Dooley, Jackie M., ed. *Encoded Archival Description: Context, Theory, and Case Studies.* Chicago: Society of American Archivists, 1998. (Articles previously published as the summer and fall 1997 issues of *American Archivist.*)

Dow, Elizabeth H. "EAD and the Small Repository." *American Archivist* 60 (fall 1997): 446-55.

*EAD Help Pages.* Maintained by the Society of American Archivists EAD Roundtable. (http://jefferson.village.virginia.edu/ead)

*Encoded Archival Description Retrospective Conversion Guidelines: A Supplement to the EAD Tag Library and EAD Guidelines.* Maintained by the Electronic Text Unit, University of California, Berkeley, for the American Heritage Virtual Archive Project and the University of California Encoded Archival Description Project. (http://sunsite.berkeley.edu/amher/upguide.html)

*Encoded Archival Description Tag Library, Version 1.0.* Chicago: Society of American Archivists, 1998.

*Encoded Archival Description Official Web Site.* Maintained by the Library of Congress. Network Development and MARC Standards Office. (http://www.loc.gov/ead)

"Encoding Standards for Electronic Aids: A Report by the Bentley Team for Encoded Archival Description Development." *Archival Outlook* 10 (January 1996): 10.

Fox, Michael. "Implementing Encoded Archival Description: An Overview of Administrative and Technical Considerations." *American Archivist* 60 (summer 1997): 330-43.

Hensen, Steven L. " 'NISTF II' and EAD: The Evolution of Archival Description." *American Archivist* 60 (summer 1997): 284-97.

Kiesling, Kris. "EAD as an Archival Descriptive Standard." *American Archivist* 60 (summer 1997): 344-54.

Lacy, Mary A., and Anne Mitchell. "EAD Testing and Implementation at the Library of Congress." *American Archivist* 60 (fall 1997): 420-35.

McClung, Patricia. "Access to Primary Sources: During and After the Digital Revolution." Keynote Address presented at the Berkeley Finding Aids Conference, Berkeley, Calif., April 4-6, 1995. (http://jefferson.village.virginia.edu/ead/literature/bfac/mcclung.html)

Meissner, Dennis. "First Things First: Reengineering Finding Aids for Implementation of EAD." *American Archivist* 60 (fall 1997): 372-87.

Morris, Leslie A. "Developing a Cooperative Intra-institutional Approach to EAD Implementation: The Harvard/Radcliffe Digital Findings Aids Project." *American Archivist* 60 (fall 1997): 388-407.

"Online Archive of California (OAC) Project: A Prototype Union Database of Encoded Archival Finding Aids." (http://sunsite.Berkeley.edu/FindingAids/uc-ead/)

Pitti, Daniel V. "Access to Digital Representations of Archival Material: The Berkeley Finding Aid Project." In *RLG Digital Image Access Project: Proceedings from an RLG Symposium.* Palo Alto, Calif.: The Research Libraries Group, 1995. (http://sunsite.berkeley.edu/FindingAids/EAD/diap.html)

Pitti, Daniel V. "Encoded Archival Description: The Development of an Encoding Standard for Archival Finding Aids." *American Archivist* 60 (summer 1997): 268-83.

Pitti, Daniel V. "Settling the Digital Frontier: The Future of Scholarly Communication in the Humanities." Paper presented at the Berkeley Finding Aids Conference, Berkeley, Calif., April 4-6, 1995. (http://jefferson.village.virginia.edu/ead/literature/bfac/dpitti.html)

Ruth, Janice E. "Encoded Archival Description: A Structural Overview." *American Archivist* 60 (summer 1997): 310-29.

Seaman, David. "Multi-Institutional EAD: The University of Virginia's Role in the American Heritage Project." *American Archivist* 60 (fall 1997): 436-45.

## Standard Generalized Markup Language (SGML), Extensible Markup Language (XML), and Related Technologies

Alschuler, Liora. *ABCD ... SGML: A User's Guide to Structured Information.* London and Boston: International Thomson Computer Press, 1995.

Barnard, David, et al. "SGML-Based Markup for Literary Texts." *Computers and the Humanities* 22 (1988): 265-76.

Barron, David. "Why use SGML?" *Electronic Publishing Origination, Dissemination and Design* 2.1 (April 1989): 3-24.

Burnard, Lou and C. M. Sperberg-McQueen. *TEI Lite: An Introduction to Text Encoding for Interchange.* Document No. TEI U 5, June 1995. (http://info.ox.ac.uk/~archive/teilite/)

Busch, Joseph A. "SGML for Cultural Heritage Information." Paper presented at the American Society for Information Science Mid-Year Meeting, Minneapolis, Minn., May 24, 1995. (http://www.oasis-open.org/cover/buschSGML.html)

Coombs, James H., Allen H. Renear, and Steven J. DeRose. "Markup Systems and the Future of Scholarly Text Processing," *Communications of the ACM* 30 (November 1987): 933-947.

Cover, Robin. *The SGML/XML Web Page.* (http://www.oasis-open.org/cover).

*Current Cites Virtual Issue: SGML Information.* Bibliography of current works produced dynamically at moment of request. (http://sunsite.berkeley.edu/SGML)

DeRose, Stephen J. *The SGML FAQ Book: Understanding the Foundation of HTML and XML*. Dordrecht, Boston, and London: Kluwer Academic Publishers, 1997.

DeRose, Stephen J. and David G. Durand. *Making Hypermedia Work: A User's Guide to HyTime*. Boston, Dordrecht, and London: Kluwer Academic Publishers, 1994.

Erickson, Janet C. "Options for Presentation of Multilingual Text: Use of the Unicode Standard." March 14, 1997. (http://www.oasis-open.org/cover/ericksonUnicode.html)

Goldfarb, Charles, Steven R. Newcomb, W. Eliot Kimber, and Peter J. Newcomb. *A Reader's Guide to the HyTime Standard*. (http://www.hytime.org/papers/htguide.html)

Goldfarb, Charles F. *The SGML Handbook*. Oxford: Clarendon Press, 1990.

Goldfarb, Charles F. and Paul Prescod. *The XML Handbook*. Upper Saddle River, N.J.: Prentice Hall, 1998.

*The Handle System* web site. Maintained by the Corporation for National Research Initiatives. (http://www.handle.net/).

Herwijnen, Eric van. *Practical SGML*. 2d ed. Boston, Dordrecht, and London: Kluwer Academic Publishers, 1994.

*Humanities Text Initiative Web Site*. Maintained by the Humanities Text Initiative, University of Michigan. (http://www.hti.umich.edu/)

Ide, Nancy M. and C. M. Sperberg-McQueen. "The TEI: History, Goals, and Future." *Computers and the Humanities* 29 (1995): 5-15.

International Organization for Standardization. *ISO 8859-1: 1987 (E). Information processing --- 8-bit Single-Byte Coded Graphic Character Sets --- Part 1: Latin Alphabet No. 1*. Geneva: International Organization for Standardization, 1987.

International Organization for Standardization. *ISO 8879-1986 (E). Information Processing --- Text and Office Systems --- Standard Generalized Markup Language (SGML)*. Geneva: International Organization for Standardization, 1986.

International Organization for Standardization. *ISO 8879:1986 / A1:1988 (E). Information Processing --- Text and Office Systems --- Standard Generalized Markup Language (SGML), Amendment 1*. Geneva: International Organization for Standardization, 1988.

International Organization for Standardization. *ISO/TR 9573-1988(E). Information processing---SGML Support Facilities---Techniques for Using SGML*. Geneva: International Organization for Standardization, 1988.

International Organization for Standardization and International Electrotechnical Commission. *ISO/IEC 10646-1: 1993. Information Technology --- Universal Multiple-Octet Coded Character Set (UCS) --- Part 1: Architecture and Basic Multilingual Plane*. Geneva: International Organization for Standardization, 1993.

International Organization for Standardization and International Electrotechnical Commission. *ISO/IEC 10744: 1992. Information Technology --- Hypermedia/Time-based Structuring Language (HyTime)*. Geneva: International Organization for Standardization, 1992.

*An Introduction to SGML.* Maintained by Benoît Marchal. (http://www.pineapplesoft.com/reports/sgml/index.html)

Langendoen, D. Terence and Gary F. Simons. "A Rationale for the TEI Recommendations for Feature-Structure Markup." *Computers and the Humanities* (1995): 191-209.

Maler, Eve and Jeanne El Abduloussi. *Developing SGML DTDs: From Text to Model to Markup.* Upper Saddle River, N.J.: Prentice Hall, 1996.

*MARC DTDs Web Page.* Maintained by the Library of Congress. Network Development and MARC Standards Office. (http://lcweb.loc.gov/marc/marcsgml.html)

Pitti, Daniel V. "Standard Generalized Markup Language and the Future of Cataloging." *The Serials Librarian* 25 (1995): 243-53. Also in: Beth Holley and Mary Ann Sheble, eds,. *A Kaleidoscope of Choices: Reshaping Roles and Opportunities for Serialists* (New York: The Haworth Press, 1995)

Price-Wilkin, John. "A Gateway Between the World-Wide Web and PAT: Exploiting SGML Through the Web." *The Public-Access Computer Systems Review* 5, no. 7 (1994): 5-27. (http://www.oasis-open.org/cover/pricewil.html)

Price-Wilkin, John. "Just-in-time Conversion, Just-in-case Collections: Effectively Leveraging Rich Document Formats for the WWW." *D-Lib Magazine* (May 1997). (http://www.dlib.org/dlib/may97/michigan/05pricewilkin.html)

"Publishing the Documents of the Future Today: XML and DynaText®." Inso White Paper. Inso Corporation. (http://www.inso.com/dynatext/dtxtwp.htm)

Rubinsky, Yuri and Murray Maloney. *SGML on the Web: Small Steps Beyond HTML.* Upper Saddle River, N.J.: Prentice Hall, 1997.

"SGML: Getting Started; A Guide to SGML (Standard Generalized Markup Language) and its Role in Information Management." Arbor Text White Paper. Arbor Text Inc., 1995. (http://www.arbortext.com/Think_Tank/SGML_Resources/Getting_Started_with_SGML/getting_started_with_sgml.html)

*The SGML Primer: SoftQuad's Quick Reference Guide to the Essentials of the Standard: The SGML Needed for Reading a DTD and Marked-up Documents and Discussing Them Reasonably.* Toronto: SoftQuad, 1991. (http://www.interleaf.com/Panorama/resources/PRIMER/primebody.html)

*SGML Resources: SGML—Your Multi-Platform Publishing and Information Management Solution.* Maintained by SoftQuad, Inc. (http://www.sq.com/resources/sgml/index.html)

Sperberg-McQueen, C. M. and Lou Burnard, eds. *Guidelines for Electronic Text Encoding and Interchange. TEI P3.* Chicago: Text Encoding Initiative, 1994. (http://www.uic.edu/orgs/tei/p3/doc/p3.html)

*The Text Encoding Initiative Home Page.* Maintained by Wendy Plotkin and C. M. Sperberg-McQueen. (http://www.uic.edu/orgs/tei)

Travis, Brian E. and Dale C. Waldt Springer. *The SGML Implementation Guide: A Blueprint for SGML Migration.* Berlin: Springer, 1995.

von Hagen, Bill. *SGML for Dummies.* Foster City, Calif.: IDG Books Worldwide, 1997.

Warmer, J. and S. van Egmond. "The Implementation of the Amsterdam SGML Parser." *Electronic Publishing Origination, Dissemination and Design* 2.2 (July 1989): 65-90.

*The Whirlwind Guide to SGML and XML Tools and Vendors*. Maintained by Steve Pepper. (http://www.infotek.no/sgmltool/guide.htm)

World Wide Web Consortium (W3C). Web site. (http://www.w3.org)

## Archival Description

Abraham, Terry. "Oliver W. Holmes Revisited: Levels of Arrangement and Description in Practice." *American Archivist* 54 (summer 1991): 370-77.

Bearman, David A. *The National Information Systems Task Force (NISTF) Papers, 1981-1984*. Chicago: Society of American Archivists, 1987.

Bureau of Canadian Archivists. *Toward Descriptive Standards: Report and Recommendations of the Canadian Working Group on Archival Descriptive Standards.* Ottawa: Bureau of Canadian Archivists, 1985.

Duchein, Michel. "Theoretical Principles and Practical Problems of *Respect des Fonds* in Archival Science." *Archivaria* 16 (1983): 64-82.

Evans, Max. "Authority Control: An Alternative to the Record Group Concept." *American Archivist* 49 (summer 1986): 249-61.

Fox, Michael J. and Peter L. Wilkerson. *Introduction to Archival Organization and Description.* Los Angeles: J. Paul Getty Trust, 1998.

Hamer, Philip. *Guide to Archives and Manuscripts in the United States*. New Haven: Yale University Press, 1961.

Hensen, Steven L. "Archival Description and New Paradigms of Bibliographic Control and Access in the Networked Digital Environment." In *The Future of the Descriptive Cataloging Rules,* edited by Brian E. C. Schottlaender. ALCTS Papers on Library Technical Services and Collections, no. 6. Chicago: American Library Association, 1998.

Hensen, Steven L. "Primary Sources, Research, and the Internet: The Digital Scriptorium at Duke." *First Monday, Peer Reviewed Journal on the Internet* 2, no. 9 (1997). (http://www.firstmonday.dk/issues/issue2_9/hensen/)

Hensen, Steven L. "Squaring the Circle: The Reformation of Archival Description in AACR2." *Library Trends* (winter 1988): 539-52.

Hensen, Steven L. "The Use of Standards in the Application of the AMC Format." *American Archivist* 49 (winter 1986): 31-40.

Hickerson, H. Thomas. "Archival Information Exchange and the Role of Bibliographic Networks." *Library Trends* (winter 1988): 553-71.

Holmes, Oliver Wendell. "Archival Arrangement—Five Different Operations at Five Different Levels." *American Archivist* 27 (January 1964): 21-41.

Library of Congress. Descriptive Cataloging Division. Manuscripts Section. *National Union Catalog of Manuscript Collections*. Washington, D.C.: Library of Congress, 1959-1993.

Miller, Fredric M. *Arranging and Describing Archives and Manuscripts.* Chicago: Society of American Archivists, 1990.

Public Archives of Canada. *Union List of Manuscripts in Canadian Repositories = Catalogue collectif des manuscrits archives canadiennes.* Edited by Robert S. Gordon. Ottawa: Public Archives of Canada, 1968.

Walch, Victoria Irons, comp. *Standards for Archival Description: A Handbook.* Chicago: Society of American Archivists, 1994. (http://www.archivists.org/publications/stds99/index.html)

Weissman, Ronald F. E. "Archives and the New Information Architecture of the Late 1990s." *American Archivist* 57 (winter 1994): 20-34. Duranti, Luciana. "Commentary." *American Archivist* 57 (winter 1994): 36-40.

Working Group on Standards for Archival Description. "Archival Descriptive Standards." *American Archivist* 52:4 (fall 1990) and 53:1 (winter 1990). The report of the Working Group on Standards for Archival Description and related background papers.

## Thesauri and Rules for Archival Description

*Anglo-American Cataloging Rules*, 2d ed., rev. Chicago: American Library Association, 1988.

*Art & Architecture Thesaurus*, 2d ed. New York: Oxford University Press, 1994. (http://www.ahip.getty.edu/aat_browser/)

Betz, Elisabeth W. *Graphic Materials: Rules for Describing Original Items and Historical Collections.* Washington, D.C.: Library of Congress, 1982.

*Canadian Subject Headings.* Edited by Alina Schweitzer. Ottawa, Canada: National Library of Canada, 1992.

*Categories for the Description of Works of Art.* The Getty Information Institute. (http://www.gii.getty.edu/index/cdwa.html)

Cook, Michael and Margaret Procter. *A Manual of Archival Description*, 2d ed. Aldershot, Hants: Gower, 1989.

*Dictionary of Occupational Titles,* 4th ed., rev. Washington, DC: U.S. Department of Labor, Employment and Training Administration, U.S. Employment Service, 1991.

Hensen, Steven L. *Archives, Personal Papers, and Manuscripts: A Cataloging Manual for Archival Repositories, Historical Societies, and Manuscript Libraries*, 2d ed. Chicago: Society of American Archivists, 1989.

*ISAD(G): General International Standard Archival Description, adopted by the Ad Hoc Commission on Descriptive Standards, Stockholm, Sweden, 21-23 January 1993.* Ottawa, Ontario: International Council on Archives, 1994. (http://www.archives.ca/ica/cds/isad(g)e.html)

*Library of Congress Name Authority File.* Available online by subscription from the OCLC or RLIN bibliographic networks.

*Library of Congress Subject Headings*, 19th ed. Washington, D.C.: Cataloging Distribution Service, Library of Congress, 1996. Prepared by the Cataloging Policy and Support Office, Library Services.

Matters, Marion E. *Oral History Cataloging Manual*. Chicago: Society of American Archivists, 1995.

*Medical Subject Headings*. Washington, D.C.: U.S. Government Printing Office, 1998.

*Moving Image Materials: Genre Terms*. Compiled by Martha M. Yee for the National Moving Image Database Standards Committee, National Center for Film and Video Preservation at the American Film Institute; coordinated by Motion Picture, Broadcasting, and Recorded Sound Division, Library of Congress. Washington, D.C.: Cataloging Distribution Service, Library of Congress, 1988.

*National Council on Archives Rules for Construction of Personal, Corporate, and Place Names*. Maintained by the National Council on Archives (U.K.). (http://www.hmc.gov.uk/pubs/pubs.htm)

*Revised Nomenclature for Museum Cataloging: A Revised and Expanded Version of Robert G. Chenhall's System for Classifying Man-made Objects*. Edited by James R. Blackaby and Patricia Greeno. Nashville, Tenn.: AASLH Press, 1989.

*Rules for Archival Description*. Prepared by the Planning Committee on Descriptive Standards of the Bureau of Canadian Archivists. Ottawa: Bureau of Canadian Archivists, 1990.

Smiraglia, Richard P. *Describing Music Materials: A Manual for Descriptive Cataloging of Printed and Recorded Music, Music Videos, and Archival Music Collections*, 3d ed. Lake Crystal, Minn.: Soldier Creek Press, 1997.

*Thesaurus for Graphic Materials*. Compiled by the Prints and Photographs Division, Library of Congress. Washington, D.C.: Cataloging Distribution Service, Library of Congress, 1995.

*Thesaurus of Geographic Names, Version 1.0*. Los Angeles: The J. Paul Getty Trust, 1997. (http://www.ahip.getty.edu/tgn_browser/)

*Unesco thesaurus: a structured list of descriptors for indexing and retrieving literature in the fields of education, science, social science, culture, and communication*. Compiled by Jean Aitchison. Paris: Unesco, 1977.

*Union List of Artists' Names, Version 2.0*. Los Angeles: The J. Paul Getty Trust, 1998. (http://www.ahip.getty.edu/ulan_browser/)

*USMARC Concise Format for Bibliographic Data,*. 1994 ed. with 3 updates through July 1997. Maintained by the Library of Congress, Network Development and MARC Standards Office. (http://lcweb.loc.gov/marc/bibliographic/ecbdhome.html)

*USMARC Code List for Countries*. Prepared by Network Development and MARC Standards Office. Washington: Library of Congress Cataloging Distribution Service, 1993.

White-Hensen, Wendy. *Archival Moving Image Materials: A Cataloging Manual*. Washington, D.C.: Motion Picture, Broadcasting, and Recorded Sound Division, Library of Congress, 1984.

# INDEX

- In keeping with the format of the *Application Guidelines*, attribute names have been rendered in SMALL CAPS and attribute values have been rendered in quotation marks.

- For the most part, attributes have been indexed under their attribute name, not under each element with which they can be used. Discussions of attributes that are accompanied by an encoded example are indicated by (example) following the page number(s).

- Elements have been indexed under their tag names (rendered with angle brackets), with cross-references from the element names. Discussions of elements that are accompanied by an encoded example are indicated by (example) following the page number(s).

- Software packages have been indexed under the software name followed by the producer's name (when available) in brackets; software producers have not been indexed separately.

- Markup languages such as SGML and XML have been indexed under their full name, but many related topics use just the abbreviation of the name so those should be checked also for complete information on a particular markup language.

- All appendices, with the exception of appendix E (examples) and appendix F (glossary), have been indexed.

- Entries made under ''Encoding'' are not meant to be definitive for each category; rather they are meant to provide users with an entry point into the element and tag names dealing with encoding a particular part of a finding aid. The relevant tag name(s) should be checked for additional information.

- When attribute and tag names are included as subentries, they are usually alphabetized by the tag name, not any preceding text.